THE BATTLE FOR
THE MEDITERRANEAN

Also available in this series

AGINCOURT – *Christopher Hibbert*

THE SPANISH ARMADA – *Michael Lewis*

BATTLES OF THE ENGLISH CIVIL WAR – *Austin Woolrych*

BATTLES OF THE '45 – *Katherine Tomasson and Francis Buist*

TRAFALGAR – *Oliver Warner*

CORUNNA – *Christopher Hibbert*

WATERLOO – *John Naylor*

BATTLES OF THE CRIMEAN WAR – *W. Baring Pemberton*

BATTLES OF THE INDIAN MUTINY – *Michael Edwardes*

BATTLES OF THE BOER WAR – *W. Baring Pemberton*

YPRES 1914: DEATH OF AN ARMY – *A. H. Farrar-Hockley*

THE IRONCLADS OF CAMBRAI – *Bryan Cooper*

CORONEL AND THE FALKLANDS – *Geoffrey Bennett*

THE BATTLE OF THE ATLANTIC – *Donald Macintyre*

THE BATTLE OF MATAPAN – *S. W. C. Pack*

THE BATTLE FOR NORMANDY – *Eversley Belfield and H. Essame*

CONDITIONS OF SALE

British Battles Series

THE BATTLE FOR
THE MEDITERRANEAN

DONALD MACINTYRE

UNABRIDGED

PAN BOOKS LTD · LONDON

First published 1964 by B. T. Batsford Ltd.
This edition published 1970 by Pan Books Ltd,
33 Tothill Street, London, S.W.1

ISBN 0 330 02525 2

Printed in Great Britain by
Cox & Wyman Ltd, London, Reading and Fakenham

CONTENTS

	List of Illustrations	7
	Acknowledgement	9
	Map of the Mediterranean	10
	Introduction	13
1	Disputed Control	15
2	Taranto and After	31
3	Luftwaffe and Afrika Korps Intervene	44
4	Greece and Crete: Triumph of the Luftwaffe	61
5	Malta Strikes at Rommel's Lifeline	82
6	Massacre on the Libyan Supply Route	99
7	The Mediterranean Fleet in Eclipse	118
8	Malta Suppressed	131
9	Tobruk Surrenders: Rommel's Fatal Blunder	148
10	The Turn of the Tide	170
11	Rommel's Supply Crisis	193
12	British Sea Power Victorious	206
	Select Bibliography	218
	Index	219

ILLUSTRATIONS IN PHOTOGRAVURE
(*between pages* 120 *and* 121)

Admiral Sir James Somerville, Commanding Force 'H'
until January, 1942
(*Courtesy of the Imperial War Museum*)

Admiral Sir Andrew Cunningham, Commander-in-Chief
Mediterranean Fleet until April 1942 and after
February 1943
(*Courtesy of The Imperial War Museum*)

Admiral Inigo Campioni, Commander-in-Chief, Italian
Fleet until December, 1940
(*Courtesy of Ministero della Difesa Marina, Rome*)

Admiral Angelo Iachino, Commander-in-Chief, Italian
Fleet from December, 1940
(*Courtesy of Admiral A. Iachino*)

The *Cavour* sunk in Taranto Harbour, November 11th, 1940
(*Courtesy of Ministero della Difesa Marina, Rome*)

An Italian troop convoy assembling
(*Courtesy of Ministero della Difesa Marina, Rome*)

Near misses by bombs on the *Ark Royal*
(*Courtesy of the Imperial War Museum*)

The *Ark Royal* sinking
(*Courtesy of the Imperial War Museum*)

The Grand Harbour, Malta, under air attack
(*Courtesy of Verlag Ullstein, Berlin*)

ACKNOWLEDGEMENT

In writing this book I have been greatly helped by Admiralty permission to consult the official Staff Histories and by the guidance of the Admiralty Historical Section headed by Lieutenant-Commander P. K. Kemp, OBE, RN.

In particular I have greatly benefited from the wide knowledge of the naval war in the Mediterranean of Commander G. A. Titterton, RN, author of the relevant Staff History on the campaign, whose advice and help are gratefully acknowledged.

D.M.

Acknowledgement is due to the authors and publishers of the following books for permission to quote from them:

A Sailor's Odyssey by Admiral of the Fleet, Lord Cunningham (Hutchinson & Co Ltd and E. P. Dutton & Co Inc), by courtesy of the Executors of the late Lord Cunningham; *Briefed to Attack* by Air Marshal Sir Hugh Lloyd (Hodder & Stoughton Ltd); *Fighting Admiral* by Captain Donald Macintyre (Evans Brothers); *La Guerra sui Mari nel Conflitto Mondiale* by Admiral Bernotti (Societá Editrice Tirrena, Livorno); *The Fatal Decisions* by Lieutenant-General Fritz Bayerlein (Michael Joseph Ltd); *The Rommel Papers*, edited by Captain B. H. Liddell Hart (Wm Collins Sons & Co Ltd).

Other quotations are from British and Italian official sources.

THE MEDITERRANEAN

0   200   400
Miles

Introduction

THE VARIOUS military campaigns and battles in and around the Mediterranean during the Second World War have been individually described by a number of authors. The factor common to all of them, the overriding importance in their outcome of control of the sea and the supply routes upon which the success or failure of the contending armies largely depended, has been less noticed.

In this the British laboured under the disadvantage of a sea supply route of some 14,000 miles round the Cape of Good Hope to Suez as compared to the Italo-German supply route of a few hundred miles across the Central Mediterranean. Yet, throughout his period of command in North Africa, General Rommel never ceased to complain that the German Afrika Korps was starved of men, weapons and supplies, particularly fuel, even during those periods in the campaigns when the opposing sides remained static.

When the Battle of El Alamein began, the British Eighth Army enjoyed a superiority of $2\frac{1}{2}$ to 1 in tanks over the Axis Panzer Army and a lavish supply of ammunition and fuel. Rommel's armoured formations, outnumbered and outgunned as they were, were further hamstrung by such a dearth of supplies that only three issues of petrol were available for them in the whole of North Africa.

It is the purpose of this book to outline how this prelude to victory was brought about by three years of bitter struggle on, above and below the Mediterranean waters; a struggle in which the British, at the outset suffering under all the disadvantages consequent upon their peacetime neglect of naval air power, ship-borne and shore-based, and facing more powerful and concentrated Italian and German naval and air forces, succeeded in exerting a stranglehold on the Axis supply lines to North Africa.

The contest revolved largely round the ability of the British to build up and preserve the little island of Malta as an offensive base in the midst of waters otherwise dominated by enemy air and sea power. This involved, on the one hand, the supply and replenishment of the fortress; on the other, the efforts by the enemy to eliminate it. It led to the principal clashes by sea.

On the outcome depended, absolutely, the success or failure of the campaigns in North Africa and hence, it can be said, of the whole war.

1

Disputed Control

UPON ITALY'S entry into the war on June 11th, 1940, although France was clearly already going down in defeat, the opposing naval forces in the Mediterranean were fairly evenly balanced. Mussolini's flamboyant directive calling for 'the offensive at all points in the Mediterranean and outside' was, therefore, tacitly ignored by his Chief of Naval Staff, Admiral Cavagnari.

In contrast, Admiral Sir Andrew Cunningham, Commander-in-Chief of the Allied Mediterranean Fleet, based on Alexandria, was determined to follow the traditional British naval policy of seeking out and destroying the enemy fleet. He was confronted, however, with a dual factor of crucial importance – the huge disparity between the two sides in submarine and air strength.

As regards the former, the Italians possessed more than 100 submarines – twice the number with which the Germans were wreaking havoc in the Atlantic. The Allied strength in destroyers, which roughly equalled that of the Italians, was divided between the two halves of the Mediterranean, leaving Cunningham with far less than the minimum required for screening his fleet as well as performing their multifarious duties of patrol and convoy. Italian submarines might thus make penetration of the central Mediterranean an unacceptable hazard.

For air support, each fleet was in the position of having to rely almost entirely upon the cooperation of an independent Air Force. Each found the situation less than satisfactory. The Italian Navy complained that the type of aircraft developed by the Air Force for reconnaissance – the single-engine Cant Z501 seaplane, with a top speed of 100 knots –

was woefully inefficient. More than 100 of them were available, nevertheless, and with this number it should have been possible to detect and shadow any large-scale movement of the enemy fleet. In striking power, the Italian Air Force was theoretically overwhelmingly powerful; but the heavy bombers in which it initially trusted, in opposition to the Navy's appeals for torpedo planes, were to prove largely ineffective.

Admiral Cunningham in comparison, so far as shore-based air support was concerned, had the services of only a handful of flying boats divided between Malta and Alexandria, too lightly armed to operate off the enemy's coasts within range of his shore-based aircraft. To be sure, he did have a carrier in his fleet, the 20-year-old *Eagle*, carrying 17 Swordfish torpedo-reconnaissance planes which provided the fleet with reconnaissance in its immediate vicinity while at sea. But this could not help him to bring the Italian fleet to action from his base 1,000 miles to the eastward of Malta. As for aerial striking power and defence, the *Eagle* represented his total resources. For the former, about half of her complement of Swordfish could be spared for attack purposes. The superior speed of Italian ships made it vitally important that they should be slowed down by air attack if a decisive naval action was to be brought about. In defence of the fleet, the *Eagle* had embarked just three Gloster 'Gladiator' biplane fighters, which Charles Keighley-Peach, her Commander (Flying) had extracted from a Fleet Air Arm store. Until he was able to instruct and give flying practice to a few volunteers from the Swordfish pilots, he constituted by himself the total fighter force of the fleet. In spite of a bullet through his thigh in one of his first combats, he had considerable success in shooting down the enemy reconnaissance machines which were shadowing the fleet.

On May 20th the First Sea Lord, Admiral of the Fleet Sir Dudley Pound, had written to Cunningham:

I am afraid you are terribly short of 'air', but . . . I do not see what can be done because, as you will realize, every

available aircraft is wanted in home waters. The one
lesson we have learnt here is that it is essential to have
fighter protection over the fleet whenever they are within
range of enemy bombers. You will be without such protection, which is a very serious matter, but I do not see
any way of rectifying it.

In spite of this, Cunningham was mainly concerned with
the problem of how to bring the Italian fleet to action.

'You may be sure that all in the fleet are imbued with a
burning desire to get at the Italian Fleet', he had written on
June 6th in reply to a message originating from the Prime
Minister, Mr Churchill, criticizing his plans as 'purely
defensive',

but you will appreciate that a policy of seeking and destroying his naval forces requires good and continuous air
reconnaissance, and a means of fixing the enemy when
located. I am far from well provided with either require-
ment, whereas the Italians have both. Indeed my chief
fear is that we shall make contact with little or nothing
except aircraft and submarines, and I must get the measure
of these before attempting sustained operations in the
Central Mediterranean.

The first hours after the opening of hostilities found the
Mediterranean fleet steaming north-westward from Alexandria for a sweep of the central Mediterranean. Cunningham hoped that he might encounter enemy naval units; but
part of his object was simply to 'try out the Italian air at the
earliest possible moment'. In the event, the only surface unit
encountered was a small minesweeper off Bardia which was
sunk, while the Italian Air Force failed entirely to put in an
appearance. An ominous occurrence there was, nevertheless,
in the loss of the old light cruiser *Calypso* to the torpedoes
of the Italian submarine *Bagnolini*.

This skilfully conducted attack might have led to a false
impression of the influence Italian submarines were to have

upon events in the Mediterranean, had not others displayed
a compensating lack of competence which resulted in ten
being destroyed before the end of June. In fact, the Italian
submarine fleet, to which an examination of 'paper' strength
would have given a dominating role in the forthcoming
campaign, was rarely to live up to its potentialities. Air
power, on the other hand, in spite of its absence on this
occasion, was to prove a decisive element.

Meanwhile, the first two weeks of the campaign saw the
opposing naval forces holding an uneasy balance. Though
the Italian main fleet lay supine in its bases, Malta was
repeatedly bombed, thus beginning its long ordeal which
was to continue intermittently for more than two years. The
Allied fleet, unable to draw its reluctant opponent to sea,
turned its guns on to the Libyan port of Bardia and employed its light forces to good effect in hunting Italian
submarines.

Then, on June 24th, the whole situation was transformed
by the collapse of France. The balance of naval power
swung heavily in favour of Italy. In the western half of the
Mediterranean, hitherto a French responsibility, there were
virtually no British naval forces. In the other half, though
Cunningham's slight (and temporary) preponderance in
battleship strength remained, he was now faced with an
Italian superiority of 7 heavy and 11 light cruisers and 61
destroyers over his own 6 light cruisers and 20 destroyers.
The British advantage in battleships was more apparent
than real, as, of Cunningham's 4 ships, 3 were unmodernized
and so outranged by the two modernized enemy ships in
service, and all were slower than the Italian ships. Furthermore, the Italian battleship strength was about to be increased by the addition of two more modernized ships and
two splendid new battleships, *Vittorio Veneto* and *Littorio*.

Fortunately, the situation in home waters following upon
the campaign in Norway made it possible for the Admiralty
to detach a powerful squadron, to be called Force 'H', to
Gibraltar to fill the vacuum in the western Mediterranean.
On June 28th Vice-Admiral Sir James Somerville hoisted his

flag in the battlecruiser *Hood* to take command of this force comprising, besides the *Hood*, the battleships *Valiant* and *Resolution*, the carrier *Ark Royal*, the light cruiser *Arethusa* and four destroyers.

The overall situation at the end of June was, nevertheless, from the British point of view, a perilous one should the Italians take full advantage of their vastly improved position.

The elimination of France did, indeed, lead to greater activity by the Italian Navy. They now, for the first time, felt able to run convoys with urgent supplies of ammunition and equipment for their armies in Libya. With Malta untenable as a naval base and still almost devoid of strike aircraft,* there was little that could be done to prevent them. The onward transport of the supplies along the coast from Tripoli to Tobruk in destroyers, however, gave an opportunity to attack them by air. RAF bomber squadrons made repeated attacks on Tobruk but it was the Swordfish of No 813 Squadron, disembarked from the *Eagle* while in harbour, which achieved the most concrete successes. Attacking on July 5th, they succeeded in torpedoing the destroyers *Zeffiro* and *Euro*, the former being sunk and the latter having her bow blown off. In the same attack a 4,000-ton transport was sunk and the liner *Liguria* damaged. In a further attack on July 20th, two more destroyers, the *Ostro* and *Nembo*, were also sunk.

But it was the large force of Italian heavy warships which came to sea from time to time to cover their convoys that would have offered the possibility of a naval engagement if the necessary air reconnaissance had been available on the British side. Without it, chance alone could bring it about. Such a chance occurred during the early days of July. It was to result in nothing more than a 'brush', but, setting the pattern for much that was to come later, it merits examination.

On the evening of July 6th, a convoy of five merchant ships for Libya sailed from Naples. Passing through the

---

* Nine Fleet Air Arm Swordfish of No 830 Squadron had arrived in Malta from Toulon shortly before the French collapse.

Straits of Messina it was in the Ionian Sea by the next morning. Covering its passage was an Italian force of 16 cruisers and the battleships *Giulio Cesare* and *Cavour*, commanded by Admiral Campioni. None of this was known to the British until, during the afternoon of the 8th, the submarine *Phoenix* and an RAF flying-boat on reconnaissance reported the cruisers and battleships, their covering mission completed, in a position 220 miles north of Benghazi.

Meanwhile, Cunningham had also put to sea with his fleet on the evening of July 7th in order to give cover to two convoys carrying civilian families and the wives and children of servicemen being evacuated from Malta to Alexandria and naval stores for the fleet. The move, though not its purpose, was known at once to the Italian high command. During the next day, when the fleet was south of Crete, heavy and continuous air attacks were delivered by the Italian Air Force. They were of a standard of uniform accuracy which was to be repeated again and again in the days and months to come. Time and again ships would be apparently smothered by the tall, black, leaping splashes from the bursts of a carpet of bombs simultaneously released. Time and again they emerged unscathed. Contrary to all forecasts, the percentage of hits, even with such accurate aiming, turned out to be, if not negligible, at least acceptable. Nevertheless, the moral effect was undoubtedly daunting. Every bomb seemed to be dropping directly on to an observer watching them. Sooner or later one must hit and on this first occasion of serious attack on the fleet one did, landing squarely on the compass platform of the cruiser *Gloucester*, killing seven officers, including Captain Garside, and 11 ratings and wounding a number of others. In spite of this the cruiser, commanded from her secondary control position, was able to remain with the fleet.

That afternoon Cunningham received the report that the Italian fleet was at sea. Even with his slower battleships he could hope to bring it to action if he could get between it and its base. He therefore steered at once for Taranto. His intentions were soon known to the enemy through their ability to decode certain messages. The Italian high command ordered Campioni to steer so as to avoid battle until noon the following day, by which time the British fleet would be within easy range of bombers from Italian shore bases.

Early the next morning Campioni's fleet was located by a flying-boat from Malta some 145 miles to the westward of Cunningham's flagship, the *Warspite*. Soon afterwards reconnaissance Swordfish from the *Eagle* made contact and remained to shadow and report their movements. Not until noon, when the two fleets were some 80 miles apart, did Campioni, badly let down by his Air Force, locate his opponent by means of an aircraft catapulted from his flagship, the *Giulio Cesare*. He had hoped that by this time bombers of the Italian Air Force would have done something to reduce Cunningham's strength. Nevertheless, he pressed on, accepting action as he could well afford to do, for his two recently modernized battleships could outrun all Cunningham's and could outrange all except the *Warspite*. His six heavy, and ten light, cruisers were opposed to five British light cruisers, one of which had been damaged and was held back in support of the *Eagle*. Cunningham, too, confidently accepted battle. 'It was not quite the moment I would have chosen to give battle', he was to write later. '. . . However, any opportunity was welcome and the *Warspite* was soon pressing on in support of our cruisers which, with no 8-inch gun ships, were heavily outgunned and outnumbered by the Italian.'

At 11.45 AM, and again four hours later, a small striking force of Swordfish armed with torpedoes was flown off the *Eagle*. As was to be demonstrated so often in the future, such a number was too small to ensure success. But it was all there was and on this first occasion of going into action it was scarcely surprising, even if disappointing, that they failed to score any hits.

Meanwhile, soon after 3 PM in clear blue Mediterranean weather, with a light breeze from the north-west flecking the water, the two fleets had come in sight of one another. A few minutes later the action opened when a squadron of Italian 8-inch cruisers opened fire on the four British cruisers led by Vice-Admiral John Tovey in the *Orion* at a range of more than 13 miles. As soon as the range of his 6-inch guns permitted, Tovey replied; but the odds were great, and to reduce the balance the *Warspite*, now far ahead of her two consorts, sent a few salvos from her 15-inch guns at the Italian cruisers. They at once turned away under smoke. A lull ensued during which the *Warspite* circled to allow the *Malaya*, held up by the slow-steaming *Royal Sovereign*, to catch up.

Then at 3.53 the opposing battleship columns came in sight of one another. The *Warspite*, her great guns elevated to maximum range, opened fire at 26,000 yards. Both sides shot well and straddled their targets almost at once. It was just 4 o'clock when Cunningham saw 'the great orange-coloured flash of a heavy explosion at the base of the enemy flagship's funnels'. The hit caused fires to break out below decks in the *Cesare* as well as other damage. The Italian fleet at once turned away under a heavy smoke-screen. A confused action followed with cruisers and destroyers appearing momentarily out of the smoke, the latter to make long-range but unsuccessful torpedo attacks to cover the withdrawal.

Meanwhile, behind his smoke-screen, Campioni was heading away south-westwards for the safety of his own protected waters in the Straits of Messina.

Cunningham was unwilling to plunge blindly through the barrier of smoke. Though, from one of the *Warspite*'s catapult aircraft shadowing the enemy, he knew that the enemy had made off to the south-westward, he had in mind the possibility of a submarine trap waiting for him. He chose therefore to work his way round to the north and windward of the smoke. By the time his first ships had drawn clear of it, the enemy had vanished over the horizon. The superior speed of the Italian ships would in any case have made a chase unproductive. The British fleet held on for a time, however, closing to within 25 miles of the coast before turning

back, in spite of the tardy arrival of the bombers of the
Regia Aeronautica.

Campioni's brief display of offensive spirit, so promptly
extinguished by the *Warspite*'s impressive shooting, had
indeed been contrary to Italian strategic policy, which saw
nothing to be gained from a naval battle for its own sake.
The purpose for which the Italian fleet had come to sea – the
protection of the military convoy to Libya – had been
accomplished. Campioni knew nothing of the British convoys, to cover which had been Cunningham's original object.
The only reason for Campioni's half-hearted challenge had
been to draw the British fleet into easy range of the bombers
of the Italian Air Force. In this he had been sadly betrayed.
Not until 40 minutes after his flagship had shuddered under
the impact of the *Warspite*'s 15-inch shell (which, fortunately
for Campioni, had only temporarily reduced his speed), did
the bombers appear on the scene.

Worse was to follow. Not only did the airmen fail to hit
any of Cunningham's ships, but a number of them, to the
fury of Admiral Campioni, chose their own fleet as their
target, continuing to bomb it even after it had entered the
Messina Straits, though without effect. Nevertheless, the
repeated attacks on the British fleet, which were to continue
intermittently for the next four days, were impressive, to say
the least. During July 12th, as the fleet was returning to
Alexandria, 22 attacks were made, more than 300 bombs
being dropped. On one occasion 36 plunged all round the
Warspite, bursting within 200 yards of her, 24 to port and 12
to starboard. The old *Eagle*, particularly vulnerable with her
outmoded design, was similarly near-missed on a number of
occasions, suffering an accumulation of minor defects which
were to put her out of action at an important moment later.
It seemed a miracle as again and again ships steamed
through the well-aimed bomb patterns without being struck.

Abortive as the bombing proved to be, it was clear that it
only required a modicum of luck for it to bring down disaster, particularly if Cunningham's solitary and vulnerable
carrier should be hit. Equally ineffective was the anti-aircraft

gunnery of the fleet, a lesson which had already been learnt during the Norwegian campaign, but which the Mediterranean Fleet had to learn by personal experience before being convinced. On the other hand, the Gladiators from the *Eagle*, flown by Charles Keighley-Peach and two volunteers from the Swordfish squadrons, brought down five enemy bombers – a score which was later to rise to 11, showing what might be accomplished by a proper fighter defence.

The safe arrival of the fleet and the two convoys at Alexandria brought the operation to an end. Material consequences were negligible; but what amounted to little more than a first brush with the enemy has been examined in some detail because it set the pattern for much that was to happen in the future. It also clearly presented the problem facing the two antagonists in the Mediterranean, though it cannot be said that either fully understood it.

To both it was demonstrated that a British fleet operating from Alexandria could not prevent the safe passage of Italian supply convoys to Africa. From the Italian point of view this supported their contention that there was nothing to be gained from sending their battle-fleet out to seek action as an end in itself. What the Italians failed to see was that this situation must sooner or later force the British to strain every nerve to restore Malta – written off before the war by the Chiefs of Staff as indefensible – as an air and naval base from which to attack their convoys to Libya. The only certain way to prevent this was by capturing it while it yet lay virtually defenceless. This the Italian Navy had urged on the Italian *Comando Supremo*. General Rommel was to do the same when appointed to command the Afrika Korps, offering to command the operation himself. But both the Italian and German Supreme Commands believed they could achieve their object merely by neutralizing the island by air attack. It was to prove a fatal mistake.

On the other hand it cannot be said that the true situation was any better understood on the British side. After the operation Cunningham wrote:

It must have shown the Italians that their Air Force and submarines cannot stop our Fleet penetrating into the Central Mediterranean and that only their main Fleet can seriously interfere with our operating there. [The operation] produced throughout the Fleet a determination to overcome the air menace and not let it interfere with our freedom of manoeuvre and hence our control of the Mediterranean.

The truth of the matter was that it was only a matter of time and the arrival on the scene of the Luftwaffe with its dive-bombers for the central Mediterranean basin to be closed to naval forces that were without the benefit of a numerous fighter defence. In those narrow waters, such aircraft carriers as might become available could not provide this in sufficient strength. Only a large-scale deployment of fighters on Malta could do so.

On the basis of the lessons learnt in the action off Calabria, Cunningham asked for the addition to his force of one of the new armoured aircraft carriers to provide fighter-defence. The *Illustrious*, carrying 12 Fulmar two-seater fighters and 22 Swordfish, would be sent to him in the following month and would perform valiant service for a time, only to fall a victim to the first onslaught of dive-bombers when the Luftwaffe came to support the Italian Air Force.

Apart from Cunningham's trust – so soon to be shown as unjustified – in the ability of 12 low-performance fighters to defend a fleet against assault by a properly equipped and trained air force, there is a basic fallacy in the idea that freedom of the Mediterranean Fleet, based on Alexandria, to manoeuvre in the central Mediterranean could achieve control of the Mediterranean. It is an example of the loose terminology which has so often befogged British naval strategic thought. 'Control of the Mediterranean', if it means anything, must mean an ability to prevent the enemy from using it for his purposes – in this case passing his convoys to and from Libya – and an ability to ensure the safe use of it by one's own shipping – in this case the passage of supply and troop convoys to Malta and to the British Army of the Nile. In these pages it is hoped to show that the accomplishment of these two objects hinged absolutely upon the availability of Malta as a sea and air base, defensive and offensive.

Malta's vital role was not to provide a base for the main British Mediterranean Fleet but for the submarines and aircraft which had even then come to dominate naval warfare. Battleships had already been relegated – though it was not yet apparent – to an ancillary position in support of naval air power. And, indeed, in the campaign in the Mediterranean the opposing battle-squadrons were never again to come within range of each other's mighty guns.

Admiral Cunningham had pressed in vain, even prior to the outbreak of war, for Malta's air defence to be built up. Had the Navy had full control of its own air component (which must logically include a shore-based element), this would surely have been done. An air force entrusted with the air defence of the homeland and starved of funds by a parsimonious government during the years between the wars cannot be altogether blamed if an apparently purely naval commitment such as the defence of Malta received sparse consideration. Consequently, the only fighters on the island at the end of July 1940 were 3 reserve Fleet Air Arm Gladiators turned over to the RAF and flown by spare flying-boat pilots, and 5 Hurricanes which had arrived, staged through France and Tunis, shortly before the French collapse. Although the Air Officer Commanding, Mediterranean, appealed in August for a striking force, saying that '15 aircraft would produce results out of all proportion to the numbers involved', the only offensive element was No 830 Squadron of the Fleet Air Arm – 9 Swordfish which had originally been based at Toulon to work with the French Navy. Similarly, though approval had been belatedly given to building up the island's anti-aircraft gun defences to 112 heavy and 60 light AA guns, only 34 heavy and eight light AA guns had so far materialized, with a solitary radar set which could not be kept in continuous operation.

The inability of the RAF and Army Chiefs of Staff to garrison Malta while there was yet time, though matched by the enemy's failure to seize the opportunity to capture the island, was to cost us dear. It was to lead also to the paradoxical situation, in the view of Admiral Cunningham, that, should he take the risk and station naval striking forces at the island, successful attacks by them on the enemy's convoys might force the Italians to mount an assault which the defences were in no state to parry. At this time he wrote:

If we are to avoid a serious threat to Malta itself, it appears necessary that in any given period the scale of attack drawn down should not be disproportionate to the state of the defences it has been possible to install. It is only logical therefore to expect the full weight of Italian attack if our light forces work effectively.

Such arguments slowly drove home the vital importance of building up Malta's fighter strength. Though the Battle of Britain was raging and though the Air Officer Commanding in the Middle East, Air Chief Marshal Sir Arthur Longmore, was equally justifiably pressing for fighter reinforcements to take care of his widespread commitments in the land campaigns about to open, 12 Hurricanes were loaded in the old carrier *Argus* and flown off to Malta from a position south of Sardinia. It was the first of many such operations by British and, later, American carriers by which Malta was eventually to be given the means to defend itself.

By land as well as by sea the months of July and August 1940 were fraught with deep anxiety for the British Commanders-in-Chief. The Italian armies in Libya, greatly superior in number to the troops at the disposal of General Sir Archibald Wavell, were known to be preparing for an advance into Egypt. Reinforcements for the British Army had been withheld at first in favour of building up the army in France. Then, at Dunkirk, equipment had been lost in such quantity that nothing could be spared for the Middle East. The RAF had been similarly denied reinforcement;

so that, at the end of May 1940, Longmore, responsible for air operations on the several fronts held by the Army in Egypt and for cooperation with the Navy in the Eastern Mediterranean and the Red Sea, including long-distance reconnaissance, had at his disposal only 96 bombers (Blenheim I) and bomber-transports (Bombay), 75 fighters (Gladiator), 24 Army Cooperation (Lysander) and 10 flying-boats (Sunderland) – a force manifestly incapable of meeting his minimum needs.

By mid-August, however, the vital needs of the Middle East had been partially acknowledged and strenuous efforts were being made to send reinforcements. A military convoy carrying troops, tanks and ammunition was dispatched by the Cape route which was expected to reach Suez by September 24th. The heavy cruiser *York* and the light cruiser *Ajax* of the escort would join Cunningham's fleet. Twenty-four Hurricanes were on their way by the same route and a further 30 were being taken in the *Argus* to the Gold Coast port of Takoradi, thence to be flown to Egypt over a route organized across central Africa. In the next three years more than 5,000 aircraft were to use this route. In addition, 24 Blenheims had reached Egypt via Malta, another 24 were being sent there by sea and six Wellingtons were being flown out.

A very useful addition to the maritime air component was a flight of three Glenn-Martin 'Maryland' long-range reconnaissance aircraft soon to be sent out to Malta, with which the Italian naval ports could be kept under observation – a task impossible for the slow and vulnerable flying-boats. On the other hand, the continued absence of any long-range fighters left the R A F still incapable of giving the fleet fighter cover except in the vicinity of its base. The arrival on September 1st of the *Illustrious* with her handful of Fulmars, together with the modernized and radar-fitted battleship *Valiant* and the anti-aircraft cruisers *Calcutta* and *Coventry*, was, therefore, most welcome.

Should the Italian battle-fleet accept action now, Cunningham would have two ships which could fire at long range, more than ever important as the enemy could by this time deploy a battle-squadron of five – the *Vittorio Veneto*, the *Littorio* and three modernized older ships. Even so it soon became apparent that, even when everything was in their favour, the Italians would not seek a fight. Cunningham had taken his fleet to sea on August 30th to meet his reinforcements off Malta and at the same time to escort a convoy of two merchant ships and a tanker carrying supplies to the island. The Italian battle-fleet, comprising 5 battleships, 10 cruisers and 34 destroyers, ordered to sea to oppose Cunningham's 2 battleships, the *Eagle*, 5 light cruisers and 9 destroyers, was located 90 miles away by a Swordfish from the carrier at dusk on August 31st.

Cunningham turned away and stationed himself in position to cover his convoy in expectation of battle the next day. Admiral Campioni, however, reversed course for the night. By morning the two fleets were so far apart that neither was able to locate the other until the Italians were finally found by a flying-boat that evening at the entrance to the Gulf of Taranto returning to base. His convoy safely delivered and his reinforcements met according to plan, Cunningham took his fleet back to Alexandria. The Italians' chance to strike while still commanding an overwhelming superiority had gone. From now onwards the air-striking force available to Cunningham would go a long way towards squaring the odds.

Commander Bragadin, author of *The Italian Navy in World War II*, blames this 'great opportunity lost' on the bad weather which prevented air reconnaissance during September 1st; but a lack of desire on the part of the Italians to risk their fleet even when circumstances were in their favour is more probable, a policy which accorded with the theory of maintenance of a 'fleet in being'. This apparently spiritless strategy was not appreciated by Italian political circles any more than it was by Cunningham, imbued with the traditional ambition of the Royal Navy to 'seek out and destroy the enemy's fleet'. Admiral Bernotti in his book *La Guerra sui Mari nel Conflitto Mondiale* writes:

The directive for the policy of our fleet, besides the protection of the traffic with Libya and Albania, laid down that it must bring the enemy naval forces to battle, whenever favourable conditions permitted. In irresponsible and incompetent political circles, signs of growing impatience were being manifested therefore in the middle of September 1940 and the Naval Chief of Staff asked the Chief of the General Staff, Marshal Badoglio, for a ruling.

The judgement of the Marshal, summed up, was that, though battle should be accepted if necessary to further an ulterior object or to prevent the enemy from achieving his object, 'the conception of a naval battle as an end in itself is absurd'. This policy, incidentally, is identical with that of the French during their naval wars with the British during the eighteenth century.

From the point of view of morale, the apparent pusillanimity of the Italians inevitably reacted in favour of the British fleet, whose confidence was to be constantly heightened by repeated refusals of the Italians to stand and fight, so that eventually the British became ready and willing to undertake the seemingly impossible in order to get supplies through to Malta. On the other hand, the continued existence of a superior Italian fleet poised on the flank of the supply route to Malta was to play an important part in bringing the fortress within sight of starvation and capitulation, and was consequently to hamper severely the capacity of the British to interfere with the supply traffic to North Africa. Which of these opposing considerations had the greater influence on the campaign for control of the Mediterranean the reader of the following chapters will be able to decide for himself.

2

Taranto and After

ON SEPTEMBER 13th, 1940, the long-expected Italian offensive across the Egyptian–Libyan frontier opened. Undertaken in accordance with a direct order from Mussolini to his unwilling army commander, Marshal Graziani, it was a half-hearted affair. Nevertheless, General Wavell, his army as yet greatly inferior in numbers and ill-equipped, contented himself with absorbing the initial blow with a light mobile screen which then fell back on the main body stationed to oppose any further advance towards the port of Mersa Matruh. Having occupied Sidi Barrani, on the coast, some sixty miles inside Egypt, the Italians halted, the impetus of their forward move exhausted. The stalemate on land thereupon reestablished itself.

Except for the sweep into the central Mediterranean to meet its reinforcements, mentioned in the previous chapter, the Mediterranean fleet during August and September remained static, though far from idle, in the east. Without adequate deep reconnaissance there was nothing to be gained by offensive sweeps towards Malta in the hope of encountering the enemy. Instead, Cunningham's ships addressed themselves to supporting the army by bombardments of the enemy supply port of Bardia and installations along the coast, while his carrier aircraft, with mines and torpedoes, reaped a considerable harvest of minor warships and transports. The exploits of No 813 Squadron from the *Eagle* have already been mentioned. On August 22nd, three Swordfish of No 824 Squadron, based ashore, achieved a brilliant success at Bomba. Their leader, Captain Oliver Patch, Royal Marines, torpedoed and sank the submarine *Iride*; the others sank a depot ship and seriously damaged a

destroyer. The *Iride* was about to proceed on an important
secret operation which will be referred to later. Her loss was
to cause a delay of eighteen months in its performance.

One effect, without doubt, of such successes was to con-
vince the Regia Aeronautica that the Italian Navy had been
right in its advocacy of the airborne torpedo for attack on
ships. Hitherto, though the Navy had developed a very
efficient aerial torpedo, the Italian Air Force had refused to
use it. During September 1940, the torpedo plane took its
place as the principal hazard run by British ships at that
stage of the campaign, beginning with the torpedoing of the
cruiser *Kent* off Bardia on September 17th, to be followed
on October 10th by the cruiser *Liverpool*.

The pedestrian pace of the naval campaign in the Mediterranean during the late summer of 1940, forced on the British
by their continued inability to use Malta, suited only the
Italians, who were able to pass their convoys to Libya unhindered across the short sea passage from Sicily to Cape
Bon and thence by inshore waters to Tripoli. On September
9th, Cunningham had been incensed by a signal from the
Minister of Defence hinting that he was being insufficiently
offensive. As he again pointed out, only constant and complete air reconnaissance, which he was very far from enjoying, could enable him to bring about a major encounter
on reasonable terms. One is inevitably reminded of Nelson's
bitter cry 'Was I to die this moment, want of frigates would
be found stamped on my heart'. Thus already Malta, as the
only possible base for such reconnaissance as well as for the
air and submarine striking force with which to cut the Italian
convoy route, was proving itself the key to the situation.
Not yet, however, was it receiving the top priority it deserved,
though reinforcements and supplies in small quantities were
becoming available. Cunningham took part of his fleet – his
'First Eleven', comprising the more modern big ships,
Warspite, *Valiant* and *Illustrious* – into the central basin at
the end of September to cover the passage of troops embarked in two of his cruisers. Admiral Campioni, with four
battleships, put to sea and was located by aircraft from the

Illustrious 120 miles to the northward. Once again, however, he held off – lacking information of Cunningham's position, according to Commander Bragadin – and by the time Cunningham had landed the troops and was ready to return to his base, Campioni had retired to Taranto.

Early in October Cunningham repeated his excursion to cover a supply convoy, this time with the whole of his fleet; but the Italians contented themselves with sending out a small force of destroyers to seek to deliver a night attack. A spirited action resulted when they encountered the cruiser *Ajax*, in which three of the Italian ships were sunk and another damaged, at the cost of seven shell hits on the cruiser.

Nevertheless, the month of October saw a sudden quickening in the pace of events. On October 28th Mussolini took the step which was, in the long run, to be so fatal to the fortunes of the Axis, by declaring war on Greece. It was also eventually to cost us dear in ships and men. At the outset, though it threw the heavy additional burden on the already fully extended Mediterranean Fleet of escorting supply convoys to the Piraeus and to Crete, it also gave Cunningham his long-standing wish for an advanced base at Suda Bay on the north coast of Crete.

A much less impressive event, but one which was to have important consequences, had taken place earlier in the month. No 431 Flight of the R A F, comprising three Glenn-Martin 'Maryland' reconnaissance aircraft, had arrived in Malta. Much faster than the Sunderland flying-boats and able to climb higher, these could keep a regular watch on the Italian naval bases. Every move by the Italian fleet was passed to Cunningham at once. He no longer had to wait for the enemy to be located out at sea to know what he was doing. A long-cherished plan now became feasible.

Cunningham had, some time back, broached to the First Sea Lord his tentative idea of launching an airborne torpedo attack upon the Italian battle-fleet in harbour, should opportunity arise. When Rear-Admiral Lyster arrived in the *Illustrious* to command the carrier squadron, he had found him to be enthusiastic about the idea. Furthermore, the

Illustrious had brought a supply of long-range petrol tanks for the torpedo planes which would permit a flying-off position sufficiently far out at sea to give a good chance of achieving surprise. Until the necessary intelligence of the enemy's movements became available, it had remained an unattainable dream. But plans had been prepared and every opportunity taken to give the aircrews the necessary training, particularly for night operations; for any idea of sending the slow, lumbering Swordfish by day against the defences of a first-class naval port was out of the question.

Now, at last, with the reports and photographic intelligence from the Marylands coming in regularly and showing the whole of the Italian battle-fleet to be concentrated at Taranto, the project could go ahead. Trafalgar Day, October 21st, was selected for it. A fire in the hangar of the *Illustrious* caused a postponement; defects on the petrol system of the *Eagle*, caused by the repeated shocks of near-miss bombs, forced her to be withdrawn; finally, a number of the *Eagle*'s Swordfish, transferred to the *Illustrious* for the operation, were lost owing to contaminated petrol in their tanks. In spite of these ominous set-backs, Operation 'Judgement' was fixed for November 11th though only 21 aircraft instead of the originally planned 30 would be able to take part.

Meanwhile, the preliminary operations were proceeding. In company with Admiral Somerville's Force 'H', reinforcements for Cunningham, comprising the battleship *Barham*, the cruisers *Glasgow* and *Berwick* and six destroyers carrying between them 2,150 troops for the Malta garrison, had sailed eastwards from Gibraltar on the evening of November 7th. Cunningham, with the *Warspite, Valiant, Malaya, Ramillies, Illustrious* and destroyers, was steering westwards from Alexandria to cover a convoy taking stores, fuel and ammunition to Greece and Crete, another of five store ships for Malta, and finally four empty store ships from Malta to Alexandria.

The Italian command knew at once of the movements of the two fleets. Admiral Campioni prepared to take his battle-

fleet to sea on the 8th when he expected to have the necessary
scouting reports from the Air Force. When no news reached
him during the forenoon of the 8th he continued to wait in
harbour. Though the shortage of oil fuel which the Italian
Navy was to suffer may already have been having its influence, this delay was surely inexcusable if a desire to join
action with the British fleet existed. When at last, during the
afternoon, air reconnaissance reported the convoy for Malta,
it was already beyond the point at which the Italian fleet,
sailing from Taranto, could intercept it. It must have been
realized that Cunningham's fleet would be somewhere in the
central basin to cover it, yet Campioni made no move.

For the next three days the British Mediterranean fleet
was manoeuvring in the central basin less than 350 miles
from Taranto, waiting for its reinforcements to join and for
various ships to refuel at Malta. Though the Italian Air
Force delivered some ineffectual bombing attacks on Cunningham's force as well as on Force 'H' to the southwards
of Sardinia, its reconnaissance reports were so confused and
conflicting that the Italian high command was completely
baffled. Many of Campioni's ships carried scouting sea-
planes on catapults. If his fleet had put to sea and used them
for an organized search, he must soon have located his
enemy; instead he remained in harbour waiting in vain for
information. He was to suffer a bitter humiliation in consequence.

By the 11th, Cunningham's reinforcements had joined
him, the convoy was safely on its way from Malta to Alexandria and he was free to bear away for the selected flying-
off position some 170 miles south-east of Taranto.

One of the *Illustrious*' aircraft had brought out from
Malta the latest photographs of Taranto obtained by the
Marylands. Five battleships could be seen in the anchorage.
Later in the day a sixth battleship was sighted returning to
harbour. All the Italian eggs were in one basket.

It was vitally important that the British force should be
unobserved that day, a task in the hands of the fighter pilots
of the *Illustrious* and the operators of the radar sets with

which the fleet was now moderately well equipped. Italian reconnaissance planes which approached were pounced on with ruthless efficiency and shot down before they could make any report or driven off before they could catch sight of the fleet. So far as the Italian high command was concerned the Mediterranean fleet had vanished and was assumed to be on its way back to Alexandria.

At 6 PM, shortly before sunset, the *Illustrious*, with an escort of cruisers and destroyers, acknowledged the signal from the fleet flagship, 'Proceed in execution of previous orders for Operation "Judgement" .' As she turned away to the north-westward a last signal winked out to her from Andrew Cunningham: 'Good luck then to your lads in their enterprise. Their success may well have a most important bearing on the course of the war in the Mediterranean.'

In the carrier's hangars final preparations were being made to the 21 'Stringbags' which were to take part. They were to be launched in two waves; the first, of 12 machines, would be led by Lieutenant-Commander Kenneth Williamson, commanding No 815 Squadron, with Lieutenant N. J. Scarlett as his observer. The remaining nine would be led by Lieutenant-Commander J. W. Hale, commanding officer of No 819 Squadron, whose observer was to be Lieutenant G. A. Carline. Not all even of this small force were to be armed with torpedoes. Six of the first wave and four of the second would carry bombs with which they would create a diversion by attacking cruisers and destroyers berthed in the inner harbour. Two of these bombers in each wave would also carry a number of magnesium flares and it would be their first duty to lay these in a line so placed as to show up in silhouette the Italian battleships in the outer harbour.

The torpedoes were something new and special. To detonate their warheads they had a new device known as a 'Duplex' pistol, so called because either a direct hit or the change of magnetic field as the torpedo passed underneath a ship would actuate it. The torpedoes would have to be set to run deep in case they were dropped outside the anti-torpedo nets known to exist. A small error in their depth-keeping would be enough to take them too deep for a direct hit. The magnetic device would then operate instead.

The prospect facing the 42 naval airmen was a daunting one. Photographic reconnaissance showed that torpedo planes would have to pass through a barrier of balloon cables to reach their dropping positions. Besides the massive volume of gunfire to be expected from the six battleships, nine cruisers and great number of destroyers and auxiliaries present, the permanent defences of the port comprised 21 batteries of 4-inch HA guns backed up by 200 automatic close-range weapons. Blinding illumination was to be expected from a large number of searchlights.

Unknown to them, however, were two factors which were to go a small way towards reducing the hazards and difficulties. Recent storms had damaged a great many of the barrage balloons. Only 27 would be aloft this night. Then the anti-torpedo net defence was not fully extended, partly on account of a shortage of material and partly because Admiral Campioni was unwilling to hamper the movements of ships in and out of harbour by hedging them closely round with heavy, unwieldy lines of nets, particularly as, assuming that Cunningham was on his way back to Alexandria, he was intending to take his fleet to sea the following morning to bombard the forward base at Suda Bay.

At 8.35 PM on November 11th, Kenneth Williamson led the first wave of Swordfish off the *Illustrious*' deck. An hour later the second wave was airborne.

There is no space in a book of this nature and scope for details of the individual exploits and experiences of the various aircrews as, for the wild, brief minutes of their attacks, they dipped and weaved through an apparently impenetrable storm of tracer shells and bullets.* It will suffice to say that, as the last Swordfish droned away and the gunfire ceased, Italy's serviceable battleships had been reduced to two, the *Vittorio Veneto* and the *Cesare*. Of the remainder,

---

* The attention of readers wishing to read of these is directed to a splendid account in *Taranto* by Don Newton and A. Cecil Hampshire (William Kimber).

the *Littorio* had suffered three torpedo hits, the *Duilio* one –
to be out of action for five and six months respectively – the
Cavour had been beached after being hit by a torpedo in a
vital spot and was never again to be seaworthy.*

The gallant leader of the attack, Kenneth Williamson, had
been shot down and he and his observer taken prisoner. The
crew of another plane destroyed were killed. By 2.50 AM on
the 12th all the remainder, some of them shot up and riddled
with holes, had landed safely on board their ship.

The scene in Taranto harbour which greeted the eye at
dawn on November 12th, 1940, marked, for those who had
eyes to see, the end of the battleship era in naval warfare.
For five months two opposing battle-fleets had faced each
other in the restricted waters of the Mediterranean, one unwilling to risk an action though superior in strength, the
other unable to force one. Neither had been able to wield
sea power over the other in the fullest sense. The Italians had
been unable to prevent supplies being sent to Malta by sea.
The British had been unable to cut the Italian supply line to
North Africa.

The relative strength of the two battle-fleets had now been
reversed in favour of the British. Only two battleships remained available to the Italians against five in Cunningham's
fleet. In his autobiography, Andrew Cunningham has said
that 'The crippling of half the Italian battle-fleet at a blow
at Taranto had a profound effect on the naval strategical
situation in the Mediterranean'. This judgement is open to
doubt. Certainly the dramatic success was a savage blow to
Italian morale and confidence and a welcome boost to that
of the British, at home as well as in the Mediterranean. It
also removed for Cunningham the risk, previously accepted,
of having to accept action with a greatly superior fleet.
Furthermore, he could now dispense with his two older
battleships, *Malaya* and *Ramillies*, which in turn brought
some relief to his overworked destroyer screen.

Basically, however, the naval situation in the Mediter-

* The *Andrea Doria*, which was undamaged, was not at this time
ready for service.

ranean remained virtually unchanged because battleships
were no longer the linchpin of sea power. Each side lacked
in some degree the element upon which control of the sea
had come to depend – naval air strength, offensive and
defensive.

The Italian Navy, forced to rely entirely upon an independent Air Force, poorly trained and wrongly equipped for
war over the sea, had, even prior to Taranto, been neutralized by the handful of aircraft carried by the *Illustrious* in
the eastern half and by the *Ark Royal* of Force 'H' in the
western half of the Mediterranean. The few, low-performance fighters in these two ships had been sufficient to take
much of the sting out of the efforts of the Italian bombers;
while the threat posed by the British naval torpedo planes
had more than compensated for the Italian superiority in
capital ships.

The British, on the other hand, though for the time being
they could operate at will in the central basin and so run
reinforcements safely through to Malta, could not take full
advantage of it owing to an inability of the Royal Air Force
to provide shore-based fighters and 'strike' aircraft – torpedo
carriers or dive-bombers – upon which, based on Malta, the
real control of the central Mediterranean now depended.
Thus were the British paying not only for their obstinate
parsimony towards defence requirements in the years between the wars, but for the mistaken policy that placed
responsibility for naval air requirements in the hands of an
independent air force which inevitably gave priority to its
independent rather than ancillary functions. For a maritime
empire, relying absolutely on sea power, it was disastrous.

For the time being, while the land campaign in North
Africa was hanging fire, soon to swing temporarily in favour
of the British, the consequences to the Mediterranean
theatre were not fatal. Though little or nothing could be
done to halt the flow of supplies from Italy to Libya, the
ineffectiveness of the Italian armies was reducing the importance of this. On the other hand, supply convoys to Greece
and Crete were being safely convoyed by Cunningham's

forces and Crete was being put into a reasonable state of defence.

As for Malta, a convoy of two large fast merchant ships loaded with motor transport and stores for the island, together with a third ship destined for Alexandria, had assembled at Gibraltar. A further 1,400 troops for the garrison were embarked in the cruisers *Manchester* and *Southampton*. Under cover of Admiral Somerville's Force 'H' – *Renown*, *Ark Royal*, the cruisers *Sheffield* and *Despatch* and five destroyers – they sailed eastwards on the evening of November 25th. At the same time the Mediterranean Fleet left Alexandria with a convoy of four more supply ships for Malta. On reaching the central basin, the *Ramillies* and the *Berwick* were to part company and carry on through the Sicilian Narrows to join Somerville.

It was now the turn of Somerville to try his hand at bringing an unwilling enemy to action. Both British moves were, as usual, known almost at once to the Italians. The Italian fleet, its battleship strength now reduced to the *Vittorio Veneto* and the *Cesare*, had been withdrawn to Naples since the disaster at Taranto. Force 'H' was thus the more convenient of the two possible objectives open to it. The High Command ordered Campioni to sail so as to be to the southward of Sardinia by the morning of the 27th. He had with him, besides the two battleships, six heavy cruisers and 14 destroyers. His orders were to seek battle only if he found himself faced by a decisively inferior force.

At about 10.40 A M on the 27th it seemed that that moment had come when a scouting plane from the cruiser *Bolzano* reported a force of one battleship, two cruisers and four destroyers off Bône. Signalling for full speed, Campioni turned south-eastwards on a course to intercept. 'I had in mind that the English forces were inferior to the Italian', he reported later. 'Furthermore, an encounter would be brought about in waters closer to Sicily than Sardinia, that is, in conditions favourable to us.'

Meanwhile, from the Sicilian Narrows, the *Ramillies* and *Berwick* were coming west at the former's best speed of 20 knots to join Somerville who had at 10.15 learnt of the presence of the Italian fleet. Sending his convoy away to the south-east, Somerville pushed ahead to make rendezvous with the *Ramillies* and *Berwick* and to interpose himself between the enemy and the convoy. The *Ark Royal* was ordered to prepare to launch a striking force of torpedo planes. When it became clear that the rendezvous would be made in time to engage the enemy with his whole force, Somerville was able to assess the relative strength of the two fleets. Reports from his scouting aircraft indicated that the enemy had either two or three battleships and at least six cruisers against his one modernized battlecruiser, *Renown*, one old, slow and outranged battleship, *Ramillies*, and five cruisers, two of which were cluttered with their military passengers and only one of which had 8-inch guns. Furthermore, the impending action would be fought well inside the range of Italian bomber forces based on Sardinia and Sicily.

This put the odds at first sight somewhat in favour of the enemy should he choose to stand and fight, as it would be difficult for the *Ramillies* to get into action effectively. But Somerville had in addition the uncertain asset of the *Ark Royal*'s torpedo striking force. Unfortunately, many of the pilots had only recently joined the ship. They lacked training and practice; and it must be remembered that at this stage of the war, carrier striking forces, thrown in, as they were, in small numbers, had as yet failed to justify themselves in action against squadrons of warships at sea.

By now Campioni also had received more accurate information about his opponent's strength which, as far as could be judged from a number of conflicting reports, contained two or three battleships and an aircraft carrier. His appeals for intervention by the Air Force had as yet produced neither fighter defence nor bombers. The two Admirals acted in accordance with the 'form' to be expected of them. Somerville decided that, 'Whatever the composition of the enemy Force, it was clear to me that in order to achieve my object – the safe and timely arrival of the convoy at its destination – it was essential to show a bold front and attack the enemy

as soon as possible'. Campioni, with Italy's only two serviceable battleships under his flag and hedged round by the high
command's strict instructions, declined to take up the
challenge. He signalled to his fleet to turn away for Naples.
Though the opposing cruisers had by this time come within
extreme range of each other, and the *Berwick* was damaged
in the ensuing exchange of gunfire, the faster Italian ships
drew out of range.

Somerville's only hope of catching the enemy now lay
with the Fleet Air Arm's torpedo planes – a situation which
was to be repeated many times during the war. Eleven
Swordfish attacked but none were successful. The Italians,
their superior speed unimpaired, drew steadily away to the
north-eastward and under cover of their own Air Force,
which now arrived belatedly on the scene. The Italian airmen
attacked with their customary accuracy, the *Ark Royal* at
times being completely obscured in the midst of a forest of
tall splashes from bursting bombs, only to emerge unharmed, her guns blazing furiously back at her attackers.

Nevertheless, it was undoubtedly air power which had
decided the course of events, the presence of the *Ark Royal*
weighing most heavily on Campioni's mind as he made his
decision to retire. The capital ships on either side again
failed to come within range of each other's guns. Meanwhile, the convoys for Malta had been left undisturbed to
reach harbour safely with their precious cargoes.

That the Italian Air Force was finding itself stretched
beyond the limits of its resources, as a result of Mussolini's
ill-judged attack on Greece, was evident from the fact that
for the first time Cunningham's fleet completed its cruise in
the central Mediterranean without a single gun being fired
by any of his ships. For the time being the Italian ability to
dispute control of the east–west route through the Mediterranean had vanished. On land, the Italian Army under
Marshal Graziani was defeated by General Wavell's Army
of the Nile in a three-day battle from December 9th to the
11th and expelled from Egypt with the loss of 38,300 prisoners.

British plans to take advantage of the new situation to run supply convoys through from Gibraltar to Malta and Greece, and from Alexandria to Malta, were at once put in hand. Already, however, movements were in train on the other side by which air power was to reverse the situation. The deteriorating situation in the Mediterranean was causing Hitler to cast a critical eye on his partner's efforts and to consider means of going to his assistance. His own failure to eliminate Britain by invasion was in any case leading him to turn his attention to the Mediterranean as an alternative theatre in which to strike at the British.

As yet Hitler had no intention of sending German troops to Africa. His aid to his ally was to be confined to air forces to strike at the British fleet and to neutralize Malta. Arrangements were pushed ahead, however, for the deployment on Sicilian airfields of Fliegerkorps X from Norway. This independent unit which included long-range bombers, dive-bombers, fighters and reconnaissance machines, in all some 450 aircraft, with its own defensive flak, transport, signals, bombs and fuel, had been specially trained and equipped for attacking ships. By mid-December it was on the move southwards through Italy. Early in January 1941 it was already established in some strength – some 300 aircraft of all types – under the command of General der Flieger Geister, spread between the airfields of Catania, Comiso, Trapani, Palermo and Reggio Calabria. It was to advertise its arrival in dramatic fashion.

3

Luftwaffe and Afrika Korps Intervene

THE IMPROVED situation in the Mediterranean brought about by the reduction of the enemy's battleship strength at Taranto and the dispersal of the Italian air effort was quickly turned to account. From Alexandria a convoy of four store ships for Malta sailed on December 16th with only the battleship *Malaya* and four destroyers as escort. Admiral Cunningham was able to spread the remainder of his force over several widely separated tasks. Rear-Admiral Rawlings, commanding the 1st Battle Squadron, was left with his flag-ship, *Barham*, in operational control of the naval forces operating in support of the army along the Libyan coast. The remainder of the fleet took the route north of Crete so that the *Illustrious*' aircraft could strike at Italian airfields on Stampalia and Rhodes. Then, after refuelling at Suda Bay on the 17th, the fleet steered north-eastward into the Ionian Sea, the cruisers going ahead to make an exploratory sweep of the Adriatic while the *Warspite* and *Valiant* hurled one hundred 15-inch shells into the Albanian port of Valona, the main supply port for the Italian Army in the Balkans. The material damage done was not great, but it served to advertise the freedom of action of the British fleet in Mussolini's *Mare Nostrum*.

Malta, too, was enjoying a respite from air attack, during which the repair facilities of the dockyard were got back into fair working order. Cunningham's flagship entered the Grand Harbour for the first time since May to a frenzied welcome by the populace which was extended to the Admiral himself as he went about inspecting naval establishments.

Only with regard to the air strength on the island was the situation unsatisfactory, falling far short in quantity and type of what had been urgently requested by Air Chief Marshal Longmore. The fighter defences were still only 16 Hurricanes, while to the original striking force of 12 naval Swordfish of 830 Squadron, only 16 Wellington bombers had been added. These, nevertheless, were having some effect, bombing the Italians in the harbours of Brindisi, Bari and Taranto whence supplies for their armies in Greece were shipped; Naples, where the serviceable ships of the Italian Navy were concentrated, and where the cruiser *Pola* and the battleship *Cesare* were damaged by them; and Tripoli, the North African terminus of the trans-Mediterranean supply line. Beaufort torpedo aircraft to attack convoys at sea had been asked for, but none were available. For long-range naval reconnaissance there were still only the four Sunderland flying-boats and four Marylands.

Meanwhile, Rear-Admiral Lyster with the remainder of the fleet cruised unchallenged in the Sicilian Channel and aircraft from the *Illustrious* sank two out of three ships of an Italian convoy on its way to Tripoli, and went on to attack the port itself and shipping in the harbour. The *Malaya*, escorting two empty store ships westward, similarly passed through the Sicilian Narrows to join Force 'H' without interference by the enemy except for a submarine attack off Pantellaria which sank the destroyer *Hyperion*.

On land the prospect seemed equally bright. The Greeks were having wide-spread successes against the Italian invaders. In North Africa the British Army of the Nile was preparing a further offensive which would drive the Italians out of Cyrenaica. Both on land and sea, however, it was to prove a false dawn. It had long been expected that Germany would feel impelled sooner or later to come south to aid and inspire her less enterprising ally. That Mussolini himself had not been satisfied with the higher direction of his Navy was indicated by the dismissal on December 8th of Admiral Cavagnari as Chief of Staff. His successor was Admiral Arturo Riccardi who, since the beginning of the war, had held commands ashore and, with no experience of action, was in no position to advocate a more spirited policy for the

Italian fleet. At the same time Admiral Campioni was replaced as Commander-in-Chief by Admiral Angelo Iachino,
an officer of great repute in the Italian Navy who had
previously commanded the Italian cruiser force which had
acquitted itself well in the inconclusive action with Force
'H' south of Sardinia in November.

However, the situation was not one which could be improved by a change in the structure of the high command.
The Italian Navy, not unreasonably, felt itself hamstrung by
the inefficiency of the air reconnaissance at its disposal and
the ineffectiveness of the striking power of the Air Force. It
was very willing to accept the aid of Fliegerkorps X. The
Italian Army, outclassed both in Africa and Greece, was
equally in need of assistance from the Wehrmacht. Hitler
was not yet contemplating a heavy involvement in either
theatre; but early in January he was to give orders for the
formation of an 'Afrika Korps' primarily equipped for
defence and which was intended to stiffen the Italian defence
of Tripolitania. In Greece, the Italian failure was soon to
imperil his plan to attack Russia and he would be forced to
intervene to secure the flank of his line of advance. Thus, as
1940 came to an end, forces were already on the move which
would dim the brighter prospects which seemed to be
opening up for the British in the Mediterranean.

A large-scale convoy movement (Operation 'Excess') had
meanwhile been planned. Following the now well-tried
practice, five ships – one with 4,000 tons of ammunition, the
equally crucial cargo of 3,000 tons of seed potatoes for
Malta, as well as 12 crated Hurricanes, and four ships for
the Piraeus with urgent supplies for Greece – were to come
from Gibraltar under cover of Force 'H'. In the eastern
Mediterranean two laden supply ships for Malta and two
convoys of empties to Alexandria would be covered by
Cunningham's cruisers commanded by the Vice-Admiral,
Light Forces, H. D. Pridham-Wippell. The Commander-in-
Chief with his carrier and two battleships would go ahead
to meet the supply convoy from the west in the Sicilian
Channel.

The operation was planned to take place late in December, but events outside the Mediterranean interposed to cause a delay. The transports sailed from England with a large convoy routed round the Cape, from which they were to break off when the latitude of Gibraltar was reached. On Christmas Day this convoy was attacked by the cruiser *Hipper* out in the Atlantic and was forced to scatter. Force 'H' was hurried to sea to the rescue. Meeting heavy weather, Admiral Somerville's flagship *Renown* received damage to her starboard bulge which spread to her side plating. Thus not only was the arrival of the transports for 'Excess' delayed, but the *Renown* had to be taken in hand for repairs before the operation could be initiated. Then one of the transports for Greece was driven ashore in a gale and could not take part. So it was not until the evening of January 6th, 1941, that Force 'H' and the four remaining transports were able to sail from Gibraltar. In the meantime, the dive-bombers of Fliegerkorps X had been given time to deploy on the airfields of Sicily.

Somerville's force comprised only the *Renown, Malaya, Ark Royal*, the cruiser *Sheffield* and six destroyers, while the new light cruiser *Bonaventure* and four destroyers formed the convoy's close escort. Though the cruisers *Southampton* and *Gloucester* from Cunningham's force were to come through the Narrows to join the convoy escort for the last part of its journey to Malta, Force 'H' was markedly inferior to the Italian fleet grouped round the *Vittorio Veneto* and *Cesare* based at Naples, in a good position to intercept it south of Sardinia. The interconnection of sea and air operations and the importance of Malta as an offensive base was clearly demonstrated when, on the night of January 8th, the small force of Wellingtons on the island raided Naples and so damaged the *Cesare* with a near-miss that both she and the *Vittorio Veneto* were hastily withdrawn to Genoa. The operations of both British fleets were thus relieved of all threat of surface opposition.

For a while it seemed as though the air threat was to be of its usual spectacular but rather ineffective nature. Ten

Savoia 79s straddled but failed to hit the *Malaya* and *Gloucester*, losing two of their numbers to Fulmars of the *Ark Royal* shortly before Force 'H' turned back to Gibraltar at dusk on the 9th. The same afternoon a force of bombers and fighters seeking Cunningham's force failed to find it and expended its bombs unsuccessfully on shipping in harbour. Sporadic attacks by small groups of bombers and torpedo planes on the various units escorting and covering the convoy during its passage of the Sicilian Channel were uniformly unsuccessful.

Dawn on January 10th found the convoy and its escort still to the westward of Malta. Covering it was Cunningham's main force – *Warspite, Valiant, Illustrious* and five destroyers. His cruisers, *Gloucester, Southampton* and *Bonaventure*, were escorting the destroyer *Gallant* which had struck a mine and was being towed into Malta by the *Mohawk*. The forenoon passed quietly. It seemed that the operation – the most ambitious and complex convoy operation so far attempted – was achieving complete success. An Italian reconnaissance plane was chopped out of the sky with deadly efficiency by Fulmars from the *Illustrious*. At 1.30 PM two torpedo planes came in low to attack the battleship. Their torpedoes were avoided; but the attempt was nevertheless to have a fateful consequence. From their station high above the fleet the Fulmars on patrol came swooping down in chase of the two Savoias. Hardly had they done so when to the northward against the clear blue of the sky was seen a host of aircraft approaching in their squadrons. These were the Junkers 87s (Stukas), the true dive-bombers which could plummet vertically out of the sky to drop their 1,000-lb bombs with great accuracy and which were now making their début in the Mediterranean theatre. Behind them could be seen further formations of twin-engine Junkers 88s, more strictly 'glide' than 'dive' bombers, but carrying a heavier load of bombs and better able to defend themselves against fighters.

The slow-climbing Fulmars, recalled from their chase, clawed their way upwards to the defence, but neither they nor fresh fighters hastily flown off by the carrier could gain height quickly enough to intervene in good time. The Stukas were the first to attack. They concentrated principally upon the *Illustrious*. Every gun in the fleet opened on them but, as had been learnt earlier in the Norwegian campaign, in the absence of fighter defence only close-range automatic weapons in numbers far greater than those mounted in British warships could offer an effective defence.

To Admiral Cunningham it was a revelation of what efficiently used and properly equipped air power could achieve in sea warfare, as bomb after bomb struck the carrier.

One was too interested in this new form of dive-bombing attack really to be frightened [he was to write later], and there was no doubt we were watching complete experts. Formed roughly in a large circle over the fleet they peeled off one by one when reaching the attacking position. We could not but admire the skill and precision of it all.

For ten minutes the *Illustrious* steamed through a hail of bombs raising their leaping brown columns of water as they exploded close alongside. Six times she shuddered under the impact of direct hits, some of which penetrated by means of the lift-wells to the hangars and lower deck spaces. Her steering gear was wrecked and, with her flight deck damaged and fires blazing fore and aft, she circled helplessly. But for her armoured flight deck, which absorbed the shock of some of the hits, the *Illustrious* must have been sunk. As it was, though hit yet again in a later attack, she was able to limp away to reach Malta dockyard for temporary repairs. On the following day the dive-bombers struck again, this time at the *Gloucester* and *Southampton* to the south-eastward of Malta where they had joined the escort of the slow convoy for Alexandria. Both ships were hit. The *Gloucester* was fortunate in that a bomb which plunged down through five decks failed to explode; but the *Southampton* was so heavily damaged that she had to be abandoned and sunk.

Thus, thunderously, the pilots of Fliegerkorps X advertised

to the world their arrival on the Mediterranean scene
and ushered in a new phase of the campaign. Benefiting from
their none too brilliant experiences in the Norwegian campaign and perhaps inspired by the demonstration of what
could be done by such properly trained dive-bombers as the
Skuas of the Fleet Air Arm, which had sunk the *Königsberg*
in a few minutes of dive-bombing, they had undergone
special training for ship attack.

The consequences seemed likely to be decisive. The several
convoys had, to be sure, reached their destinations unscathed; but the cost in ships of war had been prohibitive.
Britain's few aircraft carriers were of incalculable importance to her prosecution of the war at sea. Though the
Illustrious had reached the shelter of the Grand Harbour,
Malta's still puny defences were unlikely to save her from
further and probably fatal attacks. Carriers – by now
established as the major units of the British fleet – could no
longer be risked in the central basin of the Mediterranean.
Thus the task of disputing the control of the vital convoy
routes supplying the Italian and German forces in Africa
would now rest upon Malta, the unsinkable but still poorly
equipped carrier.

The Germans were alive to the importance of neutralizing
the island, though, except for a far-sighted few, of whom
Rommel was one, they did not appreciate the absolute
necessity to eliminate it permanently. Fliegerkorps X was
given the task, but it was not until six days after the *Illustrious* entered the Grand Harbour that they were ready to
attack in force. The breathing space was made good use of
to hasten temporary repairs to the carrier. The first massive
raid by some 60 dive-bombers on the 16th was concentrated
on the dockyard where she lay but she escaped with minor
damage from a single bomb hit. On the 18th, the attackers
turned their attention to Malta's airfields and establishments. The carrier was almost ready to sail by the following
day when another raid on the dockyard caused her further
underwater damage. Nevertheless, in spite of all the enemy
could do, as darkness was settling down over the harbour on

the 23rd, the *Illustrious* crept slowly out between the heads of the breakwater unobserved by enemy planes and was soon making 20 knots towards Alexandria on the first leg of the long journey which was to take her to Norfolk, Virginia, for repairs.

Though the *Illustrious* had thus escaped the full consequences of the new turn of events, Malta was to continue to suffer under a succession of massive blows as Stukas and Me 110s streaked in for combined dive-bombing and low-level attacks, while Ju 88s and He 111 and Savoia bombers with fighter escort bombed from on high. It was little enough that the few fighters available on the island could do in reply. At any one time about six Hurricanes comprised the total force of high-performance fighters which could take the air. In addition there might be three of the Fulmars disembarked from the *Illustrious* and perhaps one of the surviving Gladiators. Between these fighters and the gun defences of the island 16 Axis aircraft were accounted for, but it was not enough to deter them. Through January, February and March the raids went on incessantly.

Yet, though the island's defences were almost negligible, its ability to strike back was far from paralysed. The Wellingtons of No 148 Squadron bombed the Sicilian airfields, destroying a number of aircraft and damaging hangars and facilities; while the Swordfish of 830 Squadron, in cooperation with the scouting Sunderlands, had notable successes against Italian convoys bound for Libya even while the air raids were at their height. Nor did the enemy raids prevent the re-establishment of a submarine base on Malta from which, in the months to come, the most deadly menace to the Libyan convoys was to operate. Had Fliegerkorps X been able to continue to throw their full weight of attack on Malta the outcome might have been different. But events elsewhere in the Mediterranean were to intervene and to mask the over-riding importance of Malta from the Italian and German strategic viewpoint. They were also to demonstrate the closely woven interdependence of the various sectors of the Mediterranean theatre.

In North Africa the British Army of the Nile had advanced to capture Tobruk on January 22nd, and by February 6th the Italian armies had been driven from Cyrenaica. German fears for their ally's ability to defend Tripolitania had already led to Hitler's order to form an Afrika Korps, the transport of which was begun at the beginning of February 1941. As a further stiffening of Italian defence, nearly half of Fliegerkorps X, mostly dive-bombers and fighters, was transferred to North Africa. Consequently, though the supply ships supporting the British Army, and their escorts, began to suffer painful losses, the intensity of the assault on Malta began to fall away just when the situation on the island was becoming critical.

Nevertheless, the situation during March seemed grim and foreboding, owing to the air supremacy established by the Luftwaffe. Along the Libyan coast, warships of the Inshore Squadron were being lost or damaged almost daily. The naval Commander-in-Chief added his appeals to those of his Air Force colleague for reinforcements of fighter aircraft.

> There seems to be some bad misunderstanding about the state of our Air Force out here [he wrote to the First Sea Lord on March 11th]. I feel the Chiefs of Staff are badly misinformed about the number of fighter squadrons available. Longmore is absolutely stretched to the limit and we seem to have far fewer than is supposed at home. We are getting sat on by the Germans in Cyrenaica. The figures there are over two hundred German and Italian fighters against thirty of our own.
>
> [As for Malta], I have just seen the Air Vice-Marshal who is here to report. He tells me that the Germans are right on top of them. He has only eight serviceable Hurricanes left. . . He is being sent six from the shortage here; but that is no good. He ought to have two full squadrons and at once.

On hearing that he had been created a Knight Grand Cross of the Bath, Admiral Cunningham commented bitterly, 'I would sooner have had three squadrons of Hurricanes'. With a massive threat building up in the Balkans and in Libya, the air – and consequently the naval – situation was indeed desperate. Nevertheless, with the arrival on March 10th of the new carrier *Formidable* via the Suez Canal to replace the damaged *Illustrious*, Cunningham succeeded in running a convoy of four supply ships through to Malta without interference by the enemy.

On the other hand, beginning early in February, the Italians had been transporting to Tripoli the German Afrika Korps, an operation with which the British had been unable seriously to interfere. It had become possible during February to establish a few of the new small 'U' Class submarines at Malta, the nucleus of a flotilla which was to gain imperishable fame and to have in time a considerable effect on the campaign. The *Upright*, commanded by Lieutenant E. D. Norman, torpedoed and sank the Italian cruiser *Armando Diaz* on the night of February 25th; but it was not until well into March that the Malta flotilla was able to discover the best means of getting at the Libyan convoys. By that time most of the Afrika Korps, its original defensive structure transformed by the addition of a Panzer Division, had reached its destination. The German high command sent one of its few congratulatory messages to the Italian Navy: 'Particularly gratifying is the fact that this operation could be carried out with so few losses, notwithstanding the great difficulties and the dangers of enemy action.' Before the impending storm broke in Libya and in Greece upon the British armies, outnumbered and almost without air support, the Italian Navy was to take a humiliating knock and lose this new-found respect of its critical ally.

The Germans had been far from pleased with the efforts of the Italian Navy to interfere with the stream of supply ships and troop transports from Egypt reaching Greece, where their invasion was soon to be launched. As early as February 14th, at a meeting at Merano between Admiral Riccardi and Grand Admiral Raeder, the latter had urged that surface units of the Italian fleet should go over to the offensive by striking at this supply traffic. Riccardi's objections, based on the distances involved and the ability of the British, with their superior air reconnaissance, to evade any such threat, seemed at the time to have been accepted. But early in March the Germans again brought political pressure at the highest levels to spur the Italian Navy into action. From the *Comando Supremo* orders went out to the naval Chief of Staff, Riccardi, and thence to the Commander-in-Chief, Iachino, that an offensive strike was to be mounted. To meet the Navy's objections, the Luftwaffe promised extensive cooperation by Fliegerkorps X – aerial reconnaissance over Alexandria and the central and eastern Mediterranean and air cover for the fleet throughout daylight hours as far east as Cape Matapan. To ensure the efficiency of this operation, Fliekerkorps X was to carry out an escort and ship identification exercise for a large number of its aircraft over the Italian Fleet on its first morning at sea, south of the Messina Straits. The Italian Air Force promised fighter cover from Rhodes while the fleet was in Cretan waters and air attacks on the airfields on Crete. All this had as its primary object the achievement of surprise on the part of the Italian fleet and assurance against it being itself surprised by the British Mediterranean Fleet. Finally, to calm Italian misgivings, the Luftwaffe claimed that their torpedo planes had crippled two of Cunningham's battleships on March 16th – a claim with no foundation in fact.

Fortified by these assurances, though far from convinced of their reliability or of the practical value of an operation which would make a heavy drain on Italy's diminishing stocks of oil fuel, Admiral Angelo Iachino sailed from Naples on the evening of March 26th, his flag flying in the *Vittorio Veneto*. At dawn the next day he passed through the Straits of Messina in company with the four destroyers of his screen and preceded by the 3rd Division of heavy cruisers – *Trieste, Trento, Bolzano,* and destroyers. From Taranto the 1st Division – *Zara, Pola* and *Fiume* – and from Brindisi the 8th Division – light cruisers *Abruzzi* and *Garibaldi* – had sailed with their attendant destroyers for a rendezvous with the Commander-in-Chief about 60 miles east of Augusta. The Fleet then proceeded in company on a course which would take it to the vicinity of Gavdo Island to the southward of Crete.

Iachino's doubts of the efficiency of the air cooperation promised him were strengthened by the failure of any of Fliegerkorps X to appear for the exercise planned for the morning of the 27th, or to prevent a British Sunderland on reconnaissance from reporting him. Though from its report, which the Italians were able to decode, it was evident that only one division of cruisers had actually been sighted in the low visibility prevailing, Iachino knew from that moment that any prospect of achieving surprise had gone.

The flying-boat's report was correctly interpreted at Alexandria. The increased aerial reconnaissance activity by the enemy over the last few days had already suggested that some activity by the Italian fleet might be expected. Under cover of darkness that evening the Mediterranean Fleet slipped away to sea – *Warspite, Barham, Valiant, Formidable* and attendant destroyers – and steered to place itself between the enemy force and the convoy route to Greece, a course which would lead to roughly the same position south of Gavdo Island as that planned for the *Vittorio Veneto*. Vice-Admiral Pridham-Wippell, who, in the *Orion*, with the *Ajax, Perth* and *Gloucester* and four destroyers, had been operating in the Aegean, was also given a rendezvous for dawn on the 28th to the south-west of Gavdo.

Thus, through the night of March 27th–28th, the two fleets were hurrying towards a head-on clash the following morning, an encounter which was to develop into the Battle of Matapan. Full details of this action can be found in the book with that title by Captain S. W. C. Pack and need not be repeated here. It is sufficient to say that Admiral Iachino was justified in his mistrust of the air cooperation promised him, which left him unprotected against the air attacks mounted by the Royal Air Force bombers and the torpedo planes of the *Formidable* and ignorant for much of the day of the position and composition of the forces opposing him.

This mistrust led him, however, into a fatal error of judgement. Given the choice of believing either the information provided, late in the day, by a reconnaissance plane which made it clear that Cunningham's battle squadron was in close pursuit, or an estimate of Cunningham's position based on radio direction finding which placed him some 170 miles astern, he chose the latter. To the assistance of the cruiser *Pola*, hit and immobilized by a torpedo from one of the *Formidable*'s Swordfish and left behind as the remainder ran for base, he sent the cruisers *Zara* and *Fiume* and four destroyers. Running blindly athwart the course of the British battle-fleet during the night, both cruisers and two of the destroyers were blown out of the water. The *Pola* was then sunk at leisure. The *Vittorio Veneto*, also torpedoed by the Fleet Air Arm, and for a time in danger of being overtaken by the British battleships, escaped.

Once again an encounter between the two fleets had been dominated by the air element, the battleships on either side never coming within range of each other's guns. On this occasion the failure of the German and Italian Air Forces to fulfil their obligations to support the Italian fleet had permitted the handful of aircraft, RAF and Fleet Air Arm, firstly to give the British Commander-in-Chief the information necessary to bring his unwilling enemy to action, and then to cripple some of his fleeing units, delivering them to destruction by gun-fire. The Italians, in contrast, fighting blindly and without fighter protection, were perhaps lucky to escape greater losses.

Even while the Battle of Matapan was coming to its violent and bloody end, final preparations were being made by the Germans and Italians in Libya and the Balkans for massive assaults which, in the course of a few brief weeks, were drastically to alter the situation in the Mediterranean in their favour. On March 31st the Italo-German army attacked in Libya. By April 3rd Benghazi had fallen and the British army was in full retreat. On the 6th the German 12th Army crossed the frontier from Bulgaria into Greece and began the offensive which was, in less than three weeks, to give them possession of the whole of that country.

The former was to bring down on Admiral Cunningham's head unjustified exhortations, from a government not far from panic, to stop the Italian convoys carrying supplies to the German Afrika Korps. The latter was soon to involve the Mediterranean Fleet in hazardous and costly operations firstly to evacuate the Army from Greece and then to repel the enemy's efforts to invade Crete by sea, and finally to bring away the soldiers from Crete when it was captured by airborne invasion.

Cunningham had always pointed out to the Government that the interruption of the Libyan convoys was dependent upon the use of Malta as an air and sea base. Early in March the heavy losses on the ground amongst the Wellingtons of No 148 Squadron had necessitated the temporary withdrawal of the squadron to Egypt, leaving the handful of Swordfish as the only offensive air strength available. His appeals and those of his air colleague, Air Chief Marshal Longmore, for fighter reinforcements, had received scant satisfaction. A beginning was now made in building up the island's air defences by the dispatch of a dozen Hurricanes to Gibraltar in the *Argus*. There they were transferred to the *Ark Royal* which, under the cover of Force 'H', flew them off to Malta from a position south of Sardinia, on April 3rd. Though a further 23 Hurricanes were later sent by the same means on April 27th and 47 more on May 21st, for the time being Malta could do little to defend itself against the assaults of Fliegerkorps X, let alone strike at the Italian convoys in any strength.

In spite of the insecurity of the base, however, Cunningham, on April 11th, sent four destroyers of the 14th Flotilla – *Jervis*, *Janus*, *Mohawk* and *Nubian* – under Captain Philip Mack of the *Jervis*, to act as a raiding force. In an area so dominated by enemy air power, it could only operate by night. Lacking radar, interception of convoys reported by air reconnaissance was a chancy business. Nevertheless they were quickly successful.

A convoy of five transports escorted by three Italian

destroyers had been located following the route along the Tunisian coast to Tripoli. As dusk was falling on April 15th, Mack led his force to sea and steered to intercept it off the Kerkenah Banks, some 30 miles to seaward of Sfax. By 1.45 AM the flotilla had reached the estimated point of interception, and, in fact, was passing the enemy on an opposite course, all unawares, at a range of three miles. A quarter moon hung in a clear sky to the south-eastward, against which they should have been sighted by the Italian look-outs as they approached. Instead it was the British who were to enjoy the advantage of surprise when at 1.58, having turned back, they saw the convoy silhouetted against the moon-light, six miles ahead.

Steering so as to keep the enemy between him and the moon, Mack brought his ships up from astern and on a parallel course to that of his unsuspecting prey. At 2.20, the guns of the *Jervis* flashed out at the nearest Italian destroyer. This was the *Lampo*, where the startled captain had barely time to call for full speed and fire three salvos from his guns before they were put out of action and his ship brought to a standstill. His torpedoes were launched but went wide.

The next escort to be engaged was the *Baleno*. The first salvo from the *Nubian* hit squarely on her bridge, wiping out at one blow the Italian captain and all his officers. Hammered to a wreck, the *Baleno* drifted helplessly out of the fight.

While the British destroyers were now turning their attention to the transports (one of which, the Italian ship *Sabaudia*, loaded with ammunition, blew up in a spectacular explosion), the escort commander, Commander Pietro de Cristoforo, in the destroyer *Tarigo*, turned back from his position ahead of the convoy and gallantly threw himself between the attackers and their prey. Mortally wounded by the first salvo aimed at his ship, his steering gear wrecked, a storm of shells tearing his ship apart, Cristoforo retained sufficient control of his ship, in its last moments before sinking, to launch three torpedoes at the *Mohawk*. Two of them found their mark, sinking the British destroyer, in which two officers and 39 ratings lost their lives.

These were the only British casualties. The remaining four transports, all German and loaded with troops and supplies for Rommel, were sunk as were the *Baleno* and *Tarigo*. The *Lampo* drifted on to the Kerkenah Bank and was eventually salved by the Italians. The 350 men, 300 vehicles and 3,500 tons of stores destroyed in the merchant ships represented the most serious loss suffered by the Afrika Korps during its initial transport to Libya. Except for one ship torpedoed and sunk by Swordfish of 830 Squadron, the only other losses inflicted on the Libyan traffic from the beginning of January to the end of April 1941 were the work of British submarines which sank 10 ships totalling 27,168 tons during that period.

In time to come, as Malta's air strength was re-established, aircraft were to assume great importance in the struggle to cut Rommel's lifeline, and, though the submarines based on Malta were to have the greatest and most consistent successes, it is not too much to say that between them these two arms were to have a decisive influence on the battle for the Mediterranean. Details of their operations will be examined later.

Meanwhile, so far as the existing striking power of Malta-based forces allowed, everything possible was being done. The Government at home, however, suffering the consequences of their failure to equip Malta in good time, were now so alarmed at the deteriorating situation in Libya and Greece that they were demanding 'drastic measures to stabilize the position in the Middle East'. Suggestions were made that Cunningham should attempt a combined blocking and bombardment of the port of Tripoli, using the battleship *Barham* and a cruiser for block-ships. Examination of the proposal showed it to be completely impracticable. Against his own judgement, and protesting that the elimination of Tripoli's port facilities was a task for air power, as he felt he knew well from the experiences at Greek ports under aerial bombardment by the Luftwaffe, Cunningham agreed to carry out instead a bombardment of Tripoli. Achieving complete surprise and coordination with air attack by

Malta's Swordfish and Wellingtons, his fleet wreaked heavy damage on the city and withdrew without any interference by the enemy's air force based on the nearby airfield of Castel Benito.

Nevertheless the port itself suffered little and efforts by the Government to induce Cunningham to repeat an operation which, in his opinion, was not worth the very heavy risks involved, petered out, overtaken by events elsewhere which absorbed all the fleet's resources. For on the same day as the bombardment the decision was taken by the Government that British forces in Greece must be evacuated. An ordeal thus began which, with a brief interval, continued for soldiers and sailors alike, as they fought under a sky dominated by more than 500 aircraft of Fliegerkorps X and VIII, until June 1st, when the last men were evacuated from Crete.

4

Greece and Crete: Triumph of the Luftwaffe

OF THE several periods of the Second World War during which Britain's hopes of avoiding defeat seemed to have sunk almost to vanishing point, few can have been more fraught with doom than the spring and early summer of 1941. In North Africa, General Wavell's Army of the Nile, its numbers and its exiguous air strength both greatly reduced by the dispatch of assistance to Greece, had been unable to withstand the counter-attack of the enemy, now revitalized by General Erwin Rommel and his Afrika Korps. Cyrenaica, with the exception of Tobruk, was once again in enemy hands.

In Greece the British aid sent at such sacrifice had been insufficient to prevent the German 12th Army, covered by the overwhelming air superiority of Fliegerkorps VIII and part of Fliegerkorps X, from over-running the whole country in less than three weeks. By April 21st it was clear that the troops so arduously transported there would have to be evacuated. That it would have to be done by night and under conditions of daunting difficulty was stressed when, on the 21st and 22nd, the enemy's unopposed Air Force destroyed 23 ships, including a Greek destroyer and two hospital ships in Greek waters.

The general plan for Operation 'Demon', as it was named, was for the troops to make a fighting retreat to a number of beaches which could be reached by reasonably good roads. There, as soon as it was dark, the rescue ships would arrive, while a swarm of caiques, motor-boats and local craft would ferry the men off to them. These few sentences cover a complexity of organization, a degree of inspired improvisation in a constantly changing situation and an infinite variety of unpredictable events such as to require a book devoted entirely to the operation to give a full, detailed account.

Fifty-one thousand troops had to make their way under ceaseless attack by the Stukas to the various beaches allotted to them – Megara, Raphina and Raphtis near Athens, Nauplia, Tolon, Monemvasia and Kalamata in Morea. From his headquarters at Suda Bay, Vice-Admiral Pridham-Wippell directed the movements of a great assortment of ships and craft. Of warships there were 4 cruisers – his flagship, *Orion*, the *Ajax*, *Phoebe* and HM Australian Ship *Perth*; 3 anti-aircraft cruisers, *Calcutta*, *Coventry* and *Carlisle*; 20 destroyers; 3 frigates; and the infantry assault ships *Glenearn* and *Glengyle*. Under the Red Ensign were 19 medium-sized troop ships. Every available small craft was also sent to the beaches including a number of 'A' lighters, forerunners of the LCTs.

By April 24th the various columns of troops had reached their allotted beaches. Exhausted, hungry and harried as they were, their morale remained high and Rear-Admiral Baillie Grohman, the Naval Liaison officer, later recorded that 'the Army organization in rear of the beaches and the discipline of the troops were magnificent; especially considering that they had been fighting a rearguard action for some weeks, from Salonika almost to Cape Matapan'.

That night the darkened ships crept shoreward to anchor as close in as possible, and soon the first small craft, loaded to the gunwales with troops, were bumping alongside.

So began the first of three major operations in which almost the entire British Mediterranean Fleet was engaged, succouring and supporting the Army in its struggle against impossible odds. During this phase, the bomber squadrons of the Luftwaffe had not yet had time to move their bases forward. Losses amongst the warships which could get well away from the coast were consequently comparatively light. Four troopships, however, were sunk, *Pennland*, *Slamat*, *Costa Rica* and *Ulster Prince*. At one or two of the embarkation points there were wharves and jetties at which the small craft could load or the smaller ships – destroyers and troop carriers – could themselves secure. But in general it was from open beaches that the evacuation took place, a process painfully slow. Each night at 3 AM embarkation was halted and the ships hastened seawards to be away before the Luftwaffe's dive-bombers found them.

The fate awaiting any ship which lingered beyond this hour rather than abandon troops on the shore was shown in the case of the *Slamat* which did not clear from Nauplia until 4.15 on the morning of the 27th. Soon after daylight the Stukas found her and quickly sent her to the bottom. The destroyers *Diamond* and *Wryneck* were sent to her aid and picked up 700 men, being dive-bombed the while. Rescue operations completed, they steered at high speed for Suda Bay only to be set upon once again by dive-bombers who this time made no mistake, sending both ships to the bottom with the loss of all on board except one officer, 41 ratings and eight soldiers.

Nevertheless, this was the only serious loss amongst the 50,732 troops embarked from Greece, about 80 per cent of the total originally sent to that country. The majority were transported back to Egypt, but 16,000 were left to form the garrison for Crete which, it was decided, must be held at all costs.

Before this phase of the campaign began there was a pause during which Cunningham might have expected a brief respite for his hard-driven cruisers and destroyers and rest for their crews. Bombed almost continuously during daylight hours whenever they had put to sea since the operation to reinforce Greece had begun on March 5th, the ships and their machinery were accumulating damage and defects. That officers and men were also showing signs of strain is not surprising. There was to be no respite, however, and little rest. Once again the situation in the campaign on land called for urgent, large-scale efforts by the Navy to rectify it. On April 20th General Wavell had reported to the Chiefs of Staff that a German Panzer Division had been identified in North Africa. Tank reinforcements to enable him to cope with this large access of strength to the enemy were urgently required. The Prime Minister, declaring that 'the fate of the war in the Middle East, the loss of the Suez Canal, the frustration or confusion of the enormous forces we have built up in Egypt ... all may turn on a few hundred armoured vehicles', brushed aside the Admiralty's previously expressed reluctance, since the arrival of the Luftwaffe in Sicily, to run convoys through the central Mediterranean. Even before the evacuation from Greece had been completed, a convoy of five transports carrying tanks for the Army of the Nile had sailed from England, and an attempt was to be made to run them through the Mediterranean, under cover of Force 'H' as far as the Sicilian Narrows and of the Mediterranean Fleet from the Malta Channel onwards. The operation was given the code name 'Tiger' and was to be of a complex but, by now, in its main features, familiar pattern.

As usual, Admiral Cunningham was to seize the opportunity to throw supplies into beleaguered Malta by means of two convoys, a slow one of two tankers with oil-fuel and a fast one of four supply ships – each convoy with a close escort of cruisers and destroyers. In addition there would be the special supply ship HMS *Breconshire*, with oil-fuel and munitions, which had already begun her long career of hazardous voyages to relieve Malta where eventually she was to meet her heroic end. On this occasion she was to sail with the main covering force from Alexandria, comprising the *Warspite*, *Barham*, *Valiant*, the carrier *Formidable*, the cruisers *Orion*, *Ajax* and *Perth*, the fast minelayer *Abdiel* and all available destroyers. Opportunity would also be taken to send a small force to bombard Benghazi both on the outward and return journeys of the Fleet.

From Gibraltar Admiral Somerville's Force 'H' – *Renown*, *Ark Royal*, *Sheffield* and nine destroyers – would bring, besides the convoy, reinforcements for the Mediterranean Fleet in the shape of the battleship *Queen Elizabeth* and the cruisers *Naiad* and *Fiji*. A new feature in this operation was the dispatch to Malta from England of 15 Beaufighters of No 252 Squadron to give long-range fighter protection to the 'Tiger' convoy to the eastward of Malta.

Operation 'Tiger', which had seemed to the Admiralty a hazardous gamble, went off with a smoothness exceeding all expectations. Not until the morning of May 8th did the Italian air reconnaissance discover the presence of Force 'H' and the convoy, by which time they were already to the southward of Sardinia. It was too late then for interception by the Italian fleet even had the Italians been prepared to risk their only two operational battleships. Air attacks during the day were harassed and broken up by the little force of Fulmar fighters from the *Ark Royal*, though Somerville's flagship, *Renown*, had a narrow escape from an aerial torpedo.

At dusk the entrance to the Narrows was reached where Force 'H' turned back, its part of the operation completed without loss. With the *Queen Elizabeth*, *Naiad*, *Fiji* and the destroyers of its close escort, the convoy steamed on through the shallow, mine-strewn waters of the Skerki Channel. It was open, in the bright moonlight, to attack by the enemy's light forces, motor torpedo boats, submarines and torpedo aircraft; but the Italians made no effort to intervene. Only the mines took their toll. The transport *Empire Song* exploded two of them. Fire breaking out in her ammunition hold, she was abandoned shortly before blowing up and sinking. The *New Zealand Star* struck another mine but was only slightly damaged.

The following morning, the 9th, the convoy and escort came under the 'umbrella' of the Beaufighters from Malta and that afternoon made rendezvous with the Mediterranean Fleet. In poor visibility with much low cloud the bombers of the Luftwaffe and the Regia Aeronautica failed to make contact. Meanwhile, the convoys for Malta had been safely conducted into the Grand Harbour, led by the *Gloxinia*, the solitary minesweeper available, whose magnetic sweep exploded nearly a dozen mines.

These convoys and the Mediterranean Fleet had left Alexandria on the 5th and 6th. During the 7th, the cruiser *Ajax* and three destroyers had been detached to bombard

T–C

Benghazi that night. In spite of the bright moonlight and the aid of star-shells, it proved difficult to select worthwhile targets inside the harbour where the damage done was not great; fortune smiled on them, nevertheless, when two ships, fully loaded with ammunition, were encountered in the offing and were sunk. This was a bitter blow to Rommel who, that same day, was reporting on the grave consequences of any further delay of seaborne supplies and that the 'supply situation was extremely critical'. On May 1st a lone British bomber, making a daring low-level attack on Tripoli harbour, had blown up an ammunition ship, which wrecked the only quay at which tanks and trucks could be unloaded. Two days later two more ships had been destroyed when German bombs carried by one of them had spontaneously exploded.

Not until the night of the 10th did enemy bombers, taking advantage of a clear night and a full moon, succeed in attacking the 'Tiger' convoy and the fleet. Met by a tremendous gun barrage they had no success whatever. The following day, a return of the poor visibility and the capable handling of the *Formidable*'s Fulmars held them at arm's length. On the 12th the precious cargoes of 238 tanks and 43 crated Hurricanes were safe in Alexandria harbour.

Fortune had indeed favoured the bold, providing thick and cloudy weather in the central Mediterranean at a season when it was unprecedented. At home there was a tendency by the authorities to overlook this fact and to play down the hazards of operating within range of Luftwaffe bases. Neither Cunningham nor Somerville had any such illusions. As the former commented in his memoirs, 'Before long the dismal truth was painfully to be brought home to them'. It was to be indeed – in the waters surrounding Crete.

The capture of Crete was, from the strategic point of view, the logical sequel to the sweeping successes of the German Army in Greece. Such a prospect was clear enough to the German high command. A joint determination by the three armed services to achieve it in conjunction, which might have been expected to emerge, was, however, hindered partly by the division of strategic responsibilities between the two Axis partners and partly by the lack of cooperation between the services themselves, particularly between the Luftwaffe and the Kriegsmarine.

The German Navy fully appreciated the strategic importance of Crete in the struggle for control of the Mediterranean; but the arrangements between the Axis partners left naval matters in that theatre an Italian responsibility. In time to come the German Navy was to intervene, sending U-boats and light forces to the Mediterranean. At this stage the German Naval Staff confined itself to urging the Italian Navy into greater activity, but without notable success. The Luftwaffe, on the other hand, had been committed for the last five months to the major role in the campaign in the Mediterranean. The possession of Crete was of immense direct importance to it, both as a link in the most convenient air route to Cyrenaica and as a base from which to dominate the eastern Mediterranean, including Egypt.

It was natural, therefore, that the proposal to capture Crete, which was put to Hitler in the middle of April, should come from the Luftwaffe. The suggestion, however, was not for a combined operation by all three services, with the Navy transporting the assault forces under the umbrella of the overwhelming air power available, but for an airborne assault for which the Luftwaffe would be solely responsible. Only such heavy items as tanks, guns and reserves of ammunition would go by sea, under escort of Italian warships.

The author of the scheme was General Kurt Student, at that time commanding Fliegerkorps XI (Parachute and Airborne troops) stationed in central Germany. On condition that the operation would be quickly accomplished and the troops released in time for the impending attack on Russia, Hitler gave his approval, without consulting either the Navy or the Army General Staff. Air support would be provided by Fliegerkorps VIII – 228 bombers, 205 dive-bombers, 114 twin-engined and 119 single-engined fighters and 50 reconnaissance aircraft, a total of 716 – as well as certain units of

Fliegerkorps X, which were transferred from Sicily to Greece for the purpose. With such massive air strength, a combined operation on conventional lines would have been a more certain and less hazardous method of assault; but the Luftwaffe and its ambitious chief, Marshal Goering, had no wish to share the laurels with the sister services. The consequences were to be costly and to come within an ace of calamity.

With tremendous energy airfields in Greece and the Aegean islands were prepared to receive this huge force; the complex organization to overcome congestion on the airfields and to distribute the necessary fuel was set in motion. By May 16th the assembly was complete, including the 500 transport aircraft and 72 gliders of Fliegerkorps XI. In overall command of all Luftwaffe forces taking part was General Löhr, commanding Luftflotte 4. The date for the assault was fixed for the 20th.

The decision of the British Government that Crete should be held must be accounted a notable example of the still prevalent lack of understanding of what could or could not be done in the face of an absolute enemy air superiority. General Maitland Wilson, while in Crete after evacuation from Greece, was asked by General Wavell for his opinion in the matter. He replied that 'unless all three Services are prepared to face the strain of maintaining adequate forces up to strength, the holding of the island is a dangerous commitment'. 'Adequate' air forces simply did not exist. It may be that the paper strength of three R A F and one Fleet Air Arm fighter squadrons on the airfields of Heraklion and Maleme deceived the authorities at home. In fact the survivors of these squadrons had been reduced before the end of April to half a dozen Hurricanes and a dozen obsolete Gladiators, their numbers daily diminishing as their pilots went aloft to fight against fantastic odds – especially after May 14th when the Germans began 'softening-up' attacks in preparation for the airborne assault. By May 19th they had been reduced to four Hurricanes and three Gladiators.

With the concurrence of General Freyberg to whom had been entrusted the command in Crete, they were then sent away to Egypt. Thus, when the assault began at dawn on the 20th, the defenders were totally without fighter defence.

Nevertheless, General Freyberg, though he had made no bones about expressing his opinion that to hold Crete his strength, particularly in the air, was inadequate, had also told the Prime Minister that he was not anxious about an airborne attack alone, an estimate which was to err only by a narrow margin. If, however, it were to be combined with a seaborne landing, he had no illusions about the difficulties which would face him.

Thus it appeared that the key to the defence of Crete was the prevention of seaborne landings. Implicit in the Government's decision to hold the island was a belief in the ability of the fleet to operate without air support in waters dominated by an enemy air force of more than 500 bombers and dive-bombers. Cunningham knew better: his appeals for reinforcements of aircraft had gone unanswered; his only carrier, the *Formidable*, could not participate until her fighter strength, at this time reduced to four Fulmars, had been built up; but his duty was clear. On May 20th, when the assault on Crete opened, his cruisers and destroyers had for some days been committed, sweeping the sea approaches to Crete from the Aegean by night and withdrawing at daylight to the south of Crete when it was known that no enemy forces were at sea.

That morning, at 6 o'clock, the assault on Crete began with two hours of savage bombing of the area round Maleme airfield and Canea. Then at 8 A M, through the drifting clouds of smoke and dust, gliders were seen dropping down to land. Overhead the sky was full of German aircraft, bombers and fighters, ready to swoop on any British troops who left cover and exposed themselves. General Student's airborne troops nevertheless met an opposition far stiffer than anything expected. At the end of the first day's fighting, in which heavy casualties were suffered by both sides, Maleme airfield, which had been expected to fall quickly to a converging attack, remained a no-man's-land. The troops landed near Canea had made no progress whatever.

The airfields at Heraklion and Retimo were the German objectives for the afternoon of the first day; but here, too, the attacks were firmly held. The paratroopers suffered heavily and, in fact, Heraklion was not captured until it was abandoned on the night of May 28th as part of the general evacuation from Crete, while at Retimo two battalions of Australians under Colonel I. R. Campbell, cut off and isolated, resisted until the 30th, surrendering only when their food and ammunition were exhausted.

By noon on the second day, when no attempt had been made by the Germans to land the heavy equipment, artillery and tanks, which must come by sea, it seemed that Freyberg's belief in his ability to defeat a purely airborne assault was being justified. The Germans had thrown in their last available parachute troops and were being firmly held. So desperate was their situation and so slender seemed their hopes of success that General Student, held at Luftwaffe headquarters by General Löhr, suspected that this was to ensure his survival to answer to a Court of Inquiry. Possession of the disputed landing ground at Maleme, on which Student's Ju 52 transport planes, bringing reinforcements comprising the 5th Mountain Division, could alight, was the key to the situation. Two battalions of New Zealand infantry, with the aid of which the airfield could have been recaptured during the forenoon, were available in reserve near Canea. Had they been boldly thrown in to the battle without delay, the outcome of the airborne assault on Crete might have been different. Freyberg, with the knowledge of an impending seaborne attack in mind, decided that these troops could not be moved until relieved by an Australian battalion from Georgiopolis, some 20 miles along the coast to the eastward.

By the time this move had been completed it was too late. During the afternoon, disregarding artillery and mortar fire, Ju 52s landed. The 100th Mountain Regiment which they brought just turned the scales. By 5 PM the airfield was firmly in German hands, available for a massive build-up by further airborne troops. The battle for Crete was lost from that moment.

Ironically enough, the seaborne assault, threat of which had played such an important part in these events, was repulsed that night by the Navy, their gunflashes visible to the Maori troops who were waiting to go, too late, into action to retake the airfield by a night attack.

Space cannot be devoted to any account of the further land fighting which continued, with great gallantry and heavy casualties on both sides, until the 27th when victory in the area around Maleme and Suda Bay was conceded to the Germans and the decision taken to evacuate from Crete as many troops as possible. The consequences to the Mediterranean Fleet of the ill-judged decision to try to hold Crete, however, must be recounted.

At dusk on the 20th, two cruiser forces had returned to patrol to the northward of Crete, the *Dido*, *Ajax* and *Orion* with three destroyers under Rear-Admiral I. G. Glennie and the *Naiad*, *Perth*, the small anti-aircraft cruisers *Calcutta* and *Carlisle* and four destroyers under Rear-Admiral E. L. S. King. During the night no invasion convoys were encountered and at daylight they once again withdrew to the southward of the island. By this time the enemy had evidently decided they could spare bombers from the land fighting, for throughout the day the ships were kept busy beating off attacks. With only their guns to rely upon, they yet succeeded in avoiding serious damage from the German dive-bombers, though the *Ajax* suffered some hurt from near misses. Italian high-level bombers, able to make deliberate practice without interference by fighters, scored an unusual success when a bomb which hit the destroyer *Juno* penetrated to a magazine, sending her to the bottom in two minutes with heavy loss of life.

During the 21st, information came in from long-range air reconnaissance of gatherings of small craft, escorted by destroyers making for Suda Bay from the island of Milos. These were clearly the expeditions to stop which was the

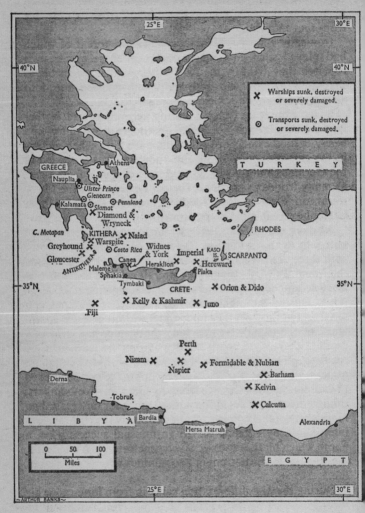

British naval losses in Greece and Crete Campaigns, 1941

fleet's primary duty. Admirals Glennie and King were told that, unless they had been located and dealt with during the night, they were to join forces at daylight and sweep northwards into the Aegean. Glennie's squadron, patrolling to the northward of Suda Bay at midnight, encountered the first convoy of 25 caiques and small steamers escorted by the Italian destroyer-escort *Lupo*. Brushing aside the gallant attempt at defence put up by the little Italian warship, the British cruisers and destroyers attacked the convoy in a mêlée lasting two and a half hours, the confusion of which was only partly resolved by the use of radar. Ten caiques were sunk, their troops killed or thrown into the sea. The remainder, with the damaged *Lupo*, turned back.

At 3.30 AM Glennie called off his scattered pack and ordered them to rendezvous with him to the westward of Crete. His cruisers had expended much of their anti-aircraft ammunition during the previous day – his flagship, the *Dido*, as much as 70 per cent. He decided that under those conditions it would be folly to linger during daylight, a target for the full fury of the German dive-bombers.

Admiral King in the meantime had been patrolling during the night off Heraklion. Having encountered no enemy, at daylight he turned northwards to search, in accordance with his orders. That air attack, heavy and continuous, would come was certain and at 7 AM it started. Nevertheless, the squadron pressed on, fighting off the bombers with their guns and successfully avoiding the bombs by violent manoeuvring. The first signs of the prey they sought came at 8.30, when the *Perth* fell in with a caique full of German troops and sank it. Then a small steamer was dealt with by the destroyers. It was not until 10 o'clock, however, that the escort of the second of the two convoys carrying reinforcements to the Germans in Crete was sighted. The convoy itself, carrying 4,000 troops to be landed at Heraklion, had already been recalled by orders of the German Admiral Schuster, commanding in the area, as a result of Glennie's action. Its escort, the destroyer-escort *Sagittario*, was rounding up stragglers when the British squadron hove in sight. She promptly laid a smoke-screen and retired, but the destroyer *Kingston*, chasing after the *Sagittario*, came in sight of a large number of caiques.

A catastrophe of some magnitude might now have developed for the Germans. But at this moment Admiral King, his anti-aircraft ammunition running low after three hours of almost continuous attack and his speed limited to that of the *Carlisle* (20 knots), decided that to continue farther north, ever closer to the airfields of the Stukas and Ju 88s, was an unjustifiable risk to his whole force. He recalled his destroyers and turned westwards for the Kithera Channel. The convoy had been stopped and all movements of troops by sea cancelled. King's action nevertheless came in for criticism from his Commander-in-Chief. Had he gone in chase of the convoy, it is probable that, though the caiques would no doubt have scattered, a great many would have been sunk with a heavy loss of life amongst the troops of the Mountain Division embarked. It would not have had a direct influence upon the struggle for Crete, but the moral effect would have been far-reaching and relations between the Axis partners would hardly have been improved by the Italian Navy's failure to provide protection. What the cost to the Mediterranean Fleet would have been can only be guessed at by consideration of the subsequent events of that day.

Retiring at its best speed to the westward, King's squadron came under continuous air attack in which the *Naiad* was damaged, having two turrets put out of action, compartments flooded and her speed reduced to 16 knots. The *Carlisle* was also hit, Captain T. C. Hampton being amongst those killed. Admiral Rawlings, who, in company with Glennie's cruiser force, had been patrolling some 20–30 miles westward of the Kithera Channel and, as he put it, 'serving a useful purpose by attracting enemy aircraft', now moved in support. At 1.30 PM the two forces were in sight of one another when the *Warspite* was hit by a heavy bomb which wrecked her starboard 4-inch and 6-inch batteries, so reducing her anti-aircraft armament by half.

Admiral King now assumed command of the combined fleet. He had not been able to gather information on the state of the various units when the destroyer *Greyhound*, returning after sinking a caique, was mortally hit by two bombs. Two other destroyers, *Kandahar* and *Kingston*, were sent to rescue her crew. The *Gloucester* and *Fiji* were left to stand by in support while the remainder of the fleet retired to the south-westward. This was a doubly unfortunate move. It again divided the fleet which, while concentrated, could put up a defence sufficient to daunt the dive-bombers; moreover, unknown to King, the two cruisers selected were the lowest in anti-aircraft ammunition, being 82 and 70 per cent short, respectively.

The *Kandahar* and *Kingston*, with devoted gallantry, had picked up the *Greyhound*'s survivors while beating off continuous low-flying bomb and machine-gun attacks when, at 3 PM, orders were received for the four detached ships to withdraw: Admiral King had now been informed of the shortage of ammunition in the cruisers. Followed by a swarm of dive-bombers, they raced westwards to rejoin the fleet. It was already in sight when at last, at 3.50 PM, the *Gloucester*, which had survived so many bomb hits in the past, received a mortal blow from a number of bombs which disabled her and set her on fire.

Being barely clear of the Kithera Channel, within easy range of the enemy's air bases, Captain William-Powlett of the *Fiji* was forced to take the agonizing decision to abandon his squadron-mate after dropping boats and life-saving rafts by her. Steaming away southward, the *Fiji* and the two destroyers beat off no less than 20 attacks in the next four hours, at the end of which the *Fiji* was reduced to firing practice shells at her tormentors. She deserved better luck than was to be her lot. At 6.45 PM a lone Me 109 fighter-bomber dived out of a cloud to drop its bomb close alongside, holing her in the engine room and bringing her to a stop. Half an hour later another single aircraft found the almost defenceless ship and delivered the *coup de grâce* with three bombs. The destroyers dropped boats and rafts before withdrawing, and, returning after dark, they were able to rescue 523 of her crew.

So ended the calamitous day. The fleet's ordeal was to continue for another eight days, the brunt of which was to be borne by Cunningham's hard-pressed and over-worked destroyers. While the land battle for Crete hung in the balance they continued to make nightly patrols off the north coast to prevent landings from the sea. On the 23rd, after such a patrol, the *Kelly* and *Kashmir* were set upon early in the morning by 24 dive-bombers and sent to the bottom, their survivors, including Captain Lord Louis Mountbatten, being picked up by the *Kipling* under further heavy attacks.

On the 24th, in reply to a request from the Chiefs of Staff at home for an appreciation, Cunningham gave his opinion that the scale of air attack made it no longer possible for the Navy to operate in the Aegean or near Crete by day. The reaction of the Chiefs of Staff was a message insisting that the fleet and the RAF must accept any losses to prevent reinforcements from reaching the enemy in Crete. In Cunningham's opinion this 'failed most lamentably to appreciate the realities of the situation'.

The facts, indeed, were that reinforcement of the enemy was going on unhindered by means of a stream of Ju 52 transport planes. The Navy could do nothing to stop it. 'It is not the fear of sustaining losses', replied the Admiral, 'but the need to avoid losses which will cripple the fleet without any commensurate advantage which is the determining factor in operating in the Aegean.' An example of the lack of appreciation of 'the realities of the situation' had occurred during the 23rd. The infantry landing ship *Glenroy*, under escort of the *Coventry* and two sloops, had set out from Alexandria with a battalion of infantry reinforcements to be landed on the south coast of Crete. The intensity of air attack south of Crete, as demonstrated by the fate of the *Kelly* and *Kashmir*, convinced Cunningham that 'it appeared to be sheer murder to send her on', and, after consultation with Wavell, he ordered the *Glenroy* to turn back during the forenoon. At 4 that afternoon the Admiralty sent her a direct order to turn north again which, if Cunningham had not countermanded it, would have meant her arriving to disembark her troops at daylight, and meeting certain destruction at the hands of the unopposed Stukas.

Nevertheless, what could be done was done. Destroyers and cruisers made night runs to Suda Bay to land supplies and ammunition for the Army and to patrol the sea approaches to the island. The *Formidable*, which had managed to build up her fighter strength to 12 Fulmars, sailed out of Alexandria with the *Queen Elizabeth* and *Barham* to launch, early on the 26th, an assault by four Albacores and four Fulmars on the enemy airfield on Scarpanto. Throughout the forenoon the remaining Fulmars fought off the enemy's efforts to take his revenge. It was not until the afternoon that some 20 dive-bombers broke through to hit and seriously damage the carrier as well as the destroyer *Nubian* of the screen. The following day the *Barham* was also damaged. A further effort by the *Glenroy* to get through with reinforcements during the 26th was foiled when she was damaged and set on fire by dive-bombers.

The whole sea area between Crete and the African coast – 'Bomb Alley' as it was to be dubbed – was by now dominated by the enemy's overwhelming air strength. Even if Crete could be held, its supply would be virtually impossible. Yet it was at this moment that the Prime Minister cabled to Wavell: 'Victory in Crete essential at this turning point of the war. Keep hurling in all you can.' But the soldiers were at the end of their endurance. They had performed miracles, inflicting such casualties on the German troops that they, too, were at the point of collapse. It was the overwhelming air superiority held by the Germans which decided the issue. A few RAF bombers from Egypt attacked the airfield at Maleme and some Hurricanes fitted with extra fuel tanks were flown to Heraklion; but the effort was too small to affect the ceaseless pounding of the British positions by the German dive-bombers.

On May 27th, therefore, the decision was taken to evacuate the island, the troops in the Suda Bay area being instructed to fall back over the mountains to the little fishing village of Sphakia on the south coast. The force at Heraklion would be evacuated from that port. Once again Cunningham was faced with the daunting prospect of exposing his ever dwindling fleet to certain losses. Already two cruisers and four destroyers had been lost in the battle for Crete; two battleships, the only aircraft carrier, another cruiser and a destroyer had been put out of action, while five cruisers and four destroyers had suffered smaller damage. There was dismay but no hesitation. 'We must not let them [the Army] down', he signalled to the fleet. When his staff bewailed the heavy cost he told them: 'It takes the Navy three years to build a ship. It would take three hundred to re-build a tradition.'

Evacuation from both points began on the night of May 28th. Four destroyers embarked 700 men at Sphakia and got safely back with them to Alexandria with no more than minor damage to the *Nizam* from a near miss. The force for Heraklion – the cruisers *Orion*, *Ajax* and *Dido* and six destroyers under Rear-Admiral Rawlings – had to pass through the Kaso Strait within 40 miles of the enemy air base on Scarpanto on both the outward and return journey, and met the full fury of the enemy. From 5 PM until darkness fell at 9, the ships raced onwards through a choppy sea with the spray whipping the exposed gun crews as they fought off a succession of attacks which began with the usual contribution of a formation of Italian high-level bombers. The more serious attacks, glide-bombers, dive-bombers and torpedo aircraft, followed.

Sneaking, twisting and turning at high speed, the ships avoided being hit; but near misses there were in plenty. One damaged the *Ajax*, which was sent back to Alexandria; another fell close under the stern of the *Imperial* without apparently doing any damage, but her steering gear had been weakened and it was to cause her loss later. Darkness at last brought relief but no rest to the tired crews. Off Heraklion harbour the cruisers stopped while the darkened destroyers crept in to secure alongside the jetty. Soon the soldiers, indignant at having to retreat from an enemy they had held and defeated, were filing aboard, some 800 to each destroyer which then left harbour and transferred 500 to a cruiser.

By 3.20, over an hour later than it had been hoped, all had been embarked and the force turned and raced for the Kaso Straits. Hardly had they settled down when the *Imperial* suddenly veered off course, narrowly missing the *Kimberley* and both the cruisers, and came to a stop. As the remainder of the force disappeared into the darkness, Rawlings sent the *Hotspur* back to find out what was wrong. When the *Hotspur* reported that the *Imperial*'s steering gear had broken down and that she was out of control, the order was given for the crew and troops to be taken off and the *Imperial* sunk. It was an hour before this could be completed and two torpedoes had given the *Imperial* her quietus. As the *Hotspur* gathered speed and headed eastwards, the chances of getting through the Kaso Strait in daylight and alone, or of escaping destruction in the Stuka-haunted waters beyond, seemed to her officers so slim, and the thought of what must happen to the 900 men crammed into the little ship was so horrifying, that it was decided to keep close inshore and to turn westwards along the south coast if the Strait was safely passed. Off the beaten track they might escape notice and if the worst occurred the ship could be beached, which would give a chance of life to many of those on board.

To those on the bridge it seemed that the *Hotspur* was doomed as dawn found her streaking through the water for the Kaso Strait alone. The relief which flooded through them as ships loomed up ahead and they realized that Rawlings had waited for them can hardly be exaggerated. They now had six other ships with whom to share the Stukas' attentions, and the gunfire of seven ships would provide a powerful deterrent.

Even so, the ordeal which followed for the next six hours was bad enough, as wave after wave of dive-bombers swooped. Quite early the destroyer *Hereward* was hit and her

speed reduced to a crawl. She had to be left to her fate.*
Then a near miss on the *Decoy* caused damage which
reduced her speed – and therefore that of the squadron – to
25 knots. It was further reduced to 21 by a near miss on the
flagship *Orion*. Her bridge was machine-gunned, Captain
Back being killed and the Admiral wounded. At 8.15 there
came a direct hit on the *Dido*'s 'B' turret. At nine o'clock it
was the *Orion*'s 'A' turret that was destroyed.

The most calamitous hit, however, was one on the flagship
at 10.45 which plunged down into the mess-decks crowded
with troops, killing 260 and wounding 280 of the soldiers
and ship's company. For a time, the *Orion* was out of control and on fire. Subsequently, when emergency steering
arrangements had been made and the fire extinguished, sea-
water contaminating her oil-fuel intermittently reduced her
speed to less than 12 knots. At last the squadron drew out of
range of the dive-bombers. Towards sundown the ships
reached Alexandria, their crews haggard-eyed with exhaustion and near the end of their endurance, and the *Orion*, with
a heavy list and her broken guns tilted awry, under tow.

For the destroyers which had escaped damage, there was
more to come. The tired-out crews moved like automata as
they went about the business of refuelling, shifting berth,
taking in ammunition and clearing up the cluttered confusion between decks. Then they were off again, this time to
Sphakia.

Fortunately, the evacuation from Sphakia, which took
place on the next three nights, during which some 12,000
troops were embarked, was a much less costly affair, fighter
cover being provided by the RAF while the ships were on
passage. The cruiser *Perth* had nevertheless to be added to
the long list of ships severely damaged, while the anti-aircraft
cruiser *Calcutta* was sunk, and the destroyers *Napier* and
Kelvin damaged.

In all, when the operation ended on June 1st, some 18,000

* She was sunk by further air attacks close to the Cretan Coast.
The majority of her crew and soldier passengers were picked up by
Italian light craft and taken prisoner.

men had been evacuated. The cost of the battle for Crete to the fleet was three cruisers and six destroyers sunk, two battleships, the aircraft carrier, two cruisers and two destroyers damaged beyond local repair, and three cruisers and six destroyers less seriously damaged.

The credit side of the account was, however, far from negligible. Fliegerkorps XI had virtually ceased to exist. So heavy had been the German casualties in Crete – a total of more than 6,000 in ten days of fighting – that the airborne attack was considered to have been far from an unqualified success. This was to have its influence when proposals for a similar assault on Malta were made later and, in fact, Operation 'Merkur', the assault on Crete, was the last major airborne operation ever undertaken by the Luftwaffe. Furthermore, with the withdrawal of Fliegerkorps VIII for Hitler's Russian campaign, Fliegerkorps X became responsible for the whole of the Central and Eastern Mediterranean area. From a purely air force point of view Greece and Crete now became the most suitable area from which to operate, putting Egypt and the Suez Canal within easy range. The broader strategic view which envisaged the prime necessity of eliminating Malta was lost to sight. The Sicilian airfields were abandoned by the Luftwaffe. For the remainder of 1941 Malta enjoyed a respite during which her defences could be built up and Rommel's supply lines disrupted. When in January 1942 the Germans realized their mistake and concentrated once again on an assault on Malta, they were to find that their opportunity had passed for ever.

5

Malta Strikes at Rommel's Lifeline

THE INTENSITY of the drama being played out in Crete and the waters surrounding it inevitably drew the attention of all eyes until the curtain fell on June 1st, 1941. It is necessary now to draw back to obtain a broader view of the whole Mediterranean scene before focusing once again on that crucial area, the central basin and the key position of Malta.

While the battle for Crete was still running its course, the hard-pressed British Commanders-in-Chief had been faced with further tasks for their slender resources. As early as April a pro-German administration in Iraq had taken steps which threatened to drive out the British forces stationed there, by long-standing agreement, to guard the vital oil interests and the pipe-line from Kirkuk to Syria and Haifa. Troops and air forces had to be sent to the area and by the end of May they had restored the situation.

In the meantime, however, the Vichy French administration, besides giving active support to the Iraq insurgents by supplying them with arms, had been permitting the Germans to use Syrian airfields to stage aircraft on their way to Iraq. It then became clear that this was only a preliminary to German occupation of Aleppo and the northern part of Syria. The danger, with its threat of a German advance on Egypt through Palestine, left the British no choice but to launch an expedition into Syria.

The operation began on June 8th and continued until July 12th when the Vichy French General Dentz capitulated. Apart from the bitter price of lives lost in battle between former allies and, indeed, between French and French, the campaign cost the depleted Mediterranean Fleet a further three destroyers put out of action.

At first sight the German occupation of Crete, involving, as it did, the loss of control by the British Fleet of all but the south-eastern corner of the Mediterranean – and consequently the cutting of the convoy route from Alexandria to Malta – and a greatly increased air threat to Egypt and the Suez Canal, spelt disaster to the British cause. Yet in fact other influences were at work to restore the balance in the British favour. Even the vast German military machine was limited in what it could simultaneously undertake. Had Hitler concentrated his available air power in the Mediterranean at this time, the consequences must have been fatal to the British position in the Middle East. But his mind was set upon Operation 'Barbarossa', the attack on Russia. All else had to be subordinated to this.

The immediate consequence in the Mediterranean was a great reduction in Luftwaffe strength in the area. Not only was Fliegerkorps VIII transferred to the Russian front but part of Fliegerkorps X also, reducing the latter to five bomber, three dive-bomber, two fighter and one heavy fighter Wings, two long-range reconnaissance and three coastal reconnaissance squadrons – a total of some 351 planes. So overworked was this reduced force, spread over a large number of airfields in Greece, Crete, the Dodecanese and Libya, that less than 200 of these aircraft could be kept operational.

In the share-out of tasks between the German and Italian Air Forces, Fliegerkorps X was made responsible for attacking Alexandria, Cairo and the Suez Canal. Had it been able to concentrate upon this the problem for the British of getting supplies through Suez to the Army of the Nile might well have been made insoluble with calamitous results upon the land campaigns. But from Afrika Korps headquarters came also forceful demands from General Rommel, whose ambitions were set on an early advance into Egypt, for the supply-line to the British garrison in isolated Tobruk to be cut and for that thorn in the flesh to be itself softened up preparatory to eliminating it in the autumn. Forced to divide its resources between these various tasks, Fliegerkorps X failed to perform any of them thoroughly.

Though repeated raids were mounted against Alexandria, Port Said and Suez, together with fairly intensive mining of the Canal, and serious delays were imposed upon the unloading of ships at Suez and the transport of supplies and reinforcements to the Army, the build-up was never entirely halted nor was the naval base of Alexandria made untenable. Similarly, though the supply of Tobruk up to the time of its relief was to cost the fleet 25 ships sunk – including one fast minelayer, two destroyers and three sloops – and nine seriously damaged, the supply route was never cut nor were Tobruk's defences breached.

Most important of the consequences of the over-stretching of the resources of Fliegerkorps X was the abandonment of the Luftwaffe's assault on Malta.

While the storm of bombs had been wrecking the airfields, runways, dispersal tracks, workshops and grounded aircraft, the island's usefulness as an offensive air-base had been reduced almost to nothing. The only concrete successes achieved by Malta's air-striking force during the first months of 1941 were to the credit of the Swordfish of the Fleet Air Arm, which sank three ships by torpedo, totalling 15,796 tons. The Wellingtons of No 148 Squadron made night attacks on Italian and North African ports, harassing and delaying the loading and unloading of transports and damaging several ships, but could claim no sinkings. Under the chaotic conditions, even if more bomber squadrons had been available, it would have been impossible to maintain them. The Wellington squadron, removed to Egypt in early March on account of the heavy attacks on Hal Far airfield, came back in April to hammer Tripoli in a series of night attacks; but, when six Blenheims arrived at the end of April to bring the more effective daylight attacks to bear on the Libyan convoys, insufficient airfield space and ground-crew strength again forced the withdrawal of the Wellingtons.

The brief, brilliant intervention of Captain Mack's destroyer flotilla has been previously mentioned. Their successors, the cruiser *Gloucester* and Mountbatten's 5th Flotilla, had had no chance to emulate them before being withdrawn to take part in the battle for Crete. Thus Malta's contribution to the vital task of harrying the Axis sea traffic was confined, for most of this period, to the work of the submarines either based there or using the base intermittently to replenish. The latter were the submarines such as the old 'P' and 'R' class, too large and unhandy for the shallow waters off the Tunisian coast, whose hunting grounds were off Italy, and the *Triton* class, all based on Alexandria.

The Malta Flotilla had gradually grown from the original force of three small 'U'-class boats, which had arrived in December 1940, and the three more which joined before the end of the year. Their size and handiness made them particularly suitable for haunting the inshore convoy route from Cape Bon to Tripoli.

First, it was necessary to discover the vulnerable points of the convoy route. Patrols by the submarines *Upright* and *Unique* in December and January off the Kerkenah Bank, which lay to the seaward of Sfax and was marked by a number of navigation buoys, established this to be a focal point for convoys to and from Tripoli. And here it was that the first important success by the Malta submarines was achieved, in combination with aircraft from the island.

A convoy for Tripoli comprising the German ship *Duisburg* and the Italian *Ingo*, escorted by an auxiliary warship the *Caralis*, sailed from Naples at 9 PM on January 25th. Rounding the western end of Sicily it followed the established route, steering for Cape Bon on the other side of the Narrows before turning to follow the coastal route to Tripoli. Up to now this had been a safe route, along which the convoys could run back and forth without loss; but off Cape Bon was waiting the submarine *Upholder*, a name which, coupled with that of its young captain, Lieutenant-Commander M. D. Wanklyn, was to spell disaster for a long list of Axis ships in the months to come.

Wanklyn on his first patrol had, however, yet to 'play himself in'. The tracks of the torpedoes he fired at this convoy shortly before midnight on the 26th were sighted and the torpedoes avoided. As soon as it was safe to do so the *Upholder* surfaced and set off in pursuit – a long, slow stern chase, as it was necessary to remain submerged for most of the daylight hours. Meanwhile, the convoy was to be harried by other means. Around noon on the 27th, a Sunderland flying-boat located it off the Kerkenah Bank. Circling on the horizon for the next three hours, it reported the convoy's position, course and speed. From Hal Far airfield, Malta, the seven serviceable Swordfish of 830 Squadron, six of them with torpedoes, took off, accompanied by two Fulmar fighters belonging to the crippled *Illustrious*. At 3.50 they arrived and swooped to the attack. The *Duisburg* swerved in time to avoid the torpedoes aimed at her, but the luckless *Ingo* was squarely struck and in a few minutes had gone to the bottom.

The lightly armed escort *Caralis* was helpless to do more than pick up the survivors and hopefully rejoin her remaining charge. Sunset came without further alarms. By dawn they were approaching Tripoli; but it was still dark when, at 5.38 AM, there came the boom of two torpedoes from the *Upholder* bursting against the *Duisburg*'s hull. She came to a standstill, down by the bow, but remained afloat. The dismayed escort commander, his ship crowded with survivors, no doubt wisely fled the scene, making for nearby Tripoli and calling for warships to go to the *Duisburg*'s assistance. The torpedo-boat *Orione* arriving on the scene, picked up the crew and passengers of the *Duisburg* from her boats. Shortly afterwards a tug was able to take the transport in tow by the stern and get her into port.

From such small beginnings was to grow, with a stubborn, patient persistence, the underwater attack on Rommel's supply line. It was less spectacular than the assault from the air but, less susceptible to the inhibition of its bases by air attack, it was to achieve more. The highlight of the month of February, however, was the sinking of an Italian cruiser which the Italian high command, influenced by their anxiety for the safe transport of the Afrika Korps, was misemploying as a convoy escort.

Starting on February 23rd, the convoy routes to Libya were thronged with important units, German and Italian, for whose safety the Italian Navy was responsible. Five fast German transports left Naples for Tripoli on the evening of the 23rd. The following evening four large Italian liners packed with German troops sailed, followed the next day by a large convoy of five Italian and five German transports. Nevertheless, the British, since the arrival of the Luftwaffe in January, had been unable to maintain any surface forces in the central Mediterranean. It was therefore unnecessary to send the cruisers *Bande Nere* and *Armando Diaz* and two destroyers to augment the close escort of four destroyers provided for the first of these convoys. Nor did Vice-Admiral Moriondo, commanding the cruiser division, take very adequate precautions against the only threat to be expected – attack by submarine.

Stationing himself close ahead of the convoy, he maintained a line-ahead formation. Zig-zagging at first, he ceased to do so when the Kerkenah Bank was reached at 2 AM on the 25th. It was a very dark, moonless and calm night with the visibility falling as the coast of Tripolitania was approached. To keep with the convoy he reduced speed to $13\frac{1}{2}$ knots. Thus Lieutenant E. D. Norman on the bridge of the submarine *Upright* was presented with the sort of target a submariner dreams of. At 3.45 the *Armando Diaz* erupted as two torpedoes hit, blowing up her forward magazine. In four minutes she had gone to the bottom with all but 147 of her crew. The subsequent depth-charging hurt the *Upright* not at all.

In March the *Utmost*, *Unique* and *Upright* all scored successes. When a heavy concentration of enemy shipping on the Tripoli route was reported on March 8th, every available boat was sent to sea. The *Utmost* (Lieutenant-Commander R. D. Cayley), recently returned from patrol, was off again after only 24 hours in harbour and on the 9th torpedoed and sank the Italian transport *Capo Vita*. The next day Lieutenant A. F. Collett in the *Unique*, whose patrol had been extended for the same reason, sank the *Fenicia*.

The *Utmost* was off the Tunisian coast again on the 19th and, falling in with a convoy of five German ships with supplies for the Afrika Korps on the 28th, torpedoed two of them, the *Heraklia* and the *Ruhr*. The former sank but the *Ruhr* was towed to port. This same convoy was further depleted on leaving Tripoli on its return journey when the *Galilea*, straggling astern of it, was torpedoed and severely damaged by the *Upright*.

During this period the submarines of the Alexandria flotilla were also hitting the Italians where it hurt them most – their scanty oil-fuel supplies. The minelaying submarine *Rorqual* called in at Malta for an outfit of mines and on the 25th and 26th March laid them off Palermo. The minefield quickly claimed its first victim in the small tanker *Verde*. Meanwhile the submarine's captain, Commander R. H. Dewhurst, disencumbered of his mines, was seeking targets for his torpedoes. The tanker *Ticino* was sent to the bottom. Then on March 30th the *Laura Corrado* was torpedoed; as she refused to sink, Dewhurst boldly surfaced and dispatched her by gunfire. The next day the *Rorqual*'s last torpedoes were expended in destroying the Italian submarine *Capponi*, which was caught rashly proceeding fully surfaced in daylight. It was a well-satisfied crew which took the *Rorqual* back to base to replenish her stock of torpedoes.

Tankers seemed to be the speciality of the Alexandria flotilla and the following month the *Tetrarch* sank the *Persiano* off Tripoli with a goodly load of Rommel's precious fuel. However, on a basis of the number of ships sunk and of tonnage, the palm must go to the handful of little 'U'-class boats from Malta (particularly, at this time, the *Upholder*), where the black-bearded lanky Scot, Malcolm David Wanklyn, had found his skill and his luck. Having left Malta on April 21st for a patrol area in the Lampedusa Channel, he was rewarded for his patience during the next four days of stormy weather in the shape of the Italian transport *Antonietta Laura*. To make sure of her he closed in to such a short range that the first torpedo of his salvo hit before the third had left the tube. Mindful of the desperate shortage of torpedoes, Wanklyn was able to save the third and fourth.

Wanklyn was now ordered to finish off the German transport *Arta*, one of those on which Mack's destroyers had swooped ten days before and which had been beached and abandoned on the Kerkenah Bank. *Upholder* was taken alongside, and the *Arta* set on fire and destroyed with her cargo of vehicles for the Afrika Korps. Five days later, around noon, as Wanklyn lay patiently waiting in heavy weather off the bank, a fat convoy of four German and one Italian transports was sighted homeward bound from Tripoli, escorted by four destroyers.

Working his way through the destroyer screen, Wanklyn saw his torpedoes explode against two of the German ships, the *Arcturus* and the *Leverkusen*, before he went deep to await the inevitable depth-charges. Shaken but undamaged by them, as the counter-attack died away, he came to periscope depth to assess results. The *Arcturus* had sunk at once but the other ship had been taken in tow by a destroyer and was making slowly for Tripoli. Setting off in pursuit Wanklyn was able to overtake and sink the *Leverkusen* with two more torpedoes.

It was Wanklyn again who, on his next patrol, brought it sharply home to the enemy that Malta still had teeth in spite of all that the Luftwaffe and the Regia Aeronautica had been able to do. His hunting ground had been shifted to the south-east coast of Sicily, a focal point for traffic using the Messina Straits. A long-range attack on a small convoy hugging the coast on May 20th brought no success and resulted in a brief but dangerous counter-attack by the escorts, at the end of which the *Upholder*'s 'ears' – asdic and hydrophones – were out of action.

Disregarding this handicap, Wanklyn remained on patrol and three days later torpedoed the Vichy French tanker *C. Damiani*, which was working for the enemy. The ordeal by depth-charge which followed intermittently until the following day was all the more nerve-racking, as the submarine could not follow the moves of the attackers, except when the thrashing of propellers directly overhead could be heard through the boat without the aid of hydrophones. The *Upholder* escaped serious damage, however, and, with only two torpedoes left and two more days of her patrol remaining, Wanklyn moved to cover the exit from the Messina Straits, a move which was to bring calamity to the Italian Navy.

At dawn on May 24th the four large ocean liners *Conte Rosso*, *Marco Polo*, *Victoria* and *Esperia*, packed with troops for Libya, had sailed from Naples. During the afternoon of the 25th they cleared the Straits of Messina and, with their close escort of four destroyers and a covering force of two cruisers and three destroyers, steered at high speed on the direct route for Tripoli.

The sun had already set when Wanklyn, looking forward to the onset of darkness (when he could surface and charge his nearly exhausted batteries) and scanning the horizon through his periscope for a last look round before the light got bad, sighted an aircraft patrolling to the north-west of him. This was very likely a convoy escort. Wanklyn remained at periscope depth searching carefully in the fading light. He was rewarded by the sight of the twin funnels of a liner silhouetted against the sunset glow.

The well-tried, incessantly drilled routine for torpedo attack was set in motion. With visibility falling, only his periscope to rely upon and only two torpedoes remaining, it had to be made at point-blank range. And as the target and her consorts approached, there came into sight the strong destroyer screen which would have to be faced. Fortunately the growing dusk, which made Wanklyn's problem difficult, helped to shroud the *Upholder*'s periscope, much of which had to be exposed in the long swell that was rolling in the otherwise calm sea. At 8.40 the submarine was in firing position.

The enemy's first realization of danger came when the senior officer of the escort in the destroyer *Freccia* saw the tracks of two torpedoes. Firing off the Very light alarm signal he swung his ship and narrowly avoided them. They sped on to find a greater target – the *Conte Rosso*, 17,879 tons, carrying 2,729 soldiers and crew and flying the flag of the Convoy Commodore, Rear-Admiral Francesco Canzoneri. The great ship was mortally hit and went down quickly, some 1,300 men being drowned.

During the next two hours the *Upholder* leapt and shuddered under the explosion of more than 40 depth charges, but she survived and by midnight was speeding on the surface to Malta. Wanklyn was to receive the Victoria Cross for his exploit.

Calamitous as the loss of this great ship was for the Italians, the attack on their merchant shipping supplying Libya up to the end of May 1941, restricted as it was to the work of the British submarines only, could not reach serious proportions. With the beginning of June, however, and the departure of Fliegerkorps X, Malta's airfields, no longer broken up by incessant raids, were quickly repaired and enlarged. The Blenheim bombers, hitherto virtually immobilized, now began to hit at the Axis convoys by day, both at sea and in harbour. The Fleet Air Arm torpedo planes had been forced to abandon daylight operations after their early successes, when the convoys were given escort by fighters or Junkers 88s against which the slow, defenceless Swordfish were helpless. Until July 1941, when they began to receive airborne radar equipment, their usefulness at night was principally to lay mines in the harbour approaches. When the Wellington bombers returned to Malta in August, the Italian convoys would be harried continuously, night and day, at sea or in harbour, the three types of air strike being successively employed round the clock. In addition, the 8th Submarine Flotilla, which was based on Gibraltar and comprised British and Dutch boats, began to haunt the Tyrrhenian Sea and the Gulf of Genoa; while the reinforced 1st Flotilla at Alexandria, besides attacking the enemy's traffic using the port of Benghazi, was able to spread its operations to the Aegean and the approaches to the Dardanelles. The Italians were thus forced to disperse their anti-submarine forces over a wide area. Morale of the crews of escorts and

transports, overworked to the point of exhaustion, began to
suffer from the increasing certainty of attack from below and
above whenever they put to sea.

From the beginning of June 1941, indeed, hardly a convoy
crossed to Libya without suffering some form of attack.
Many were driven off or evaded, the escorts displaying a
skill which must excite admiration in view of the fact that
they had no radar and that an asdic set had only been
developed since Italy's entry into the war and not all her
destroyers and torpedo boats were fitted with it or trained
in its use. For every damaging attack made on Axis convoys,
accounts of some of which are given in the following pages,
there were a greater number of safe arrivals. In the detailed
account of what the Italian official history calls 'the battle
of the convoys', the same ships are found repeatedly shuttling
back and forth, running the gauntlet with a dogged persistence and surviving the assaults which rarely ceased for long
either at sea or in harbour.

Courage of a high order was displayed on either side.
Indeed, the British submarines, operating in the clear,
shallow waters of the central basin, liberally strewn with
mines and under the constant surveillance of anti-submarine
aircraft, accepted almost suicidal risks of destruction each
time they launched a torpedo at the heavily escorted convoys. Between April and August 1941 five of Malta's submarines were lost – *Usk*, *Undaunted*, *Unison*, *P32* and *P33*.

The nervous strain on the crews mounted with each
patrol. The supreme quality of submarine captains such as
Wanklyn lay, as much as anything, in their ability to exude
calm confidence during the nerve-racking counter-attacks
when there was nothing to be done but wait passively as the
depth charges sank down through the water to explode with
hull-hammering violence. Even so, in the *Upholder*, after the
attack on the *Conte Rosso*, a signalman was so deranged
temporarily as to try to open the conning tower hatch while
the submarine was at a depth of 150 feet. It was in the *Urge*,
where another outstanding officer, Lieutenant E. P. Tomkinson, commanded, that a Leading Stoker would walk up and

down loudly reciting the Lord's Prayer during depth charge attacks.

In the air, too, appalling losses were accepted in fulfilment of the task given to the Royal Air Force on Malta 'to sink Axis shipping sailing from Europe to Africa'. Lacking a dive-bomber and until torpedo planes became available, this devolved upon the Blenheims of Nos 105 and 107 Squadrons. The ineffectiveness of high-level bombing against shipping had forced them to develop a system of attack which was highly effective but costly to a degree beyond anything that could have been demanded of them, had not the objective been of decisive importance. The target was approached on a straight course, at masthead height, and the bombs were released at point-blank range, so that they travelled on to hit the ship's side and blow a hole in her hull. In the face of the heavy volume of machine-gun fire which could be put up by the transports, as well as by the escorts, the chances of survival were slim. Yet day after day the crews of the Blenheims took off with gay insouciance to earn in this fearless fashion the bottle of Plymouth Gin awarded to the unit for each ship sunk by Air Vice-Marshal Lloyd, the Air Officer Commanding.

The effectiveness, as well as the risks, of their methods was early demonstrated when, on May 27th, a convoy of six merchantmen with an escort of eight was intercepted in the Sicilian Channel. Six Blenheims roared in to the attack. In the hail of machine-gun and barrage fire which met them, two aircraft crashed into the sea; but the steamer *Foscarini* was squarely hit by bombs, damaged and set on fire. But luck was with the Italians. The damage was not fatal and the *Foscarini* was taken to Tripoli in tow; while the bombs which hit another of the convoy, the *Venice*, failed to explode.

So began the long succession of daytime air attacks on the Axis convoys which, in combination with attacks by submarines and torpedo planes, was to lead to what the official Italian history describes as 'one of the worst periods for the sea communications between Italy and the colonies. During the months of the late summer and autumn especially, the

Italian Merchant Navy suffered perhaps the worst losses of the whole struggle'. A few examples of the experiences of the convoys will be given; but it must be remembered that for every one mentioned here there were many more, with widely varying degrees of success or failure.

Let us follow the fortunes of a series of convoys during June. The first, of six ships with a close escort of five destroyers and a covering force of two cruisers, left Naples for Tripoli on June 1st, routed through the Sicilian Channel and down the coast of Tripolitania. Overhead orbited two Caproni 42 fighters and a Cant Z 501 seaplane. It was the latter which sounded the first alarm early on the 2nd, reporting a submarine lying in wait ahead. The convoy was diverted clear of the danger.

About the same time a Sunderland flying-boat sighted and reported the position of the convoy to Headquarters, Malta. Soon after noon five Blenheims took off and swung away on a westerly course to intercept. By 2 PM the convoy was in sight. Spotting the two Italian fighters, the leader decided to play a waiting game, and to hold off until the Capronis reached the end of their endurance and went home. In the convoy the Blenheims had been briefly sighted low down on the horizon; air attack by day was, however, as yet almost unheard of, and they had been taken for Ju 52 transport planes on their way to Libya. There was no uneasiness, therefore, when the Capronis departed at 2.30 PM. Surprise was complete when, at 2.45 PM, from the direction of the sun and skimming low over the water, the five Blenheims were seen streaking for the convoy. Machine guns opened fire. One aircraft was hit, lost height and splashed into the sea; but the remainder came steadily on. As they pulled up to clear the masts, bombs left their bellies and flew on in a gently falling curve towards the ships. The steamer *Montello* carrying ammunition erupted in a cataclysmic explosion and in a few seconds had sunk, leaving only scattered debris to mark her passing. At the same time the *Beatrice Costa* had taken a bomb amidships which set her cargo of cased petrol ablaze. Abandoned by her crew, she circled out of control until a destroyer of the escort sent her to the bottom.

Reduced to four, the convoy steamed on, arriving without further damage at Tripoli on June 4th. For the next week efforts were made to get the cargo unloaded by means of the scanty facilities available after the incessant air raids, which were interrupted by four further night raids during their stay. On the 11th, when the holds were still far from cleared, the ships were ordered out to make room for the next convoy which was due on the following day.

This convoy, comprising six merchantmen with an escort of three, was also suffering attack, having been intercepted by two Blenheims south of Pantellaria. The target they selected was the motorship *Tembien*, a veteran of the Libya run, bristling with machine guns. The leader of the Blenheims was so shot to pieces that it failed to pull up and crashed into the *Tembien*'s mast, to fall blazing into the sea. Its bombs went wide as did those of the other aircraft, which fled chased by the air escort, a Savoia 79 and two Capronis.

Revenge was soon to be taken on the *Tembien*. With the rest of the convoy she sailed for home after unloading at Tripoli. On the 22nd, six Blenheims were sent in to the attack. Two were shot down but the *Tembien* and the German ship *Wachtfels* were hit and brought to a standstill heavily damaged, though they were later got into port by tugs. While the escorts were busy with their salvage there came a submarine alarm. A feverish hunt ended when apparent evidence of a kill was seen in the shape of disturbed water and oil on the surface. It was greeted with enormous enthusiasm and cries of *Viva l'Italia* from the exuberant destroyer crews – but in fact no British submarine was lost at that time.

Such were typical experiences of supply ships on the Libya run. Besides these slow convoys which followed the route to the west of Malta where they could be given an air escort throughout daylight hours, another group of ships which shuttled to and fro were a constant lure for Malta's air and submarine striking forces. These were the big ocean liners which were employed as troopships and which, on account

Axis convoy routes to Libya, July 1941–December 1942

AXIS CONVOY ROUTES
In second half of 1941
In second half of 1942

—ARTHUR BANKS—

of their high speed and their need for plenty of sea room in which to manoeuvre if attacked and in the hope of keeping outside the range of torpedo planes, followed a route to the eastward of Malta. The sinking of one of them, the *Conte Rosso* by the *Upholder*, has been related. Others were the *Oceania*, *Neptunia*, *Esperia*, *Marco Polo*, *Vulcania* and *Victoria*.

Strenuous efforts were made by Malta's air striking forces to sink these valuable ships. They were to be unsuccessful at this time, and it was to the torpedoes of British submarines that three of them were soon to succumb.

Though the 'big fish' continued to elude the aviators, it was not so with the equally vital supply ships. With the supply of radar to the Swordfish, moonlight was no longer necessary for locating the convoys which were kept under attack night and day: often torpedo planes would come in after dark to finish off ships damaged by the bombers, or on the following morning Blenheims would sink ships which had been crippled by the Swordfish.

On July 22nd a slow convoy of three Italian and one German transport, with the tanker *Brarena* following astern and intending to join it, was intercepted at dusk by the Blenheims. In the attack which followed, the German ship *Preussen* carrying ammunition was set on fire and blew up. At the same time the *Brarena*, hit by incendiaries, blazed up and her crew threw themselves overboard. When the fire had later burnt itself out, the crew were put back on board and the tanker taken in tow by one of the Italian destroyers. Hardly had this been achieved when the sight of flares and the throb of aircraft engines announced the arrival of the torpedo planes. The tow was slipped. A torpedo slammed into the helpless tanker which once again burnt fiercely. The *Brarena*, abandoned, drifted on to the Kerkenah bank where she became a total loss.

Again in August the Italian steamer *Maddalena Odero*, torpedoed by Swordfish but not sunk, was towed to Lampedusa Island, only to be bombed and blown up by a Blenheim the next day. Hardly a day passed without a merchant ship on the Libyan route being sunk or so damaged as to be out of action for a long time. Supplies arriving for the Afrika Korps, of which a minimum of 50,000 tons was required to keep it fully efficient, had dropped to 32,000 in July and to 28,400 tons in August. Thus, though Rommel had been able to defeat a British offensive (Operation Battleaxe) launched prematurely in the middle of June as a result of pressure on General Wavell from home, he was incapable of going over to the offensive himself, even to the extent of attempting to capture Tobruk which was still holding out behind his lines.

This partial strangulation of the Libyan supply route was greatly assisted both by the work of submarines from Alexandria, which patrolled off Benghazi and attacked the coastal sea route along which much of the supplies for the Afrika Korps was brought forward, and by the almost nightly raids on the ports of unloading, principally Benghazi, by the RAF bomber squadrons based in Egypt. But it was the striking power of Malta which played by far the greater part in what was the key to the whole campaign in the Mediterranean. To sustain the effort, supplies in large quantities were required, petrol, ammunition, oil-fuel, spare parts as well as food for the garrison and population of the island. We must turn, therefore, from the battle of the Libyan convoys to consider the problems involved in supplying Malta and to see how they were met.

6

Massacre on the Libyan Supply Route

NOTHING COULD have more clearly exposed the changed shape of naval warfare than the situation which existed in the Mediterranean after the fall of Crete in June 1941. The Mediterranean Fleet, though reduced by action damage and losses to two battleships, two cruisers, one anti-aircraft cruiser and 17 destroyers, was still unchallenged by an enemy fleet in the eastern half of the Mediterranean. But with that half of the sea, except for a small area in the east, flanked by enemy airfields and outside the range of fighter protection from British airfields, the fleet could exercise no control whatever. The 15-inch guns of the *Queen Elizabeth* and *Valiant*, impressive in their steely might to a beholder, were useless to affect the situation.

Conversely, in the central basin, where no British naval surface forces could operate, the Italian Fleet, with four battleships and more than a dozen cruisers, was equally unable to exercise effective control. It could do nothing to prevent the heavy and continuous loss of merchant ships to the bombs and torpedoes of British aircraft and submarines. Only a resumption of the massive and sustained aerial bombardment of Malta and, eventually, its capture, could do this.

Each side was faced with the problem of running supply convoys which, though not seriously threatened by the enemy's surface forces, were in extreme peril from attack from above and below the surface. The problem would not have been greatly affected if the battle squadrons on either side had been eliminated – as, indeed, was to happen to the Mediterranean Fleet. The success or failure of convoy operations would depend to a great extent upon the effectiveness of anti-submarine and anti-aircraft defence, either by fighters or gunfire, and upon the severity of casualties which the attacking submarines and aircraft were prepared to accept in order to achieve their object.

We have seen how this applied to the Axis convoys to Libya. The anti-submarine defences, in spite of their numerical strength – often as many escorts as merchant ships – and of the far from ideal conditions in which the submarines were forced to operate, failed to inflict unacceptable casualties. The anti-aircraft defences, principally guns in the convoys and escorts, certainly inflicted against the low-flying day attacks a proportion of casualties – often more than 30 per cent – which could only be accepted by aircrews imbued with sublime courage and instilled with an unquestioning belief in the vital importance of their task. So nearly suicidal, indeed, was this form of attack that it was abandoned as soon as the Royal Air Force could supply torpedo planes to take the place of the Blenheim bombers.

Let us now examine the reverse of the coin. As vital to the British as the supply of Rommel's army was to the Axis, was the supply and victualling of Malta. Since January 1941 and the arrival of Fliegerkorps X, no convoys from the west had been attempted. From February to May, 13 ships had been slipped into Valetta from Alexandria, usually under the cover of fleet movements. The 100,000 tons they brought had kept Malta fed, its few aircraft flying and armed, its submarines fuelled. Now, however, the depleted fleet could no longer contemplate trying to fight even single convoys through Bomb Alley between Crete and Cyrenaica. As a desperate stop-gap the larger submarines of the Alexandria flotilla were pressed into service as transports. Between June and December 1941, sixteen such trips were run, a typical load being 24 personnel, 147 bags of mail, two tons of medical stores, 62 tons of aviation spirit and 45 tons of kerosene. These trips were to continue until November 1942.

Without them Malta's capabilities of offence and defence would have virtually disappeared. Nevertheless, the supplies brought were only a fraction of the requirements. Furthermore, they included no foodstuffs. It was decided, therefore, that a July convoy of six fast store ships must be run from the west. Admiral Somerville's Force 'H', which at this time comprised only his flagship, the battlecruiser *Renown*, the *Ark Royal*, the cruiser *Hermione* and six destroyers, was reinforced by the battleship *Nelson* and a detachment called Force 'X', under Rear-Admiral Syfret, composed of the cruisers *Edinburgh*, *Manchester* and *Arethusa*, the fast mine-layer *Manxman* and eleven destroyers. This latter force was to accompany the convoy through the Sicilian Channel to Malta while the big ships of Force 'H' would await its return to the westward of the Narrows.

Though the Italian battle-fleet at this time included four battleships and three divisions of cruisers, it made no move. It was left to the Italian Air Force to strike at Force 'H' and to a small force of torpedo boats to attack the convoy during its night passage of the Sicilian Channel. During the 23rd a simultaneous attack by high bombers and torpedo aircraft achieved a measure of success. The high-level bombers aimed their bombs with their customary accuracy and lack of concrete result; but they engaged the attention of the defending Fulmars from the *Ark Royal* which climbed up to shoot down two and damage others; and meanwhile six torpedo aircraft, coming in low, sank the destroyer *Fearless* and crippled the *Manchester*, which was forced to return to Gibraltar.

It was a skilfully delivered attack, in which the achieve-ment of the torpedo planes compared favourably with any similar daylight efforts by Fleet Air Arm Swordfish. Never-theless, the hot reception they received and the casualties they suffered evidently had a daunting effect. Successive waves of aircraft were driven off by the handful of Fulmars which the Italians complimented by taking for Hurricanes. No further damage was inflicted on convoy or escorts, and that evening they passed into the narrow waters of the Skerki Channel. There during the night two of the MTBs succeeded in attacking and escaping unscathed after torpedoing the *Sydney Star*. The transport was not sunk, however, and, in spite of efforts by German dive-bombers and Italian Savoias to finish her off, she reached Malta on the afternoon of July 24th soon after the remainder of the convoy. The island base was, for the time being, once again viable.

The price could still have been made a painful one had the Italians really been prepared to use their surface fleet offensively. Syfret's Force 'X', after re-fuelling at Malta, had still to make the return passage through the Sicilian Channel. In addition six empty merchant ships and that veteran of the Malta run, the *Breconshire*, were also sent westwards from Malta on the 23rd. An Italian cruiser squadron deployed in the Sicilian Channel might have caused havoc; but the cruisers remained supinely in harbour. Syfret's force rejoined Force 'H' early on the 25th without interference while the empty transports suffered only one damaged as a result of air attacks off the Tunisian coast. As James Somerville commented, 'It was an amazing affair. They had Palermo and Messina packed with cruisers and destroyers and not a move! And so home to bed.' It was indeed a surprising conclusion to an operation which in prospect had seemed so hazardous that Somerville had issued an exhortation to his force preparing them for a hard-fought battle and concluding with the words 'The Convoy Must Go Through!'

Without the massive support of the Luftwaffe, the Italian High Command had little stomach for taking the necessary risks to maintain the siege of Malta. That great courage existed in the fighting units of the Italian Navy was demonstrated by a heroic attempt to attack the Grand Harbour and the submarine base, on the night of July 25th, by means of explosive motor-boats and human torpedoes, which will be described later with the other exploits of the organization known as the Tenth Light Flotilla. It was in Rome that the courage was lacking, the courage to risk much to bring Malta to its knees. Consequently the island's striking forces, now re-supplied, were able to go ahead, with ever-increasing success, with cutting the Libyan supply line. Rommel, poised on the Egyptian frontier, his eyes on the glittering prize of Cairo and the Suez Canal, remained in frustrated immobility.

Through the summer and autumn of 1941, while Rommel fretted at the insecurity of his sea communications and suffered from a chronic shortage of fuel and supplies, British strength on land, fed by the long Cape route and, with regard to aircraft, by the trans-African route from Takoradi to Egypt, steadily increased. Great difficulties remained in building up the strength and efficiency of the Royal Air Force in the Middle East on account of a lack of maintenance facilities and of trained aircrews. The sister services complained of inadequate air support, a situation, particularly in the case of the Navy, which was attributable to pre-war policy with its over-emphasis on the independent strategic role of the Royal Air Force. Not until October 1941 was a Naval Cooperation Group set up at Alexandria, the aircraft of which were normally to be employed under the naval Commander-in-Chief and not to be diverted to other tasks without prior consultation with him.

Nevertheless, during these months the grinding shortages of aircraft of all types, under which Air Chief Marshal Longmore had laboured, were to a great extent overcome, so that within reasonable range of its own air bases the RAF could face the enemy on at least equal terms. At the same time the air strength of Malta was built up, Hurricane fighters being transported in aircraft carriers to within flying-off range. In mid-August the serviceable aircraft on the island comprised 69 Hurricanes, 18 Blenheim IV, 17 Wellington, 12 Swordfish and seven Marylands. In September a second squadron of Blenheims was flown in from Gibraltar simultaneously with another reinforcement of Hurricanes flown off the *Ark Royal* and *Furious*. In October, as well as yet more Hurricanes, No 828 Squadron, Fleet Air Arm, Albacore torpedo planes, joined the island's striking force. Another addition to Malta's air-striking capabilities was supplied by the arrival of radar-equipped Wellingtons fitted with a radio homing device which could lead the night-flying Swordfish to their targets.

By September the need to re-supply Malta had again become urgent. A convoy of nine ships was assembled and passed through the Straits of Gibraltar during the night of the 24th. Operation 'Halberd', as it was called, followed the general lines of 'Substance', Force 'H' being composed of the *Nelson* (Admiral Somerville's flagship), the battleships *Prince of Wales* and *Rodney* and the *Ark Royal*, while a Force 'X' of five cruisers and nine destroyers under Rear-Admiral Harold Burrough would again take the convoy through the Sicilian Channel to Malta.

Efforts to deceive the Italian intelligence service succeeded in concealing the presence of the convoy for a time, but the departure of Force 'H' to the eastward from Gibraltar warned the Italian High Command that something was afoot. The same deceptive measures gave the impression, however, that Somerville's force included only one battle-ship. An Italian fleet, composed of the battleships *Littorio* and *Vittorio Veneto*, five cruisers and fourteen destroyers, was therefore assembled under Admiral Iachino's flag and sent forth to intercept.

Thus in the afternoon of the 27th, while Somerville's ships and aircraft were beating off a succession of aerial torpedo attacks (in which the *Nelson* was unlucky to be hit on the stem and damaged by a torpedo steering an exactly opposite course), information reached him of an enemy fleet approaching from the north. With his flagship reduced to 18 knots, Somerville directed Vice-Admiral Curteis to move out with the remainder of the force to engage and the *Ark Royal* to launch a torpedo striking force. A fleet action on something like equal terms seemed imminent. But Iachino was bound by orders not to join action unless he enjoyed a clear superiority of strength. When it appeared that more than one battleship as well as the *Ark Royal* opposed him, he turned back. Some radio confusion and low visibility combined to prevent the *Ark Royal*'s torpedo planes finding their target and the day ended with the Italian fleet making off for their base at Naples.

Though one of the convoy, the *Imperial Star*, was sunk by a torpedo from an Italian aircraft which made a moonlight attack during the passage of the Sicilian Channel, the remainder arrived safely at Malta to scenes of immense enthusiasm from the inhabitants of Valetta massed on the battlements. Malta was now re-stocked, with the exception of coal, fodder and kerosene, with sufficient supplies to last until May 1942.

What this meant for Axis supplies to Libya can be judged from the experiences of some of their convoys during September – of, for example, the four ships which sailed from Naples on the 1st of the month with an escort of five destroyers. In the hope of keeping outside the range of the dreaded Fleet Air Arm torpedo planes, against which they were so helpless, the convoy was routed through the Straits of Messina and thence due eastwards, before turning south to cross the Mediterranean far to the eastward of Malta – the same route as that invariably followed by the fast troop convoys of ocean liners.

They were for a time vulnerable, nevertheless, after debouching from the Straits; and it was here that soon after midnight of September 2nd–3rd, in bright moonlight, the Swordfish found them, and swooped in to the attack. Smoke billowing from the merchantmen and escorts spread a covering shroud, and a multitude of guns opened up in a blind barrage. It did not prevent torpedoes finding their mark in two of the transports, the *Andrea Gritti* and the *Barbaro*. The former quickly foundered; the *Barbaro* was got back to Messina in tow, where she was out of service for a long time, while her urgently needed cargo had to be laboriously unloaded and trans-shipped.

On the 10th another convoy of six ships left Naples with six escorts, to try its luck on the alternative route to the west of Malta. Air Headquarters on the island, kept informed by its ever watchful reconnaissance planes, prepared to hit it hard. Swordfish of 830 Squadron were the first to go out. However, when they attacked soon after 3 AM on the 12th, they found the enemy alert and wary. Twisting and turning under cover of the blanket of smoke, the merchant ships avoided all the torpedoes aimed at them. When dawn broke, bringing with it an escort of fighter aircraft, the convoy was

still whole and undamaged. The forenoon went off quietly
while the convoy was passing the Kerkenah Bank, with its
stranded wrecks offering grim mementos of previous actions.
Then, at 2 PM, came the alarm as eight Blenheims came
streaking in low from the west. White water frothed under
the sterns of the escorts as they picked up speed and turned
to bring all their guns to bear. Streams of machine-gun
tracer bullets and shells converged on the bomber formation,
interspersed with the black bursts of shells from the bigger
guns. Three Blenheims fell flaming into the water but the
remainder came remorselessly on to release their bombs as
they zoomed over the mastheads and sped away low over
the water, chased ineffectively by the Caproni fighters of the
escort.

It was a heavy price but not paid in vain. The steamship
Caffaro was left crippled, blazing with a fire which threatened
her cargo of ammunition. Her crew incontinently abandoned
ship, and none too soon as she shortly blew up and disintegrated. The remainder plodded on and as darkness fell,
with the prospect of reaching port the following morning,
hoped that the worst was over. But at 1 AM there came again
the muffled roar of the Swordfish prowling near by. Flares
blossomed along the port side lighting up the drifting clouds
of smoke in which the ships sought shelter. Then the guns
opened their wild cacophony aimed at aircraft, heard but
unseen, coming in on the starboard side. Ships turned this
way and that to present bow or stern towards the expected
torpedo tracks. None were seen, however, and suddenly it
was all over and quiet descended on the scene. Not a ship
had been hit. Masters breathed a sigh of relief and steered
their ships to reform convoy. The British, it seemed, had
shot their bolt.

But, in fact, the convoy's trials were not yet over. The
Swordfish pilots, failing to achieve surprise, had found the
smoke shroud too heavy for them to aim their torpedoes
and, remembering their failure on the previous night, had
launched none. Withdrawing to a distance they waited for
the air to clear. At 3.45 they came in again, the leader circling

to lay a line of flares beyond the convoy so that it stood out in silhouette. Before the smoke had accumulated sufficiently to hide all the ships, torpedoes were on their way, the phosphorescent pencils of their tracks reaching for their targets. Once again the convoy formation broke up as ships swung sharply to avoid them. Luck had run out for one veteran of the Libyan run: the *Nicolo Odero* shuddered under an explosion and came to a stop with flames pouring from her cargo.

As the sound of aircraft died away and the rest of the depleted convoy reformed, a destroyer took the crippled ship in tow while a devoted party fought the flames. It was to no avail. The fire was gaining on them and spreading towards a hold packed with ammunition. Abandon ship was ordered and the tow was slipped shortly before the *Nicolo Odero* blew up and sank. One third of its number lost, the convoy gained the precarious shelter of Tripoli harbour, which was lashed nightly by the bombs of the Wellington bombers. Their cargoes unloaded, the weary ship masters sailed again to face the same hazards on the homeward run.

They had, indeed, been fortunate in not also having to run the gauntlet of the Malta submarines. But these were after bigger game. Air reconnaissance had reported a troop convoy preparing to sail from Taranto, the ocean liners *Oceania*, *Neptunia* and *Vulcania*, which had survived a number of efforts to eliminate them. The *Conte Rosso* had succumbed to the torpedoes of Wanklyn's *Upholder*; and in August the *Esperia* had been sunk, in spite of every possible precaution and form of defence, by a brilliant attack carried out by Lieutenant A. R. Hezlet of the *Unique* in the swept channel leading to the port of Tripoli.

In expectation that the troop convoy, to keep outside the range of torpedo planes from Malta, would follow the usual easterly route and make landfall 100 miles to the eastward of Tripoli, an ambush by four submarines was set up. At the expected point of landfall was the *Unbeaten*, with *Upholder* and *Upright* along the coast towards Tripoli at 10-mile intervals. At the entrance to the swept channel, 30 miles east of Tripoli, was the *Ursula*.

Late on September 16th the three great liners sailed with their five destroyer escorts and headed at high speed across the Mediterranean. Twice during the following day submarine alarms sent the convoy swerving away while the destroyers dropped depth charges. There were no submarines in fact, but nerves were stretched taut aboard all the ships. There were no further alarms, however, and when at 3.30 AM the following morning Woodward of the *Unbeaten* sighted the convoy against the glow of the rising moon, too far off for him to reach an attacking position, the Italians were unaware of the train of events which was now started by *Unbeaten*'s radio report.

It was taken in by the *Upholder* in time for Wanklyn to steer on the surface to intercept. Half an hour later the bulky shapes of the liners were in sight. Still surfaced, Wanklyn moved in to the attack. He was some way off track and with such fast-moving targets he would be forced to fire at long range. The *Upholder*'s gyro-compass had chosen this moment to break down; the little magnetic compass, surrounded as it was by steel, had small directional force. In the choppy sea the helmsman had difficulty in steering and the boat yawed from side to side. Thus when the time came to fire, at a range of 5,000 yards, there was more than the usual need for Wanklyn's personal skill and 'seaman's eye', with the submarine's bow swinging across the firing course. As it swung back he fired again, judging the time lag between barking the order and the moment the torpedo left the tube – until four torpedoes were away on their long run to the target. Satisfied, Wanklyn dropped down through the conning tower hatch as *Upholder*'s bow dipped in a hasty dive.

Luck rewarded his skill. At the angle on which the torpedo tracks met that of the convoy, two of the liners overlapped making virtually one huge target. One torpedo hit the *Oceania* right aft, wrecking her propellers and bringing her to a standstill. Two others travelled on to tear a mortal wound in the side of the *Neptunia*. With a single attendant destroyer, the *Vulcania* put on her best speed and fled towards Tripoli. The *Upright*, which had also received *Unbeaten*'s report, had at once hurried south to get on the convoy's track but, going too far, had the galling experience of seeing the *Vulcania* race by out of range to the north. The *Ursula*, on the other hand, was able to attack but underestimated the liner's speed – she was much the fastest of the trio – so that her torpedoes missed astern.

Meanwhile, the destroyers of the escort were so occupied in taking the passengers and crew off the sinking *Neptunia* and trying to get the *Oceania* in tow that Wanklyn had been able to surface amongst them in the moonlight to survey the situation. Having decided to wait for sunrise before delivering the *coup de grâce* to the wounded *Oceania*, he dived again to make for a position up sun. At the same time, unknown to him, the *Unbeaten*, which had been pounding after the convoy ever since it had passed her, was making for the same position. *Upholder* reached it first and Wanklyn was about to fire when he was forced to go deep by an approaching destroyer. He therefore took *Upholder* under his target and, coming to periscope depth on the far side, put two torpedoes into the *Oceania* which sank her in eight minutes.

While Wanklyn's star was shining out so brilliantly (though soon to be extinguished for ever), Woodward's was in heart-breaking eclipse. Arriving on the scene soon after sunrise, he saw the *Neptunia* slide beneath the surface without any assistance from him. He had just squared up to launch his torpedoes at the *Oceania*, when, through the periscope, he saw the tall columns of water leap up as *Upholder*'s torpedoes robbed him of his victim.

Though the loss of life in this double catastrophe was relatively small, 384 men being lost from the two ships, the destruction of two such valuable and irreplaceable ships almost in sight of Tripoli, in the same month in which supply convoys suffered more severely than ever before, flashed a clear warning to the high commands of the Axis that drastic remedial action was needed if the battle for the Mediterranean was not to be lost.

Cries of alarm came from Admiral Weichold, the German liaison officer with the Italian Naval Staff in Rome, as a result of which the German General Staff informed the German Supreme Command in September:

> The situation as described is untenable. Italian naval and air forces are incapable of providing adequate cover for the convoys. . . . The Naval Staff considers radical changes and immediate measures to remedy the situation imperative, otherwise not only our offensive but the entire Italo-German position in North Africa will be lost.

The 'immediate measures' necessary were primarily a reinforcement of the Luftwaffe in the Mediterranean: if powerful air forces were again stationed in Sicily they could deny the central basin to British ships and neutralize Malta. But, obsessed with the overriding importance of the campaign in Russia, Hitler for the moment refused to divert any further air strength to the Mediterranean. Instead he ordered Fliegerkorps X to be diverted from its offensive task of attacking enemy ships and supply bases in Egypt to that of protecting convoys to North Africa. This might have had a serious effect on air operations from Malta had not Goering contrived to have the order modified, so as to restrict the activities of the Fliegerkorps to protection of convoys running between Greece and Benghazi and along the coastal route between Benghazi and Derna. Hitler also overrode the objections of the German Naval Staff by ordering six U-boats to the Mediterranean.

The inadequacy of these measures was soon dramatically demonstrated. The increased security of the Malta base, and the success which had attended the passage of the two supply convoys in July and September, had satisfied the Admiralty that the time had again come to station there a striking force of surface ships. On October 21st, 1941, the cruisers *Aurora* and *Penelope* from the Home Fleet and two destroyers detached from Force 'H', the *Lance* and *Lively*, arrived to form Force 'K' under the command of Captain W. G. Agnew of the *Aurora*.

Their arrival, which was at once known to the Italian Naval Staff, coincided with a temporary stoppage of all convoys for Libya owing to the heavy losses. With Rommel preparing an offensive such an embargo could not be long maintained; but it was nearly three weeks before a suitable target for Force 'K' offered itself. This was a convoy of seven freighters which the Italian Naval Staff, under heavy pressure from the Army command, felt obliged to dispatch despite the risk it was bound to run. Powerful protection was arranged for it. Six destroyers under Captain Bisciani of the *Maestrale* formed the close escort, while the heavy cruisers *Trieste* and *Trento* and four destroyers acted in close support, commanded by Vice-Admiral Bruno Brivonesi. To give warning if Force 'K' should come out, several submarines were stationed to seaward of Valetta harbour.

Debouching from the Straits of Messina around midday on November 8th, the convoy was given an air escort of eight Italian and German aircraft until dusk. These were unable to prevent a Maryland on reconnaissance from Malta sighting and reporting the convoy at 4.40 PM. An hour later Force 'K' was leaving harbour. No enemy aircraft marked their leaving, nor did the Italian submarines see or hear them. Soon they were racing eastwards, under a clear night sky, through a sea gently ruffled by a light breeze from the north-west.

By midnight the moon had risen and was shining brightly in the east. Forty minutes later, the unsuspecting convoy was sighted at a range of six miles. The British squadron was in line ahead with the *Aurora* leading; and now Captain Agnew signalled for speed to be reduced to 20 knots and led round to the north-east, so that his targets would be silhouetted against the moon, before turning starboard on to a southerly course parallel to that of the convoy.

No inkling of the devastating blow that was about to strike them had as yet alarmed the merchantmen or their guardians. Admiral Brivonesi, unwilling to keep his squadron down to the slow speed of the merchant ships and so expose himself an easy target to any prowling submarine, had been patrolling north and south on the western flank of the convoy – between it and the likely direction of any attack coming from the direction of Malta. Unlike the British squadron he had no radar. Nor were his ships well equipped or his crews well trained for night action. Thus, though Agnew had dimly sighted him to the north-eastward during his approach but had ignored him to concentrate on the main object, the convoy, Brivonesi knew nothing of the presence of the British squadron. A little while earlier he had turned north. He had reached a position some three miles astern of the convoy and was now turning back on to the southerly leg of his patrol when suddenly the horizon ahead was lit up by the bright flashes of gunfire.

Convoy and escort alike were taken completely by surprise. The destroyer *Grecale* bringing up the rear was immediately hit and brought to a stop, out of action. The *Fulmine*, on the convoy's starboard quarter, survived hardly a minute of the fire from *Aurora*'s 6-inch guns before sinking. The other destroyer on the starboard side, the *Euro*, turned to attack, but, on seeing the dark bulk of the British cruisers, came to the conclusion that they were Italian and that some dreadful mistake was being made. He countermanded the order to fire torpedoes and turned away to seek his senior officer in the *Maestrale*. There Captain Bisciani, under the impression that the convoy was being attacked by aircraft, had given the order for all ships to make smoke. He realized his mistake when the mast with his radio aerial was shot down, thus cutting him off from communication with his squadron. The two destroyers to port of the convoy, the *Libeccio* and the *Oriani*, could not make out what was going on amidst the smoke which blew down over them and were unable to take any useful action.

Similarly, the Italian cruisers could make little of the mêlée. They briefly opened fire at their half-seen target but no shell splashes were seen from the British ships. Brivonesi then turned north in which direction he estimated he would be able to intercept the British squadron as it withdrew. Certainly he was too late to prevent the massacre of the convoy, which had been quickly reduced to a number of sinking or burning ships as Agnew led his force in a wide circle, pumping shells into his helpless prey. But a northerly course was a peculiar choice, to say the least of it, as Malta lay to the south-west and it was in that direction that Agnew steered when, a few minutes after 2 AM, the last merchant ship had been disposed of.

Nothing remained for the Italian escorts but to take the crippled *Grecale* in tow by the *Oriani* and to pick up survivors from the sunken merchant ships. While this was going on, towards dawn a last misfortune befell the ill-starred Italian forces: the submarine *Upholder* put a torpedo into the *Libeccio* which later sank. Not unreasonably, scapegoats were sought amongst the Italian commanders. Admiral Brivonesi and Captain Bisciani were both deprived of their commands, though the former was later exonerated. Responsibility for the disaster could, indeed, not fairly be laid at the door of any individual, arising as it did from the Italian Navy's neglect of night-action training and equipment, as well as from its lack of radar.

This lightning blow by Force 'K', devastating as it was, was only a highlight of the campaign to destroy Axis supply ships which was being waged by British aircraft, submarines and surface ships. September 1941 had seen the loss of 28 per cent of all cargoes shipped for Libya, October 21 per cent. Now in November it rose to 63 per cent. The situation had become intolerable, not only for the Italians whose merchant marine was being wiped out, but also for Rommel and the Afrika Korps whose planned offensive to capture Tobruk had already had to be postponed from September to October, then to November. Before it could be implemented the British Eighth Army struck, on November 18th. The Afrika Korps, its power of resistance weakened by shortages of every sort of supplies, suffered a resounding defeat.

T—E

Meanwhile, however, the Italian Navy made strenuous efforts to bring succour to the hard-pressed Axis armies. Cruisers were brought into service as petrol carriers. A few merchant ships, sailing singly or in pairs, reached Benghazi by coasting down the west of Greece to Crete before crossing to the African shore. A more important convoy of four ships from Naples was sailed on November 20th and was given the powerful escort of seven destroyers and a supporting force of three heavy cruisers, two light cruisers and seven destroyers. Its air escort could not prevent one of the ubiquitous scouting Sunderlands from reporting it as it emerged from the Messina Straits the next day. That evening RAF Wellington bombers, together with the Swordfish and Albacores of 830 and 828 Squadrons from Malta, attacked. The cruiser *Duca degli Abruzzi* was torpedoed and forced to limp back, badly damaged, to Messina. During the night the submarine *Utmost* joined the attack and torpedoed the cruiser *Trieste*, which was also forced to turn back. Thereupon the convoy, with its desperately needed cargoes, was recalled and the operation abandoned.

Other small convoys which had taken the easterly route for Benghazi, hoping to slip through while British attentions were concentrated on the bigger operation, were also recalled; but one of them, composed of two German ships *Procida* and *Maritza* and escorted by the torpedo boats *Lupo* and *Cassiopaea*, failed to receive the order. During the afternoon of the 24th it was intercepted by Force 'K'. Both merchant ships, carrying ammunition and bombs as well as petrol and motor transport for the Afrika Korps, were blown up and sunk.

Out of all the ships which had set forth in this widespread effort to bring supplies to the armies in Africa which were now fighting desperately to halt the British offensive, only two got through, one to Tripoli and one to Benghazi. On November 29th the Italians tried again, using the same method of dispatching a number of small convoys on different routes and adding a battleship to the covering force of four cruisers and nine destroyers. The outcome was no more successful. Blenheims from Malta sank the Italian merchant ship *Capo Faro* and crippled two others. On December 1st Force 'K' caught and sank the auxiliary cruiser *Adriatico*, carrying ammunition, artillery and supplies, and then went on to sink the tanker *Iridio Mantovani*, previously damaged by the Blenheims, and to blow up her escorting destroyer *Da Mosto*. To replenish Rommel's fast-dwindling supplies only one ship of all those that sailed reached Benghazi on the 2nd.

For the Axis the situation was almost catastrophic. In North Africa, since the opening of the British offensive on November 18th, fortunes had swayed back and forth. The British Forces achieved complete tactical surprise: while one Army Corps, the XIII, surrounded and held the enemy forces on the Egyptian-Cyrenaican frontier, the other Corps, the XXX, made a wide sweep to Sidi Rezegh, 20 miles south-east of Tobruk. A period of confused fighting ensued in which both sides suffered very heavy tank losses. By November 27th the Tobruk garrison and the relieving force had joined hands at Sidi Rezegh, thus establishing an en-circling corridor inside which lay the Afrika Korps. Mean-while, Rommel had struck eastwards with almost all his armour, and by the 25th reached a position well inside the Egyptian frontier; he then turned north to the rescue of his beleaguered forces on the frontier. By this bold move, which threatened the British supply lines, he hoped to panic the British command into a withdrawal from the area south-east of Tobruk. He was unsuccessful, meeting not only a steady defence by units of the XIII Corps, but a sustained assault by the R A F bombers. Mounting tank losses and administra-tive and supply difficulties brought an end to Rommel's spectacular stroke. News of the junction of the Tobruk garrison with General Freyberg's New Zealand Division, which with the 1st Army Tank Brigade had captured Sidi Rezegh, forced him to turn back westward to restore the situation. Heavy fighting resulted around Sidi Rezegh during the last days of November, and by December 2nd the town was again in German hands and Tobruk was once more cut off.

By now, however, the Afrika Korps and its Italian allies had almost shot their bolt. Supplies were dangerously short and there was no reserve of fresh troops. Rommel was thrown back on the defensive while the British, able to bring in fresh troops and rely on ample supplies, were preparing to renew their interrupted offensive. It was at this moment that information reached Rommel which put an end to his hopes of halting his opponents. For some time past both he and his official Italian superior, General Bastico, had been appealing for reinforcements and a greater flow of supplies of all kinds. On December 4th there arrived Colonel Montezemolo, head of the Operations Branch of the *Comando Supremo* in Rome, with the dire news that nothing but a trickle of fuel, food and medical stores could be expected. The British naval and air operations were stopping all else.

It was small comfort to Rommel that at last Hitler had woken up to the seriousness of the situation and the importance of the Mediterranean theatre as a whole, and had ordered a Fliegerkorps again to Sicily. This could not affect the supply situation before the end of December. Meanwhile, Rommel declared, it was no longer possible to hold Cyrenaica. Two days later he abandoned the siege of Tobruk, together with all plans for relieving the troops in the Egyptian border positions, and began a fighting retreat to a position at El Gazala, west of Tobruk. By December 17th that position was, in its turn, abandoned; and by January 12th Rommel was back on the borders of Tripolitania, and all Cyrenaica was once again in British hands.

The defeat of the Axis armies and the raising of the long siege of Tobruk painted, to a superficial and landward-looking view, a bright picture of the situation of the British in the campaign for the Mediterranean. In truth, however, the principal factor which had led to this great success had already been removed. This had been the reduction of German air strength in the area, particularly in the Central Mediterranean, with the resultant build-up of the offensive and defensive capabilities of Malta, and the virtual strangulation of the Libyan supply line. It was sea power – the ability to use the sea for one's own purposes and to prevent the enemy from doing the same – which, passing into the hands of the British with the withdrawal of Fliegerkorps X from the decisive area, had been the key to the dramatic reversal of fortune in North Africa.

But even while the fruits of British successes, above, beneath and on the surface of the sea, were being gathered in the deserts of Libya, the tree on which they had grown was withering. Within two weeks of Rommel's decision to retreat to El Agheila on the border of Tripolitania, he was once again in a position to mount a successful offensive. This resulted partly from successful German counter-attacks, while Rommel was still holding his Gazala position, which inflicted heavy defeats on the British armoured formations. This offensive could not, however, have been even contemplated by Rommel but for a dramatic change in the situation at sea.

7

The Mediterranean Fleet in Eclipse

IN THE previous chapter the desire to show the close
connexion between events at sea and the land campaign in
North Africa focused attention on the severe losses inflicted
upon the Italian supply convoys to Libya. These losses and
delays reached their peak in November during which 63 per
cent of the cargoes which set out failed to arrive. Little was
said about the reactions of the Axis dictators to this catastrophic set-back to their plans – reactions which had already
begun, during November, to redress the balance of sea power
in the Mediterranean.

In response to mounting appeals for aid from the army
commanders in Libya, from the German Naval and General
Staffs and from Mussolini personally to Hitler, the latter
had turned from his all-engrossing preoccupation with the
campaign against Russia to see what could be done. His
first step was to order four more U-boats to the Mediterranean in addition to the six already sent there in September.
These quickly achieved two resounding successes. On
November 13th the *Ark Royal*, returning to Gibraltar with
Force 'H' after yet another sortie into the central Mediterranean to fly off Hurricane reinforcements for Malta, was
torpedoed and sunk in a skilfully delivered attack by U-81,
commanded by Lieutenant Guggenberger. The loss of this
famous ship, so often attacked and so often claimed by the
Germans to have been sunk, was a severe blow, coming at a
time when the *Illustrious* and *Formidable* were still repairing
battle damage in the United States, and the *Indomitable* had
recently been damaged through running aground off Kingston, Jamaica, while still working up her squadrons and
ship's company. Thus no modern carrier was available to

take her place. Without one, the ability of Force 'H' to take further convoys to Malta had gone.

Twelve days later it was the turn of the Mediterranean Fleet to suffer a calamity. It will be recalled that on November 24th Force 'K' from Malta was at sea intercepting a convoy to the north of Benghazi. Simultaneously a detachment from the Mediterranean Fleet, known as Force 'B' and comprising the 7th and 15th Cruiser Squadrons, had been out seeking prey, though without success. In support, Admiral Cunningham had taken his battle-squadron – *Queen Elizabeth*, *Barham* and *Valiant* – to sea with a screen of eight destroyers.

Some 60 miles north of Sollum, U-331, commanded by Lieutenant-Commander von Tiesenhausen, intercepted the battle-squadron, penetrated its strong screen of destroyers and hit the *Barham* with three torpedoes. She at once took a list to port, which quickly increased until she was lying on her beam ends. A minute later there was a cataclysmic explosion in which the great ship disintegrated. When the smoke and spray cleared, she had disappeared, taking with her 56 officers and 812 ratings.

These two successes by the newly arrived German U-boats were the beginning of a succession of severe blows suffered by the Royal Navy in the Mediterranean.

Meanwhile, ten days after his order for the re-deployment of U-boats, Hitler issued, on December 2nd, 1941, his Directive No 38, which was to have a vital influence on the battle for the Mediterranean. In it he gave instructions that Fliegerkorps II, under General Lörzer, should be transferred from the Russian front to Sicily and North Africa. Together with Fliegerkorps X, which was responsible for the eastern Mediterranean sector, it would form Luftflotte 2 under the overall command of Field-Marshal Kesselring, who was concurrently Commander-in-Chief (Air), South, and in command of all German armed forces in Sicily. The task given to Kesselring was a double one:

(a) to achieve air and sea mastery in the area between

southern Italy and North Africa and thus ensure safe lines of communication with Libya and Cyrenaica. The suppression of Malta is particularly important in this connexion;

(b) to paralyse enemy traffic through the Mediterranean and to stop British supplies reaching Tobruk and Malta.

Thus was set on foot a re-disposition of German strength which was to reverse the balance of sea power in the Mediterranean and subject Malta to an ordeal by bomb and a siege to which she nearly succumbed and which, if it had been carried through with single-minded vigour to its conclusion, must have made the victory at El Alamein impossible.

While Fliegerkorps II was still moving into Sicily, however, and before its effect had begun seriously to be felt, the Italian Navy recorded one of its blackest days as a result of renewed efforts to get supplies through to Africa. At the height of the British offensive a supreme effort to bring aid to Rommel was ordered. On December 13th, five supply ships sailed from Taranto, in three separate convoys. In addition to their close escort of eight destroyers, with each of two of these groups was a *Duilio* class battleship, two or three cruisers and three destroyers in close support, while the *Littorio* and *Vittorio Veneto* were sailed with a screen of four destroyers in general support.

Meanwhile, at Palermo, cased petrol in large quantities had been loaded on board the two light cruisers *Da Barbiano* and *Di Giussano*, which sailed on the evening of December 13th, in company with the torpedo-boat *Cigno*, for a high-speed dash across the Sicilian Straits to Cape Bon and thence along the coastal route to Tripoli. Their departure did not escape the watchful eye of British reconnaissance planes. Coming eastwards from Gibraltar at high speed was a force of four destroyers under Commander G. H. Stokes of the *Sikh*, with the *Maori*, *Legion* and HM Netherlands Ship *Issac Sweers*. A signal went out to him from Admiral Ford, commanding at Malta, that the cruisers of Force 'K' were

Admiral Sir James Somerville

Admiral Sir Andrew Cunningham

Admiral Inigo Campioni

Admiral Angelo Iachino

The *Cavour* sunk in Taranto Harbour, November 11th, 1940

An Italian troop convoy assembling

Near misses by bombs on the *Ark Royal*

The *Ark Royal* sinking

The Grand Harbour, Malta, under air attack

being dispatched to intercept the Italian ships 90 miles south of Cape Bon and that torpedo aircraft would also attack during the night. It was estimated that Stokes could not reach Cape Bon in time to take part but he was told to be prepared for the enemy to break back towards him.

A little later the sailing of Force 'K' was countermanded owing to Malta's shortage of oil-fuel, the last few tons of which had to be reserved against any dire emergency. Thus the Italian cruisers would have had only the torpedo aircraft to contend with had they kept to their planned schedule. For some reason, however, although Vice-Admiral Toscano commanding the squadron had been warned of the approach of the British destroyers, he was more than an hour late in his arrival off Cape Bon. Thus Stokes as he came pounding up from the westward, sighted flashing lights and then the outline of two ships which disappeared behind the steep bulk of the headland.

It seemed as though he was just too late. But luck was running on the British side that night. Toscano had just rounded Cape Bon when he heard overhead the sound of aircraft in formation which he guessed to be torpedo planes. To foil them he reversed his course, so that as the *Sikh* drew clear of the headland Stokes saw his enemy steering towards him and approaching rapidly. He at once led away to get between the Italians and the shore so that he would remain unseen against the black backdrop of the headland.

The Italians were thus taken completely by surprise, when at 2.23 AM the destroyers' guns flashed out and torpedoes splashed as they were sent on the short run to the target. A few wildly aimed salvos from the Italians dropped their shells on the shore beyond their target, but their gunfire soon ceased as three torpedoes hit the *Da Barbiano*, sending her quickly to the bottom, and another hit the *Di Giussano* whose cargo of petrol blazed up. All was over in a few minutes and the destroyers resumed their passage to Malta, leaving the *Di Giussano* to sink an hour later while the *Cigno* picked up survivors.

While this vivid demonstration of the Italian Navy's

fighting inadequacy by night was taking place, the heavily
escorted convoys from Taranto, mentioned above, were
getting under way. These movements were at once known to
Admiral Cunningham, who ordered the 15th Cruiser
Squadron – *Naiad, Galatea* and *Euryalus* and nine destroyers
from Alexandria – to proceed to intercept the enemy. From
Malta Force 'K' sailed to cooperate. Cunningham had
insufficient destroyers for screening purposes to allow him
to take his battleships to sea. Though these cruiser forces,
mounting only 6-inch guns, were prepared to fight at such
odds at this critical moment of the land campaign, Cunningham resorted to a ruse which he hoped would make it unnecessary. While strict radio silence was enjoined at Alexandria, the fast minelayer *Abdiel* was sent out to create a
radio diversion and give the impression that the battle-
squadron was at sea.

The ruse was successful. On the evening of the 13th, the
Italian convoys were recalled. Even so, they did not escape
disaster. Two of the supply ships collided, thus putting each
other out of action for some months. Two more were torpedoed and sunk by the submarine *Upright*. Finally, the
Vittorio Veneto, returning to Messina, was torpedoed and
severely damaged by the *Urge*. It would be several months
before the battleship could operate again.

However, the losses were not entirely one-sided in this
operation. Lying in wait for the 15th Cruiser Squadron on
its return, off the swept channel into Alexandria, was U-557,
which torpedoed and sank the *Galatea*. Her loss, indeed,
following that of the *Ark Royal* and *Barham*, was another
step towards the eclipse of British sea power in the Mediterranean, being closely followed by a series of disasters as well
as the opening of the Luftwaffe's renewed assault on Malta.

With the Libyan convoy route once again cut, as it
seemed, the immediate concern of Admiral Cunningham
was to get fresh supplies of oil-fuel to Malta where the
shortage was restricting the movements of the cruiser
striking force. That gallant veteran of so many Malta 'runs',
the *Breconshire*, was chosen to carry them, and late on

December 15th she sailed with the two surviving cruisers of Rear-Admiral Vian's 15th Cruiser-Squadron, the anti-aircraft cruiser *Carlisle* and eight destroyers. Off the Benghazi 'bulge', the cruisers of Force 'K' and four destroyers would come to reinforce the escort during December 17th and remain with the *Breconshire* when Vian turned back after dark that evening. Like the Italians, the British found it necessary now to press every available ship into service to escort even a single ship through the no-man's-land of the Central Mediterranean. As with the Italians, too, battleships were really necessary to give protection against attack by similar ships of the enemy. However, Cunningham's shortage of destroyers made this impossible.

Thus, when the Italians decided at the same time to make yet another supreme effort to get a convoy through to Libya, Admiral Vian was faced with the possibility of having to oppose the Italian battle-fleet with four cruisers and 12 destroyers. Nevertheless, sending back the *Carlisle* on account of her lack of speed, he pressed on with the *Breconshire*, hoping to pass ahead, across the track of the Italian forces known to be coming south in support of their convoy.

The *Aurora*, *Penelope* and four destroyers duly joined Vian on the morning of the 17th. At 10.25 AM came the expected report from a reconnaissance plane. Two battleships, two cruisers and seven destroyers were 150 miles NNW of him, steering south at slow speed. This was the Italian supporting force, actually the *Littorio*, flying the flag of Admiral Iachino, the *Doria* and *Cesare*, two heavy cruisers and 10 destroyers. Some 60 miles to the westward the convoy and its powerful close escort – the *Duilio*, three cruisers and 11 destroyers – were also coming south but had not at this time been located. At almost the same moment Iachino learnt of the presence of Vian's force (though his reconnaissance planes reported the *Breconshire* as a battleship and continued to do so throughout the day). Iachino now turned to the south-west and worked up speed to the maximum of his two older battleships – 24 knots. He was hoping before sunset to intercept the British force which he imagined to be out for the express purpose of attacking his convoy.

An opportunity thus presented itself to the Italian admiral to bring a greatly inferior British force to action. Two factors combined to prevent it – the Italian policy of refusing to take any risks with their fleet and the unfitness of their ships for night action. Making contact with Vian's squadron at sunset, Iachino turned away under threat of a torpedo attack by the British destroyers. Contact was soon lost in the gathering darkness after which the Italian admiral contented himself with covering his convoy, leaving the *Breconshire*, of whose presence he was unaware, to reach Malta safely. Vian, whose ships had survived unscathed more than 20 attacks by torpedo planes and bombers during the day, returned to Alexandria without further hindrance.

The Italian convoy, after turning about for a few hours, resumed its course for Tripoli without further interference. As Commander Bragadin has put it, 'The night, which had begun with so full a threat of every peril, passed instead amid an incredible calm for the Italian ships – a calm such as no convoy had enjoyed in many months' – a statement which, in view of the forces deployed on either side, is an indication of the moral ascendancy which had been established by the British in the central Mediterranean. It was to continue to have its effect for some time after the teeth of the British naval forces had been drawn in the events to be described, for the Italian fleet continued to put to sea in full strength to protect the Libyan convoys from a surface threat which no longer in fact existed.

Meanwhile, the convoy, which had enjoyed such unwonted immunity during the night of December 17th and during the following day, arrived off Tripoli after dark on the 18th to find the port undergoing air attack during which magnetic mines were laid by Wellington bombers. Torpedo planes from Malta had attacked the ships, an Albacore of 828 Squadron obtaining a hit on the steamer *Napoli* which had had to be taken in tow. The convoy therefore anchored off the port for the remainder of the night, but was got safely in during the 19th.

In the hope of catching it still outside, Force 'K', composed of the cruisers *Neptune*, *Aurora* and *Penelope*, with the destroyers *Lance*, *Lively*, *Havelock* and *Kandahar*, was meanwhile racing through the night from Malta. Soon after midnight disaster struck as they ran into a dense field of mines, long-established but until now unknown to the British. In the next four hours, the *Neptune* was lost with all hands but one leading seaman, and the *Aurora* and *Penelope* were both damaged, the former severely, but reached Malta under their own power. The *Kandahar*, while trying to take the *Neptune* in tow, had her stern blown off and eventually had to be sunk. Force 'K' had virtually ceased to exist.

Even while Force 'K' was suffering this calamity, a heroic exploit off Alexandria was similarly eliminating Cunningham's battle-squadron. It was the crowning success of the Italian 10th Light Flotilla, previously mentioned and whose story, briefly summarized, may best be told at this point.

The flotilla specialized in the type of individualistic operation in which the Italian seems to excel – one-man explosive motor-boats (EMB), skin-diving frogmen and two-men 'chariots', called by the Italians 'slow-speed torpedoes', or more familiarly, 'pigs'. These last were submersible craft on which the crew, wearing breathing apparatus, sat astride. On reaching their objective, the explosive head was detached, clamped to the keel and a time-fuse set. Experiments with chariots had been begun as long ago as 1935 by two Engineer Lieutenants, Toschi and Tesei, and when Italy entered the war, operational craft and trained operators were available and three submarines had been adapted to carry them. No time was lost in sending the first of these, the *Iride*, on a mission to attack the Mediterranean Fleet in Alexandria harbour. This was the submarine which, as it lay in the Gulf of Bomba, near Tobruk, making final preparations, was torpedoed and sunk by Captain Patch, Royal Marines, flying a Swordfish, as recounted in Chapter 2. Patch thus scored a more important success than was realized at the time.

At the end of September 1940 the other two submarines, *Sciré* and *Gondar*, were dispatched on similar errands to Gibraltar and Alexandria. They were recalled when it was discovered that both harbours were empty. The *Gondar* was sunk while returning and her crew, including the Flotilla Commander Giorgioni, was taken prisoner. The *Sciré* was more fortunate and, under the command of Lieutenant-Commander Valerio Borghese, enjoyed a long and successful career. Four times between October 1940 and September 1941 she successfully launched chariot attacks against shipping in Gibraltar harbour. On the first three occasions the attacks themselves failed owing to defects in the early type of chariot; but on the fourth attempt, though the charioteers failed to reach their primary objectives, the *Ark Royal* and *Nelson* of Force 'H', they succeeded in sinking three merchant ships, including the large naval tanker *Denby Dale*. The charioteers, with one or two exceptions, succeeded on each occasion in reaching the Spanish shore whence secret agents arranged for their return to Italy.

Between these operations the 10th Light Flotilla engaged in other exploits with EMBs. Attempts against the Greek ports of Corfu and Santi Quaranta in the spring of 1941 achieved nothing; but on the night of March 26th six EMBs, commanded by Lieutenant Faggioni, penetrated the net defences of the anchorage at Suda Bay and sank the cruiser *York* and a merchant ship.

The next target for the 10th Light Flotilla was Malta. An attack had been planned for some time. The arrival of the large convoy in the last week of July 1941 set it in motion during the night of the 25th. Eight EMBs were loaded in the auxiliary warship *Diana*, which set off accompanied by two MTBs each towing a chariot. The plan was for a chariot piloted by Lieutenant Tesei, the designer of the weapon, to go in first and blast a way through the obstructions in the boat passage at the inner end of the breakwater – a passage spanned by a footbridge. The EMBs would then dash through to find their targets in the Grand Harbour.

The Italians showed a surprising lack of appreciation of

the capabilities of Malta's radar in devising this plan which, indeed, was doomed to failure from the start. The presence of the *Diana* was known at once; the MTBs were likewise detected. The harbour defences were fully on the alert and ready to open fire at the first signs of any craft approaching the shore. Meanwhile, something had gone wrong with Tesei – it will never be known what, for he was never seen again. As the dawn approached without the expected explosion, two of the EMBs were ordered in to carry out his task. With sublime heroism the EMB pilots, to ensure success, blew themselves up with their boats. The resultant explosion, however, brought down the footbridge, effectively blocking the passage. And now the guns opened up with devastating effect on the remaining craft as they dashed in. All the EMBs were destroyed, while the retreating MTBs were caught and sunk at daylight by Malta's Hurricane fighters. Only the *Diana* escaped to tell the tragic tale.

The achievements of the 10th Light Flotilla had hitherto been of comparatively minor importance. It was now to strike a blow which was of great consequence in the struggle for control of the Mediterranean. At 9 PM on the evening of December 18th, 1941, in a position 1.3 miles from the lighthouse on the mole at Alexandria, Borghese brought the *Sciré* gently to the surface. Three chariots, their rubber-suited, helmeted and goggled crews astride of them, set off towards the harbour entrance. The submarine sank back into the depths and turned for the open sea.

The pilots of the three chariots, Luigi de la Penne, Antonio Marceglia and Vincenzo Martellotta, were all veterans of the exploits in Gibraltar Bay. Good luck aided their skill, for, as they were contemplating the net defences and preparing to negotiate them, they saw them obligingly drawn open to permit the entry of destroyers of Admiral Vian's force, which were returning from the encounter with the Italian fleet. Narrowly escaping being run down by the destroyers, the chariots passed into the harbour with them.

During these eventful moments the three charioteers lost touch with each other; but each had his assigned target and carried on independently. De la Penne's was the *Valiant*. Negotiating her anti-torpedo net he arrived alongside her safely, but, when submerging, his craft went out of control and plunged to the bottom. Meanwhile his diver, Bianchi, fainting from the long exposure, had lost touch. On coming to, he swam to the mooring buoy and climbed unseen on to it. De la Penne was now faced, single-handed, with the task of hauling his whole craft with its warhead to a position directly beneath the battleship. After superhuman efforts, blinded by the mud stirred up, he succeeded, set the fuse and surfaced, to be taken prisoner with Bianchi.

Refusing to enlighten his captors on the purpose of their mission until shortly before the time set for the fuse to function, they were confined in the hold and were still there when the *Valiant* shuddered under the effect of a terrific explosion. They escaped unharmed, however, to witness the damage they had caused, from which the great ship sank until she was resting on the bottom.

Shortly before this a similar explosion had blown off the stern of the tanker *Sagona*, Martellotta's objective, and badly damaged the destroyer *Jervis* lying alongside her. Martellotta and his companion Marino had reached the shore but were arrested at the dockyard gate. As De la Penne reached the crippled *Valiant*'s deck another violent explosion under the fleet flagship *Queen Elizabeth* told him that Marceglia had been equally successful. With his companion Schergat, he too reached the shore and they were able to make their way into Alexandria and thence to Rosetta off which a submarine was to be lying to pick them up. But the use of English £5 notes with which they had been supplied, currency not in use in Egypt, betrayed them before they could get away and they were taken prisoner.

Thus six brave and resourceful men eliminated at one stroke Cunningham's battle-squadron at a time when replacements were not available. For, eleven days before, the Japanese had delivered their treacherous attack on Pearl Harbor. The battleship *Prince of Wales* and battlecruiser *Repulse* had gone down before the torpedo aircraft of the

Japanese Navy. With what remained of her naval strength Britain turned to defend her eastern Imperial possessions.

By the losses suffered between December 14th and 19th, Cunningham's fleet had been suddenly reduced, apart from destroyers, to the three light cruisers of Vian's 15th Squadron, *Naiad*, *Euryalus* and *Dido*, and the anti-aircraft cruiser *Carlisle*. At Malta were the *Penelope* and *Ajax*, the latter out of action with defects. Opposing this small force the Italians had four battleships, three heavy and three light cruisers besides a great superiority in destroyers and submarines. On the face of it, therefore, the British fleet could no longer operate in the central Mediterranean. In fact, as events were to show, Cunningham's inability to 'field' a battle-squadron was of far less significance than his lack of adequate air support either from a carrier or from shore bases. In the absence of the former, so long as the Cyrenaican airfields were in British hands, Vian's squadron still was able to escort supply ships to Malta under the noses of the Italian fleet preoccupied with the task of protecting its own convoys to Libya from the striking forces on Malta.

During the first week of January the fleet auxiliary H M S *Glengyle* was run safely into Malta from Alexandria with replenishments of oil and the empty *Breconshire* brought away under the escort of Vian's cruisers. Fighter protection was available for the entire voyage and the whole force enjoyed a welcome freedom from air attack. Plans were now made to run a convoy of four or five ships to Malta each month from Alexandria. The first of these sailed on January 16th – four ships with a close escort of the *Carlisle* and eight destroyers covered by Vian's cruiser squadron. One merchant ship, the *Thermopylae*, developed engine-room defects on the 18th and was ordered back to Alexandria under escort of the *Carlisle* and two destroyers. Following a route outside cover by single-engined fighters, she was bombed and set on fire and had to be sunk. The remainder, though attacked on a number of occasions, were effectively protected by Beaufighters of Nos 252 and 272 Squadrons of the Naval Cooperation Group, RAF, which also provided full and efficient air reconnaissance, and arrived safely at Malta under the protection of Hurricane fighters from the island.

The success of this convoy operation in the teeth of opposition by Fliegerkorps II, which had by now got into its stride, was a demonstration of what a properly constituted naval force with its own air component could achieve. Or, as Admiral Cunningham was to comment, 'The work of the RAF 201 Naval Cooperation Group was strikingly efficient and valuable . . . It showed what could be done with aircraft trained to work over the sea.' It had, alas, taken 18 months of war in the Mediterranean for such an essential component of the British fleet to emerge. Between January 24th and 28th the *Breconshire* was yet again run safely into Malta and the *Glengyle* and another empty ship brought out.

It must not be thought that this brief period in January 1942 when the replenishment and reinforcement of Malta went on unimpeded was a period of British control of the central Mediterranean. Simultaneously with the re-opening of the sea route from Alexandria to Malta as a result of the Eighth Army's advance, Fliegerkorps II had gone into action, striking particularly hard at the airfields of Malta whenever an Italian convoy operation was in progress. Thus at this time each side was finding itself able to use the central Mediterranean for its own purposes but, unable to prevent the enemy from using it, neither could claim to control it.

This period of uneasy balance was now to come to an end. As Rommel in North Africa and Fliegerkorps II in Sicily began their offensive the British were thrown back on a desperate defence in which their retention of Egypt and the Suez Canal was largely to depend upon whether Malta could survive an assault far heavier than anything previously experienced.

8

Malta Suppressed

ROMMEL'S FINAL withdrawal to El Agheila on the Tripolitanian frontier in the last days of 1941 had been a voluntary
one. The Eighth Army had outrun its supplies and was in
no state to press on with its offensive. Indeed, its armoured
formations had suffered two sharp defeats on December
28th and 30th, whereupon Rommel had disengaged and
withdrawn to reorganize and supply his troops. Supplies,
particularly of petrol, were the principal preoccupation on
either side, both on land and in the air. But, whereas the
British were now handicapped by the wrecked condition of
the Cyrenaican ports, the shortage of shipping and escorts
and the length of their lines of communication, Rommel's
army, though considerably exhausted, had reduced its supply
line to the short haul from Tripoli.

On January 5th a large convoy, bringing a quantity of fuel
and 54 tanks and their crews, reached Tripoli. Escorted by
the entire Italian fleet it crossed the Mediterranean unmolested. With Force 'K' reduced to a single light cruiser
and three destroyers and Malta's airfields rendered unusable
by raids of more than 400 aircraft between December 30th
and January 5th, the island's striking power was for the time
being at an end. The situation in the central Mediterranean
was thus completely transformed by the British fleet's calami-
ties on December 18th and 19th and the return of the Luftwaffe to Sicily. The immediate effect gave Rommel a local
superiority in armoured strength which he decided to exploit
by delivering a 'spoiling attack' to prevent the Eighth
Army from resuming its offensive. The attack which
began on January 21st far exceeded Rommel's expectation and the over-extended Eighth Army was soon in

full retreat. Benghazi was retaken by the Axis forces on January 29th and by February 6th the Eighth Army was back on the Gazala–Bir Hacheim line to the west of Tobruk – a situation which was to remain stabilized until the end of May while each side refitted and prepared for a renewal of the offensive.

So far as the Axis was concerned this depended primarily upon achieving permanent security for the lines of communication across the Mediterranean. All the authorities concerned were in agreement in this; but the lengths to which it would be necessary to go remained in dispute. Early in 1942 Italian opinion, as represented by General Cavallero, heading the *Comando Supremo* in Rome, had come round to recognizing the necessity of capturing Malta. Kesselring concurred and orders were issued to prepare a combined air and sea invasion. At the same time Grand Admiral Raeder, pressing on Hitler the advantages to be gained from a quick victory in the Mediterranean, which the weakened state of the British fleet made possible, also advocated the capture of the island.

Hitler and the German Supreme Command, however, remained dubious about the necessity for the operation which would require the employment of land and air forces that, in their view, were better employed on the Eastern front or in Cyrenaica. For the time being, though plans and preparations for Operation 'Hercules', as it was called, went ahead, they contented themselves with ordering an all-out assault by the Luftwaffe to neutralize the island. Such an intensified air effort was formulated by the German Supreme Command early in February and planned to begin on March 20th. It was expected that three weeks should suffice to knock Malta out after which a lower scale of effort would keep her prostrate.

From December 21st, Fliegerkorps II had already been subjecting Malta to an air assault far more severe than anything previously experienced. During Fliegerkorps X's occupation of the Sicilian airfields the average monthly count of air raids had been 93. In December 1941 it rose to 169. In

January 1942 there were 262 raids, 73 of them by night. Not a single day and only eight nights passed without a raid. Carried out by comparatively small numbers of aircraft, the Germans classified them as 'minor' raids. Not until February did they begin to intensify their operations and the really big raids did not begin until March. In January and February many of the raids were mounted in direct support of Italian convoy operations with the object of knocking out the airfields and grounding the dreaded air.striking forces.

The small force of Hurricanes took off day after day from the cratered, hastily repaired runways, to take a steady toll of the attackers; but their numbers inevitably dwindled. By the end of January, 28 serviceable aircraft remained. On February 15th the number was down to 11. The odds they accepted were rarely less than 10 to 1. Herculean efforts by ground crews and soldiers of the garrison working night and day would repair the devastated runways again and again, only to have their work undone almost immediately.

Thus, when the Italians again dispatched a battleship-escorted convoy on January 22nd, Malta's air effort against it was reduced to an unsuccessful attack by four torpedo-carrying Swordfish. This convoy became, instead, the target for a massive effort by the aircraft of No 201 Naval Co-operation Group working from airfields in Cyrenaica and Egypt. No 201 Group by this time included Flying Fortress, Wellington and Blenheim bombers, Beaufort torpedo planes of the RAF, and Albacore torpedo planes of the Fleet Air Arm. Unfortunately, it contained no dive bombers – the type most successful in the ship-bombing role until the production of the rocket-firing fighter – because no such aircraft had been developed by the British. In its absence the RAF had been forced into employing the almost suicidal method of low-flying attack used by the Malta Blenheims, abandoned now that Beaufort torpedo planes had arrived on the scene. The RAF also persisted, however, with the high-level attack, which had already so often been proved ineffective against ships at sea. Thus out of 53 aircraft of all types sent out against this convoy, it was the torpedo planes, Beauforts and

Albacores, which achieved the only success.

Located by a reconnaissance plane early on the 23rd, the Italian force was shadowed throughout the afternoon in spite of an air escort of nine Ju 88s. At 4.15 that afternoon, the first attacks began, bombs bursting near the ocean liner *Victoria*, which with three cargo-boats comprised the convoy, and around the cruisers of the escort. They did no harm, but Admiral Bergamini, commanding the operation, called for reinforcements to his air escort which was soon increased to 12 Ju 88s. Then, at 5.25, in the eye of the setting sun, three twin-engined aircraft were seen coming in low. In the face of a tremendous volume of gunfire, they turned away at a range of some 3,500 yards. Splashes seen below them were taken for bombs being jettisoned. But these were torpedo-carrying Beauforts making their début in the Mediterranean. When the torpedo tracks were seen from the *Victoria* it was too late to take avoiding action. Hit on her starboard quarter, the great liner came to a stop.

Though crippled she was in no immediate danger of sinking, and in the gathering dusk her soldier passengers were disembarked into lifeboats and taken aboard the destroyers of the escort. While this was going on, two Albacores of No 826 Squadron, led by the squadron commander, Lieutenant-Commander J. W. S. Corbett, came droning in, their slow speed and antiquated biplane appearance belying their deadly effectiveness. The leader was shot down, indeed, and the crew taken prisoner, but the other, flown by Lieutenant H. M. Ellis, came steadily on to send its torpedo squarely into the *Victoria* to sink her. The loss of the *Victoria* – 'the pearl of the Italian merchant fleet' as Count Ciano described her in his diary – was a painful blow to the Italians; but the safe arrival of the remainder of the convoy, in spite of all that aircraft of No 201 Group could do to stop them, was a consoling indication to them of the improved situation brought about by the Malta 'blitz'.

Within a few days the airfields of Western Cyrenaica were once again in Axis hands. From that time onwards, for a long time to come, the British efforts to cut the Libyan convoy route were reduced to negligible proportions, on the one hand by the remoteness of the airfields available to No 201 Group, on the other by the difficulties of operating from the Malta base while under continuous air attack. A number of sorties were made and there were occasional successes as when Wellingtons from Malta raided Palermo and sank three German ships in the harbour there. But on the whole results were very meagre. The 10th Submarine Flotilla continued for a time to haunt the Libyan convoy route with success, but from early in March so many submarines were damaged in harbour and the refit and replenishment of the remainder so interrupted that the number at sea quickly dwindled, until at the end of April the Flotilla was forced to shift its base to Alexandria for fear of being penned in port by mines laid in the approaches.

British aims were now reduced to attempting to supply Malta with the means to survive and to defend herself until the storm blew over. Convoys from the west were out of the question since the loss of the *Ark Royal* had reduced Force 'H' to one battleship, one light-cruiser, a few destroyers and the small and ancient, non-operational carrier *Argus*. A convoy from Alexandria had been successfully passed through in January under the fighter 'umbrella' of No 201 Naval Cooperation Group. Though such protection would no longer be available for the crucial part of the voyage when the convoy was off the Benghazi 'bulge' with its enemy airfields, and though Malta's exiguous force of Hurricanes could give the ships little protection once arrived, Admiral Cunningham felt bound to try again during the dark of the moon in February. At the same time the *Breconshire* and three other empty ships would be brought away.

Accordingly, on the evening of the 12th the fast freighters *Clan Chattan*, *Clan Campbell* and *Rowallan Castle*, all veterans of the Malta run, sailed from Alexandria and headed westward with their close escort, the *Carlisle* and eight destroyers. Air attacks began the next morning and continued intermittently throughout the day. They were frustrated by the fighter cover provided from the shore bases

and the gunfire of the escorts until the evening, when a
Ju 88 dive-bomber broke through to hit and damage the
Clan Campbell. Her speed reduced, she was ordered away to
Tobruk. The following morning Rear-Admiral Vian's cruiser
force joined the escort for the critical day when little or no
fighter cover could be expected. Already it had been necessary to ration the ammunition for the anti-aircraft guns
which had been used up at a great rate on the previous day.
Now, throughout the afternoon high-level and dive-bombers·
kept up a continuous series of attacks. During one of them
the *Clan Chattan* took a bomb in her hold and was soon
ablaze with ammunition exploding. Destroyers took her
crew and service passengers off, and sent her to the bottom.

With the last surviving merchantman Vian met Force 'K'
and the four empty ships from Malta during the afternoon.
Amidst a hail of bombs the *Penelope* and her six destroyers
took over the escort of the *Rowallan Castle* while Vian
turned back for Alexandria with the empty ships. Twenty
minutes later the *Rowallan Castle* came to a halt as a near
miss disabled her engines. She was taken in tow by the
destroyer *Zulu*; but progress was slow. Air attacks continued
without respite. They were all foiled; but it was soon clear
that by the following morning the *Rowallan Castle* would
still be outside the range of Malta's Hurricane fighters and
would receive the full fury of the Luftwaffe from Sicily as
well as North Africa. On orders from the Commander-in-
Chief, she was sunk after dark. The convoy had ceased to
exist.

This calamity had not been unexpected. On paper the
object of the operation had been impossible to accomplish.
Apart from the overwhelming air threat, the Italian Navy
was able to interpose itself in superior strength and, in fact,
on the morning of February 15th a force of four cruisers
assembled to the eastward of Malta to bar the passage of
the convoy had it still existed.

To demonstrate further the shift of control of the central
Mediterranean from the British to the Axis, a week later the
Italians were able to run a large convoy of their own with

battleship and cruiser cover. Efforts by aircraft from Malta, as well as those of No 201 Group, to attack it were frustrated by a series of misfortunes which for the most part showed British capabilities in a poor light compared to those of the enemy air forces.

The convoy, six freighters with the usual escort of a battle-ship and cruisers, was first located on the night of February 21st by a radar-equipped Wellington. A force of naval Albacores took off from Malta but failed to make contact and was recalled when an error of 100 miles in the Welling-ton's report was discovered. During the next day No 201 Group organized a dawn-to-dusk operation in which Fortresses, Beauforts and Blenheims set off to the attack. Out of 25 aircraft that took off, only one, a Fortress, reached the target and bombed it – though without success. The remainder either turned back with engine trouble or radio failures, or failed to locate the convoy. Similar mishaps occurred during the following night. Although the only Wellington at Malta which survived the day's raids took off to home a force of Wellingtons of No 205 Group on to the target, it, too, had to return to base with engine trouble. Thus of the bomber force only one aircraft, which was late in taking off, found the enemy – by chance – and bombed him – without results.

Such a chapter of accidents can be ascribed, so far as the aircraft from Malta were concerned, to the appalling con-ditions under which the ground and air crews were being forced to work by the continuous air raids, that reduced workshops and dispersed areas to rubble and robbed the men of any regular rest. Though they laboured on doggedly, getting what aircraft they could into the air in the face of shortages of all types of equipment and of spare parts, and saw the aircraft they had so painfully repaired destroyed or damaged time and again before they could be flown, they refused to despair. But their ability to strike back at the enemy had been all but destroyed. The failure of the aircraft from the mainland cannot be so easily explained away and serves to stress once again the need for aircrews specially trained for operations at sea. Those based on Malta, employed continuously on shipping strikes, had come to be so trained. They were *naval* airmen, whatever uniform they wore, and their achievements, up to the time Malta was laid prostrate, were so consistent that the Axis seamen learnt to fear them mightily. But Fliegerkorps II, by hammering away at their airfields, had, for the time being, knocked them out of action.

It is not surprising that the impotence of the British naval and air forces at this time, either to protect their own convoys from attack or to inflict damage on the enemy's, should have led the Commanders-in-Chief to doubt whether they could afford to continue the attempt of supplying Malta. 'It appears useless to try to pass in a convoy until the air situation in Malta has been restored and the military situation in Cyrenaica improved', they told the Chiefs of Staff. The reply they received was categorical: 'Malta is of such importance as an air staging point and as impediment to the enemy reinforcement route that the most drastic steps are justified to retain it... No consideration of risk to ships need to deter you.'

In a belated effort to build up Malta's fighter defences, for which no reinforcements had been flown in since the *Ark Royal*'s last trip in November, the Air Ministry at last allocated Spitfires to the island where the Hurricanes had long been outclassed by the Me 109s of Fliegerkorps II. On March 7th, Force 'H', now commanded by Admiral Syfret, came east from Gibraltar with the veteran carriers *Argus* and *Eagle*. From the latter, in a position south-east of Majorca, 15 Spitfires were flown off and arrived safely. It was the first of a succession of such operations, 16 more Spitfires being flown in on March 21st and 29th.

Once again, therefore, Cunningham prepared a convoy. It included – inevitably – that old war-horse, the *Breconshire*, and three fast freighters, *Clan Campbell*, *Pampas* and the Norwegian *Talabot*. On March 20th it sailed with a close escort of the *Carlisle* and seven destroyers while Admiral Vian again provided the covering force with the 15th Cruiser

Squadron and four destroyers. His flag flew in the newly-joined *Cleopatra* which had replaced the *Naiad*, torpedoed on March 11th off Alexandria. To distract the attention of the Italian and German Air Forces in Cyrenaica, various units of the 8th Army operated to create a diversion. Raids were made by the Long-Range Desert Group on landing grounds far behind the enemy lines while other landing grounds were shelled and sabotaged. Number 201 Group R A F made widespread raids on western airfields also. These activities undoubtedly helped to restrict the enemy's air activity against the convoy and for the first two days it enjoyed an unusually quiet passage.

They had not, however, gone unnoticed by the enemy. Italian submarines on patrol and Ju 52 transport aircraft, flying along the route between Greece and Cyrenaica, reported them. At Taranto Admiral Iachino prepared to intervene with his flagship, the splendid *Littorio*, two heavy cruisers *Gorizia* and *Trento*, the light cruiser *Bande Nere* and four destroyers.

Early on March 22nd, Vian was joined by the *Penelope* and a destroyer from Malta. Vian's force had passed through 'Bomb Alley' between Crete and Cyrenaica without suffering any air attacks; but fighter cover had been overhead during the previous day. Now the convoy was beyond the range of British fighters and during the 22nd must rely only upon the guns of the escort for protection. And, as had been foreseen, soon after midnight the Italian squadron had put to sea, its passing noted and reported by the submarine *P36*. Vian estimated that it would intercept him during the afternoon. He aimed to hold the enemy off until dark by the use of pre-arranged diversionary tactics and the lavish use of smoke which, experience had shown, the Italians were wary of entering.

Meanwhile, there were some torpedo attacks by Italian S 79s to occupy his attention. The heavy volume of fire developed by the escorts deterred them from pressing their attacks home, and the torpedoes, fired at long range, were avoided. Then, at 1.30 PM, an aircraft released signal flares and Vian knew his testing time was at hand. It was confirmed at 2.27, when from the *Euryalus*, Captain Bush reported four enemy ships in sight to the north-east. Vian at once set in motion his pre-arranged tactics. While the convoy and its close escort turned away to the south-west, Vian's cruisers and destroyers steered so as to spread a smoke-screen between them and the enemy. In the rising south-easterly wind it steamed out effectively.

The Italian cruisers – at first thought to be battleships – opened fire at Vian's ships as they moved out towards them, but soon turned away to the north-west. At this, Vian also turned to overtake the convoy which he could see under a sky filled with black shell-bursts as its escort fought off a heavy attack by Ju 88s. To the Commander-in-Chief he signalled that the enemy had been driven off. This was premature. The Italian cruisers had, in fact, only fallen back on the *Littorio* on orders from their Admiral, and at 4.40 PM their whole force came in sight to the north-east.

Once again Vian moved out in defiance, opposing the 5.25-inch guns of his three cruisers and 4.7-inch guns of his destroyers to the 15-inch, 8-inch and 6-inch guns of the Italian ships. But other factors were in Vian's favour. The south-east wind was steadily increasing to a gale, whipping up a heavy sea. Lacking radar the Italians relied upon optical range-finders which, lashed by spray, were not very efficient. At the same time the smoke from the funnels of the British ships spread in a dense fog between the opposing squadrons. Both sides thus had only fleeting views of their targets as the British cruisers and flotillas emerged briefly from the smoke to fire guns or torpedoes. Nevertheless, the *Cleopatra* was hit on the bridge by a 6-inch shell and the *Euryalus* was swept by splinters as a 15-inch shell burst alongside her.

Iachino, anxious to get at the convoy but unwilling to go through the smoke, had the choice of circling the smoke-screen either to leeward by continuing on his south-westerly course or to windward by turning south-east into wind and sea. The rising sea into which his ships would have had to head deterred him from the latter alternative – a decision which the course of the battle was to prove a mistaken one. The smoke, drifting north-westward on the wind, extended so far that it was not until nearly 6 PM that he was able to turn south towards the convoy, by which time dusk was approaching, with all its perils for the Italians, lacking, as they did, radar and night fighting capabilities.

Nevertheless, the situation at this time was extremely critical for the British. Vian, suspecting that a portion of the enemy might have made what his seaman's sense told him was the correct move and circled to windward, had taken half his cruiser force to the eastward and thus run temporarily out of the action. His flotilla commanders, Captain Micklethwait and Captain Poland, by boldly moving out to attack with torpedoes and closing to within 6,000 yards to do so, saved the situation. The destroyers *Havock* and *Kingston* were hit and damaged by heavy shells and others had narrow escapes, as they raced ahead through a forest of shell splashes to loose their torpedoes. The torpedo threat and the gathering darkness brought the battle to an end as Iachino swung his ships away to the northwards and disengaged.

The Second Battle of Sirte, as it came to be called, thus ended as a tactical and moral triumph for Admiral Vian's force. Though the Italians had suffered but a single hit by a light shell on the *Littorio* which caused only superficial damage, the bold and skilful delaying tactics of the British ships and flotillas had held off their powerful armoured opponents until darkness came to their aid. The convoy, as yet unharmed by the numerous air attacks it had undergone, had been saved. Its four ships were now dispersed and, each with a destroyer escort, ordered to make their best speed for Malta. Meanwhile, the Italians were suffering more from the weather than they had from the enemy. On their way back to Taranto, two of their destroyers foundered in the gale, the *Littorio* shipped thousands of tons of water and the *Bande Nere* was damaged. The latter had to be sent to Spezia dockyard for repairs; on passage she was torpedoed and sunk by the submarine *Urge*.

Nevertheless, Iachino had partially achieved his aim. The diversion of the convoy to the southward, under the threat posed by his approach, had caused just enough delay to prevent the ships from reaching Malta at first light on the 23rd. They were thus exposed to some hours of air attack before they could reach harbour. Malta's fighter aircraft, their airfields potholed and their numbers reduced by four days of ceaseless, massive attacks, gave what protection they could.

From the moment they came within Hurricane and Spit-fire range [Air Marshal Sir Hugh Lloyd, the Air Officer Commanding in Malta at that time, has written] the only occasion when all the available fighters were not over them was when they were flying back to the aerodromes to be re-fuelled and re-armed or to pick up relief pilots. For the last ten miles to the Grand Harbour there was not a moment's respite. Every aeroplane in Sicily seemed to be flying round the island.

The *Talabot* and *Pampas*, in spite of continuous attacks since dawn, reached the Grand Harbour between 9 and 10 A M, un-harmed except for two bomb hits on the *Pampas* which failed to explode. From the battlements of Valetta the populace, regardless of their own danger from bombs directed at the harbour, watched breathlessly as the ships approached through the leaping bomb splashes and gave them a delirious welcome as they steamed past to their unloading berths.

Meanwhile, however, the gallant *Breconshire*, survivor of so many previous perilous journeys, had been hit and dis-abled when eight miles from harbour. In the heavy seas running she could not be towed and Captain C. A. G. Hutchison anchored her. An hour later the *Clan Campbell*, 20 miles out, was sunk by a bomb and the destroyer *Legion*, damaged by a near miss, had to be beached.

Even so, up to this time, losses had not been exorbitant and certainly less than might have been expected. But Malta was now cowering under the intensified air assault which had begun, as planned, on March 20th. The three supply ships gave the Stuka pilots easy targets and an added incentive. Three hundred and twenty-six bombers and fighters of Fliegerkorps II were expressly directed to their destruction. The outnumbered Hurricanes and Spitfires fought valiantly to protect them and for three days succeeded; but the end was inevitable. On the 26th both *Talabot* and *Pampas* were hit, the former having to be scuttled as fire threatened the ammunition in her hold, while the latter had all but two of her holds flooded. On the following day the *Breconshire*, which in spite of continuous attacks had been towed into a harbour on the south coast of the island, at last succumbed and sank, as did the *Legion* which had been got to the same anchorage. Of the 26,000 tons of cargo which had left Egypt in the convoy, only 5,000 were unloaded.

It was a tragic anti-climax to the gallant deeds performed by ships and aircraft and a bitter disappointment to the almost desperate defenders of Malta. But so long as virtually the whole strength of Luftflotte II could be devoted, during the lull in the campaign in Libya, to the reduction of the island, little better could be hoped for.

March 20th, as previously mentioned, had marked the opening of the grand assault. A few figures are necessary to show what this meant. During February, when no less than 222 attacks were made on the island's airfields alone, Fliegerkorps II had flown 2,497 sorties. In March this figure rose to 4,927 and in April, when Fliegerkorps X also joined the attack, it was 9,599. During April more than 6,700 tons of bombs were dropped on or around the island.

The schedule for the grand assault as laid down by Field-Marshal Kesselring called firstly for a neutralization of the air defences by forcing the batteries to exhaust their ammunition and their personnel. This was to be followed by mass attacks on airfields and grounded aircraft. Finally, the main weight was to be directed against the naval forces, dockyards and installations until they were destroyed. The first of these aims was never achieved. Though ammunition was rationed as a long-term precaution, there was never an actual shortage. As to the second, though the activities of Malta's air striking forces were brought practically to a standstill, more than 350 sorties were flown during April by the fighters which accounted for about half of the 37 Axis planes lost over the island during the month.

The naval dockyard had been a favourite target for the bombers from the start, but, though by February the damage had reached serious proportions, few ships were hit during the early stages of Fliegerkorps II's operations. Only the destroyer *Maori* was sunk at her buoy on February 11th and the *Cleopatra*, arriving en route to join the Mediterranean Fleet, was dive-bombed and hit by a 1,000-lb bomb, which fortunately did not explode. Similarly, the submarines escaped the enemy's attention until March when the *P39* was sunk and two others damaged. From this time they were kept submerged all day, manned by spare crews.

At the end of March the full fury of the enemy descended on the dockyards. All surface warships that could steam were evacuated directly after the arrival of the March convoy. There remained the *Penelope* and the destroyers *Kingston* and *Gallant*, all damaged in various degrees. Both the latter were destroyed. The story of the *Penelope*'s repair is a fantastic one of courage and dogged endurance under incessant attack, during which fresh damage accumulated while the original was being repaired; during which, too, 6,500 rounds of 4-inch ammunition were fired by her guns, wearing out the new gun-barrels fitted shortly before. It ended with the cruiser, her riddled side plating sprouting hundreds of wooden plugs, slipping away on the night of April 8th for Gibraltar. The foiled enemy sent torpedo planes and bombers after her as she passed along the coast of Tunisia but she arrived without further damage on the 10th.

At the submarine base, April 1st saw the beginning of a calamitous period. On that day the *Pandora*, fortunately cleared of the supplies she had brought, was sunk by two direct hits. The *P36* was damaged beyond repair, while the *Unbeaten*, though lying submerged, was so damaged that she had to be sailed for Gibraltar for repairs. Withdrawal of the flotilla was proposed but Captain Simpson, in command, gave his opinion that this 'virtually meant stopping offensive operations against Rommel's supplies; also since the 10th Flotilla was the only remaining means of preventing the enemy from bombarding Malta by heavy surface forces and mindful of the effect of our withdrawal on local morale . . . a further effort seems imperative'.

On April 4th the Greek submarine *Glaucos* was sunk and the Polish *Sokol* was so damaged that, after leading a hunted life under camouflage in various corners of the dockyard while temporary repairs were made, she was finally sailed for Gibraltar on the 13th with 200 holes in her upper casing. The rest camps of the submarine crews were daily machine-gunned and bombed. It became almost impossible to service the boats between patrols. (On April 14th it was known that Wanklyn's *Upholder* had been sunk with all hands on her twenty-fifth patrol.)

By April 12th the Admiral Superintendent of Malta Dockyard was reporting that 'practically no workshops were in action other than those underground; all docks were damaged; electric power, light and telephones were largely out of action'. Between the 15th and the 30th there were no less than 115 raids, the daily average of bombers attacking being 170. Great hopes were placed in the effect that the big reinforcement of 46 Spitfires, flown in from the US Carrier *Wasp* on the 20th, would have. But Fliegerkorps II watched their arrival on their radar scans and immediately pounced on the airfields. Within three days almost all the Spitfires had been either destroyed or damaged on the ground and the number of serviceable fighters was down to six.

Under these conditions the work of the submarine base was brought almost to a standstill. The decisive factor, however, which made it no longer feasible for the boats to operate from Malta was the inability to give the few remaining minesweepers the fighter protection they needed if they were to keep the harbour approaches clear. The density of the minefields daily increased – between April 24th and 27th no fewer than 123 moored mines with explosive floats

T—G

and anti-sweeping obstructions were laid by the German 3rd E-boat Flotilla. To avoid being hemmed in, Simpson was at last forced to recommend withdrawal, which was agreed to by the Commander-in-Chief on April 26th. By May 10th all submarines had gone. They were not to return for three months. The correctness of the decision was painfully confirmed by the loss of the *Urge* on April 27th to one of the newly-laid mines; this was a submarine which under the command of Lieutenant E. P. Tomkinson had gained a reputation second only to that of the *Upholder*.

Field-Marshal Kesselring may perhaps be excused for thinking that by this time Malta was totally neutralized and the Libyan convoy route made safe, though his opinion was no doubt influenced both by Rommel's impending offensive to capture Tobruk and demands for air reinforcements, and by the pressure being put on him to release some of Luftflotte II for the Russian front. Indeed, he had already made it known that he intended to transfer elsewhere two Groups of Ju 88s and two Groups of the Me 109s. Replacement by Italian bombers and fighters would permit, he considered, a sufficient weight of attack to prevent Malta from recovering.

His Italian colleagues were far less confident. Although the results of the grand assault had been good, they said they had not been up to the expectations of Kesselring. Judging by reports from Luftflotte II and the Sicilian Air Force concerning anti-aircraft fire and searchlights, the neutralization was far from complete. Furthermore, the blockade of the island, though very efficient, was not total. Above all, it was proving impossible to stop air reinforcements. In conclusion they gave their opinion that neutralization was only partial and temporary, and that it was necessary to continue and increase blockade operations lest the island should recover and re-assume the offensive.

They were to prove more correct than Kesselring. On May 9th a massive reinforcement of 60 Spitfires reached the island flown off from the *Wasp* and the *Eagle*. This time the ground crews were well prepared to receive them. Though they arrived in the middle of a raid, they were so speedily refuelled that some of them were off the ground and going into action within 35 minutes of their arrival. The following day, on which Kesselring reported to Berlin that 'the neutralization of Malta was complete', for the first time for many months the enemy were met by a superior fighter force. Efforts by the German airmen to hit the fast minelayer *Welshman*, which had arrived with Bofors anti-aircraft ammunition, aircraft spares and ammunition, were foiled and in the process the Germans lost twelve aircraft for the price of three Spitfires.

The transformation in the situation was, indeed, sudden and dramatic. The Malta War Diary records that 'such casualties were inflicted on the enemy that daylight raiding was brought to an abrupt end'. This is something of an exaggeration and presumably refers only to the dockyard area, as there were many more daylight raids recorded else-where in the island. Nevertheless, it reflects the wonderful feeling of relief and hope that was suddenly abroad. During May, German and Italian aircraft losses over Malta in-creased to 40 against a British loss in combat of 25. Still more significant, British aircraft destroyed on the ground numbered only 6 as compared to 30 in April.

The crisis of Malta's ordeal by bombs had been passed. But months of suffering still lay ahead of her. Unless supplies could reach her within a reasonable time, the island would fall without need for further effort by the enemy. Plans to attempt a convoy in May had been abandoned. Everything now depended upon the June convoy which was promised. Before that time came much would have happened.

9

Tobruk Surrenders: Rommel's Fatal Blunder

FIELD-MARSHAL KESSELRING's confident assertion that
'the neutralization of Malta was complete' was not simply
an airman's over-estimate of the result of aerial bombardment. It was rather the outcome of wishful thinking coloured
by the progress of the war elsewhere, by the mercurial
nature of General Rommel's belief in his own prospects of
victory and by the need for Luftflotte II to take part in the
offensive being prepared in Libya. Furthermore, the intention to capture Malta in due course still held good. In the
meantime, Kesselring considered, the Italian Air Force in
Sicily should be able to maintain a scale of attack which
would keep Malta quiescent.

It will be remembered that Rommel's 'spoiling attack' at
the end of January 1942 had been so unexpectedly successful
that the Eighth Army had been forced to withdraw to the
Gazala–Bir Hacheim line to the westward of Tobruk. Here
both sides had been gathering strength to mount a renewed
offensive. At this time Axis strategy called for the capture of
Malta to precede any further offensive and German partici-
pation had been promised. By the beginning of April,
however, the progress made by the British in re-grouping
and reinforcing the army in Eastern Cyrenaica was giving
Rommel doubts about his ability to hold out so long against
the growing concentration of British force. He wished to
forestall any British offensive.

When, therefore, Kesselring visited him during the first
week of April, Rommel persuaded him to urge that his
proposed assault on Malta should be postponed until after
he had mounted an offensive designed primarily to capture
Tobruk. Kesselring's report led to an agreement between

Mussolini and Hitler being reached at the Berghof on April 30th, whereby the dates for Rommel's offensive and the assault on Malta were fixed for May 26th and July 10th respectively. As a guard against Rommel's tendency to short-sighted opportunism, it was stipulated that the Axis armies should not advance farther than the Egyptian frontier and the offensive was not to be prolonged beyond June 20th, when the main effort was to be turned against Malta. For Operation 'Hercules' – the capture of the island – three Italian parachute battalions would be joined by a German parachute division and an armoured unit of captured Russian tanks. The German Navy would provide landing craft in which, immediately after the air invasion, Italian troops would be transported to the south coast of Malta and German troops to the south-east coast. In all some 35,000 troops were to be involved. Then, when the supply line to Libya had been made permanently safe, Rommel could move on to occupy the Nile Delta.

Rommel's fear that the Eighth Army would forestall him, particularly if Operation 'Hercules' was not postponed, was well founded. Since the end of February the Prime Minister and the Chiefs of Staff had been pressing on General Auchinleck the necessity for an offensive and an advance in Cyrenaica. Their primary reason was the need to regain possession of the airfields of Western Cyrenaica so that a convoy to Malta could have the fighter cover without which its chances of getting through were slight. Auchinleck insisted that the Army was not ready and refused to undertake a premature offensive, the failure of which would result in the piecemeal destruction of the new armoured formations being built up and would leave Egypt wide open to the resultant counter-attack. In March, Winston Churchill, refusing to accept this, sent Sir Stafford Cripps and Lieutenant-General Nye, the Vice-CIGS, to bring pressure to bear and to inquire into matters on the spot. Their report fully supported the Commander-in-Chief's contention that the middle of May was the earliest possible date for an offensive.

Though the Chiefs of Staff reluctantly accepted this, they

continued to press for speed while at the same time demanding the transfer of certain Middle East air units to Ceylon to meet the Japanese threat in the Indian Ocean. So black was the picture of the situation painted by the Chiefs of Staff, with its threat to the security of the supply lines to the Middle East through the Indian Ocean, that Auchinleck suggested that, rather than prepare for an offensive, he should stand on the defensive, so that everything possible could be spared for the defence of India. Told in reply that the greatest help the Middle East could give to the whole war at this juncture would be to engage and defeat the enemy in the Western Desert, Auchinleck now gave mid-June as the earliest date by which comparative tank strengths would make an offensive justifiable. The Prime Minister thereupon insisted that a major battle should be fought, if possible during May but at the latest in time to provide a distraction to help the passage of a convoy to Malta in the dark of the moon in mid-June. Given virtually the choice of complying or resigning, Auchinleck agreed to carry out his instructions. Before the time came to do so, Rommel had struck.

With the advantage of hindsight, it must be held that Auchinleck was right to resist the pressure on him to attack prematurely. Instead it was Rommel who attacked on May 26th with inadequate resources and, lured on by early success, ended up by over-extending himself.

The accumulation and maintenance of supplies was, as always, at the heart of Rommel's problem. Though convoys to Tripoli and Benghazi were now running largely unmolested, a growing shortage of suitable shipping restricted supplies to little more than the bare minimum required. A further problem was that of getting supplies to the front. Much had to be transported all the way from Tripoli owing to the poor unloading capacity of Benghazi. The latter was greatly improved at this time as a result of organizational and personnel changes; but even so there were still more than 200 miles to be covered even before the Axis armies began their advance. A chronic shortage of trucks made the long coastal road an inadequate route. At a conference on

the forthcoming operations held at Rommel's headquarters
on May 17th, Rommel proposed, as the only possible solu-
tion, that supplies should be shipped east by sea from
Benghazi. The Italian Admiral in Libya objected that this
was beyond his resources. The German Navy thereupon
assumed responsibility and achieved a remarkable improve-
ment. Whereas in April only 2,400 tons of German stores
were unloaded at Derna, in May the figures rose to 7,500
tons and in June to 11,000 tons. Meanwhile, as the day for
opening the offensive approached, there had been accumulated in Cyrenaica four large ammunition dumps, 11,000
tons of fuel and food for 30 days – sufficient for the purely
local offensive to recapture Tobruk which was all that was
envisaged, at any rate by the high command. Rommel's
strength in tanks was 584, against some 800 British, but the
inferior quality and mechanical unreliability of the latter
more than squared the odds. In air strength the Axis held the
advantage both locally in the Western Desert and in the
theatre as a whole. Furthermore, many of the British fighters
were obsolescent, compared with the German Me 109F.

Such, broadly, was the situation when the Battle of Gazala
opened on May 26th, a battle which was to end four weeks
later with the fall of Tobruk. It opened with Rommel's
favourite gambit – an attempt to encircle the British army.
This failed and for a time the Axis forces, pinned between
minefields and the British armour and short of fuel and
ammunition, were in grave danger of defeat. The attack
launched on them failed, however, and the British forces
were forced to withdraw with considerable losses. In the
south, Free French forces under General König conducted
an epic defence of Bir Hacheim against superior forces, from
May 26th to June 10th, when the garrison was withdrawn by
orders from General Ritchie. In the rest of the battle fortunes swayed back and forth until the 18th when, with its
armoured elements defeated, the Eighth Army was withdrawn to the Egyptian frontier, leaving Tobruk once again
surrounded.

Rommel lost no time in attacking, and the assault opened

at dawn on the 20th with a massive aerial bombardment in which 85 bombers, 21 Stuka dive-bombers and 40-50 fighter-bombers with 150 fighter escorts, shuttling back and forth from nearby landing grounds, dropped some 365 tons of bombs, stunning and neutralizing the defenders. Early on the 21st Tobruk surrendered. It was a tremendous personal triumph for Rommel who was immediately promoted to Field-Marshal in recognition of it. The objective laid down for his offensive had been achieved. The enemy was back on the Egyptian frontier, much shattered. According to Mussolini's directive of May 5th (Axis forces in North Africa were subject to the Italian *Comando Supremo*), the time had now come for a halt to be made while all efforts were transferred to Operation 'Hercules'. But for Rommel, the opportunist, his confidence and *élan* at full flood after his quick victory, Egypt and the Suez Canal and all that they entailed were beckoning. Amongst the booty captured at Tobruk had been 1,400 tons of petrol, large quantities of ammunition, both British and German, 2,000 serviceable vehicles and 5,000 tons of provisions. It seemed that all his problems of supply had been solved at one blow. Acting on his own initiative and by-passing the *Comando Supremo*, he radioed to the German Supreme Command that:

The morale and condition of the troops, the quantity of stores captured and the present weakness of the enemy make it possible for us to thrust onwards into the heart of Egypt. Therefore request that the Duce be prevailed upon to remove the present restrictions on movement and that all troops now under my command be placed at my disposal to continue the offensive.

Hitler took little persuading and on June 23rd wrote to Mussolini strongly supporting Rommel's views. The lightning success at Tobruk did not blind the Duce to the same extent that it had the victor himself. Though he agreed that an opportunity to go through to the Suez Canal was presenting itself, he did not fail to point out that the problems facing an attack on Egypt lay more in the safe passage of supplies across the Mediterranean – for which the Italian Navy was responsible – than in the progress of the fighting on land. The air forces in Sicily would have to be built up from Libya and elsewhere so as to neutralize the resurgent Malta once again. In the meantime Operation 'Hercules' would have to be postponed until September. Thus it may be said that Rommel's unexpected and rapid triumph at Tobruk, disastrous and ignominious for the British as it seemed at the time, saved Malta from an assault it might well have been unable to resist, with incalculable consequences to the course of the whole war.

Cavallero, now promoted to Marshal to keep pace with his German subordinate, consulted Kesselring and found him in a somewhat doubtful frame of mind. Faced with the problem of providing the aircraft for the renewed 'blitz' on Malta as well as for the support of Rommel's adventures, he preferred to compromise. He agreed to an advance into Egypt but no farther for the time being than El Alamein. When Cavallero and Kesselring arrived at Rommel's headquarters at Sidi Barrani on June 26th for a conference, they found him bubbling with confidence, about to launch an attack on Mersa Matruh and guaranteeing that his troops could be in Cairo by the 30th. Nothing must interfere with his exploiting his victory to the utmost. Intoxicated by the recent quick successes, he had forgotten his own warning made to Berlin in February 1941, on taking up his command, that 'Without Malta the Axis will end by losing control of North Africa'.

Nevertheless, the directive which Cavallero now issued in the name of the *Comando Supremo*, though it declared that any successes must be fully exploited, gave warnings of serious supply difficulties which could be expected and insisted that any advance beyond El Alamein would have to be decided upon in the light of the general Mediterranean situation. Meanwhile air forces must be transferred to Sicily for the attack on Malta. The following day, however, June 27th, Mussolini, by now caught up in the excitement of

Rommel's swift advance, issued another directive which authorized an advance to the Suez Canal. Two days later the Duce arrived in Cyrenaica to prepare for his triumphal entry into Cairo. Rommel, in fact, had already anticipated the permission to press on across the Egyptian border. By June 27th the Panzer Army, as Rommel's Italo-German Command had become known, using captured vehicles, provisions and fuel, had passed Mersa Matruh and by the end of the month had reached the El Alamein position. Only 60 miles away across the bay was Alexandria and the Mediterranean Fleet, on the edge of the rich Nile Delta which was beckoning the young Field-Marshal and holding out promises of decisive, brilliant victory. He at once hurled his forces against the British defensive position. The breakthrough he sought nevertheless eluded him. On July 3rd he made a further all-out attempt which again failed – with severe losses. When British counter-attacks were then similarly beaten back, the offensive power of both German and Italian troops had for the time being been exhausted. That night Rommel gave the order for the Panzer Army to go back on the defensive.

Between July 15th and 21st the Eighth Army struck back and, though the attacks in general failed, they were sufficient to make Rommel report that 'if the enemy succeeds in penetrating any farther our Alamein position will become untenable'. He appealed for reinforcements. Amongst those rushed over to him by air were German and Italian airborne regiments which had been standing by in Sicily for the invasion of Malta. On July 20th, Mussolini, disappointed of his triumph, returned to Italy. The next day Operation 'Hercules' was finally cancelled.

A lull now ensued in the campaign on land, while both armies, exhausted and much shattered, recuperated. It was to last until August 30th. It is time, therefore, to turn back to examine events which had been taking place at sea.

In his directive of June 26th, Cavallero had insisted on 'a quick transfer of air forces from Africa to Sicily in order to increase the attack on Malta again'.

Thus Malta, apparently brought to its knees in May, already again threatened the flank of Rommel's supply line. In the interval its defensive powers had been greatly increased by the many Spitfires which had been flown in from aircraft carriers, with the result that the July 'blitz' on the island was to be a total failure. At the same time the withdrawal of strong units of Luftflotte II to Sicily from North Africa had left Rommel's air force inferior to the enemy, a factor which was to play an important part in his failure to break through at El Alamein. Sea power in Italian hands, from January to June 1942, had enabled Rommel to exploit the technical and tactical superiority of the Panzer Army, and inflict a humiliating defeat on the Eighth Army. The Italian Navy had, however, been unable to take full advantage of this sea power delivered to it by the Luftwaffe. Partly owing to a chronic shortage of oil fuel, for which the Italians had to rely upon their ally, but basically owing to the continued policy of a fleet-in-being and a refusal to challenge enemy surface forces even when they could do so in superior strength, they had permitted Malta to be replenished and its air defences to be reinforced. Time and again British and American carriers had been allowed to penetrate to the central Mediterranean, fly off their deck-loads of Hurricanes or Spitfires and withdraw unmolested. Now, as sea power and control of the central basin became once again in dispute, the Italian surface fleet was at last to exert itself in some measure, but too late and too irresolutely.

Malta, for all its obstinate, fighting spirit, could not survive much longer without a replenishment. Its inhabitants, reduced to a bread ration of ten ounces daily, were being kept from starvation by communal feeding centres. There was no fuel for light and power. The disasters of the supply convoy in March had led to a decision to send no more supply ships until the island's fighter strength had been reinforced. Since then, however, a total of 198 Spitfires had been flown in from aircraft carriers, and it was decided to make a major effort to get supplies through in June.

The plan arrived at was to run convoys through from east

and west in a simultaneous operation. From Gibraltar were to come five freighters, the British *Troilus*, *Burdwan*, and *Orari*, the American *Chant*, the Dutch *Tanimbar* and a tanker, the American *Kentucky*. Their warship support would be divided, as on previous occasions, into two forces. The covering force, composed of the *Malaya*, the old carriers *Eagle* and *Argus*, the cruisers *Kenya*, *Liverpool*, and *Charybdis*, and eight destroyers, would go no farther east than the entrance to the Skerki Channel. The close escort – the anti-aircraft cruiser *Cairo*, five large and four small destroyers – would then take the convoy on to Malta. The operation was given the code-name 'Harpoon' and was commanded by Vice-Admiral A. T. B. Curteis, flying his flag in the *Kenya*.

At the same time from the east, under cover of the Mediterranean Fleet cruisers and destroyers, reinforced by three cruisers and some destroyers from the Eastern Fleet, was to come a convoy of no less than 11 freighters. The code-name for this part of the operation was 'Vigorous'. Apart from the inevitable air attacks to be expected by both these expeditions – in the Sicilian Channel and in the notorious 'Bomb Alley' respectively – there were Italian surface forces well placed to intervene. At Cagliari in Sardinia was a division of 6-inch cruisers and destroyers. If they were boldly handled and prepared to accept a measure of air attack from Malta, they would comprise a very serious threat to the 'Harpoon' convoy after Admiral Curteis' larger ships had parted company with it. The main Italian fleet, grouped round the modern battleships *Vittorio Veneto* and *Littorio*, was at Taranto, only 19 hours' steaming from the route of the 'Vigorous' convoy. Admiral Iachino could intercept it in the early hours of the long calm summer day. This time Admiral Vian would not have the assistance of either darkness or heavy weather to slip the convoy past such an overwhelming threat. On the other hand, Malta could now provide a striking force of Beaufort day and Wellington night torpedo planes, while from Egypt could come more Beauforts and some US Army Air Force Liberators equipped with the secret bomb sight of which great things were hoped. Shore-

based air power as a substitute for a battle-fleet was thus to
be relied upon. In all, 40 torpedo planes and eight Liberators
were to be employed – sufficient, perhaps, if thrown in in
massed attacks, but not, as experience already indicated, if
employed in small units, as their widely separated bases
dictated. Nevertheless, the attempt had to be made. To
control Operation 'Vigorous' Admiral Harwood, the naval
Commander-in-Chief who had succeeded Andrew Cunningham, and the Air Officer Commanding-in-Chief, Air Marshal
Tedder, set up a 'combined operations room' in the headquarters of No 201 Naval Cooperation Group.

Dawn on June 14th, 1942, found the 'Harpoon' force about
120 miles south-west of Sardinia and so within range of
attack by the 20 bombers and 50 torpedo planes which, with
a numerous fighter escort force, were based there. The
Italian 7th Cruiser Division – the *Eugenio di Savoia*, flying
the flag of Admiral da Zara, and the *Montecuccoli* with
destroyers – had sailed from Cagliari the previous evening.
Da Zara had hoped to intercept the speedy minelayer
Welshman, which was known to have sailed with the convoy,
laden with supplies and, as on previous occasions, would be
sent ahead to Malta to unload. Finding nothing he had now
returned to Palermo to await further orders.

In the other half of the Mediterranean the 'Vigorous'
force was well inside 'Bomb Alley' but, thanks to fighter
cover detached by the Royal Air Force from the land battle
in full swing in Cyrenaica, it was to proceed unmolested
until the late afternoon when it passed out of range of
British-held airfields. Nevertheless, it had suffered losses
earlier. One transport had been damaged by dive-bombers
and had been detached to Tobruk, and another had been
sent back as too slow. Now another ship, the Dutch *Aagtekirk*, had to be sent away to Tobruk for the same reason and
before she could reach port was set upon by forty dive-
bombers and sent to the bottom. The convoy was thus down
to eight by this time.

At Taranto, Iachino had known during the previous day
of the 'Vigorous' convoy. During the forenoon of the 14th,

his fleet prepared for sea and at 2.30 PM it sailed, in time to intercept Vian's force at 9.30 the next morning. Thus the various forces were in motion or poised ready to move towards a clash in the disputed central basin of the Mediterranean; on the result of this clash could depend the survival of Malta and perhaps the whole struggle for the Middle East.

For clarity it is necessary to follow separately the fortunes of the two convoys for Malta, the first of which to see action was 'Harpoon'. The Italians had absorbed the lessons of the past which taught the need for air attacks to be delivered *en masse*, and they had the numbers available to do so. Out of the 16 Sea Hurricanes and 4 Fulmars embarked in the *Eagle* only a very modest fighter defence could be kept airborne. Though they were to perform valiantly during the day, shooting down 17 enemy aircraft for the loss of 7 of their own number, they were too few to deter the swarms of attackers escorted by an almost equal number of fighter aircraft.

An early attack by Italian fighter-bombers did no harm. But when at 11.30 AM a coordinated attack by 28 torpedo planes and 10 high-level bombers developed, escorted by 20 fighters, the defences were swamped. The freighter *Tanimbar* was sunk and the cruiser *Liverpool* damaged, both by torpedoes. The cruiser, taken in tow by the *Antelope* and steering for Gibraltar, was for some time an irresistible lure for 26 bombers and 8 torpedo planes, but escaped without further damage. For the remainder, the afternoon passed uneventfully and it was not until 6.20 PM that the next attack came – this time by Ju 88s of Fliegerkorps II in Sicily. They were set upon by the Fleet Air Arm fighters and their efforts to hit the carriers were foiled.

An hour and a half later came another coordinated, mass attack by Italian torpedo planes and German Ju 88s and Stukas. A wild, thunderous scene of diving planes, bursting bombs and a storm of gunfire was made further chaotic by the boom of depth-charges loosed on what was believed to be a submarine's periscope. From it all the convoy and escort

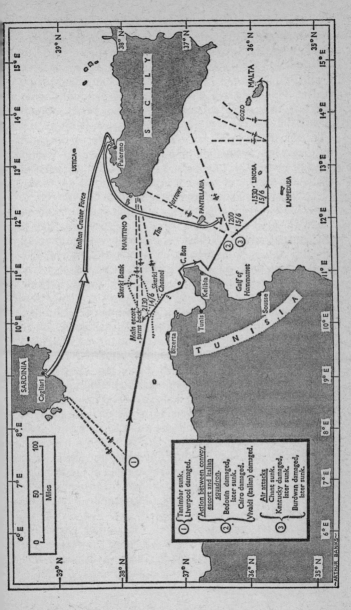

Track of British convoy in Operation 'Harpoon', June 14th–15th, 1942

emerged unscathed, though the *Argus* only narrowly avoided several torpedoes.

There was to be one more unsuccessful attack in the dusk by which time the convoy and escort had entered the restricted waters of the Skerki Channel and Admiral Curteis and the covering force had parted company. The five remaining ships of the convoy were now kept company by the *Cairo*, nine destroyers – of which four were of the little 'Hunt' class mounting only (like the *Cairo*) 4-inch guns and primarily equipped for anti-aircraft fire – four minesweepers and six minesweeping motor launches. In command of the force was Captain C. C. Hardy of the *Cairo*. The night passed quietly and dawn found the force 30 miles south of Pantellaria with Malta less than 12 hours' steaming ahead. Beaufighters from Malta were promised at first light and by noon the convoy should be under cover of Spitfires. The outlook which thus seemed reasonably hopeful was suddenly transformed when, at 6.30 AM on June 15th, Captain Hardy saw that the way ahead was barred by enemy cruisers. A few minutes later they opened fire at a range of over 10 miles, far outside the capability of any of the British guns.

Though the departure of Da Zara's squadron from Palermo had been known the previous evening, subsequent shadowing had been impossible owing to a dearth of reconnaissance planes at a time when all attention was being devoted to the Italian battle-fleet coming south from Taranto. Judging from previous form it had been assumed that Da Zara was going to join Iachino rather than operate in the Sicilian Channel. Captain Hardy turned a bold face to this unexpected and disconcerting development. His five fleet destroyers, led by Commander Scurfield of the *Bedouin*, raced out to offer battle while the convoy turned back under cover of a smoke screen laid by the *Cairo* and the four 'Hunt' class destroyers.

Da Zara, steering south across the convoy's route to Malta, divided his fire between the *Cairo*, which was steering a parallel course and screening the convoy with smoke, and the advancing British destroyers. Undistracted at first by fire from the still out-ranged British guns, the Italian cruisers made good shooting. The *Cairo* was twice hit, though she escaped serious damage. The *Bedouin* and the next ship in the British destroyer line, the *Partridge*, were both hit and disabled. On the other hand the two rear ships, *Matchless* and *Marne*, were able to turn their guns with good effect on two of the Italian destroyers, *Vivaldi* and *Malocello*, which had been ordered to break through to get at the convoy. Hit in the boiler-room, the *Vivaldi* came to a stop, on fire, and the *Malocello* stayed to go to her assistance.

Meanwhile, Captain Hardy had called for his four 'Hunt' class destroyers to support him in staving off the surface threat. Thus all the ships with good anti-aircraft capabilities were otherwise engaged when at 7 AM eight Stukas screamed down on the convoy. No fighters had opposed them, the original patrol of Beaufighters having returned to Malta and their reliefs having not yet arrived – a common defect of shore-based, as opposed to carrier-borne air defence. With little gunfire to distract them, the Stukas made good practice. The *Chant* was sunk and the *Kentucky* disabled.

As the fight between the two surface forces ran south and the Italian cruisers showed no inclination to penetrate the smoke-screen, Hardy turned back towards the convoy. He was followed by Da Zara, so that, when he found the convoy steering slowly south-eastward for Malta with the *Kentucky* in tow of the minesweeper, *Hebe*, he ordered it to reverse course again. The position of the convoy nevertheless seemed extremely perilous with the Italian cruisers' 6-inch guns about to come into action to make short work of the merchantmen, when at 8.40 AM Da Zara suddenly reversed course and made off to the eastward. For some reason he had come to the conclusion that the convoy's course would shortly take it northward to pass clear of a mined area which lay ahead, and he therefore made for the gap between the minefield and Pantellaria to await its arrival. There he waited until noon, being twice attacked – unsuccessfully – by torpedo planes from Malta.

By 9.40, Hardy had gathered in his escorts, except for the

Bedouin and *Partridge* which had repaired her damage sufficiently to take the *Bedouin* in tow, and the convoy was again on course for Malta but at the slow speed dictated by the disabled *Kentucky*. Long-range Spitfires had arrived and at 10.40 drove off some German bombers. Once again, however, they had gone back to base and their reliefs had not arrived when the next attack came in, which disabled the transport *Burdwan*.

With Malta still 150 miles away and the air and surface threat undiminished, Hardy now decided that he must cut his losses if he wished to get his last two undamaged ships, *Troilus* and *Orari*, to port. Leaving the *Hebe* to sink the *Kentucky* and the 'Hunt' class destroyer *Badsworth* to sink the *Burdwan*, he ordered the remainder to increase to their maximum speed. Two hours later, from the *Hebe*, following some 25 miles astern of the convoy after unsuccessfully trying to sink the *Kentucky*, Hardy heard that the Italian cruisers had returned to the scene and had damaged the minesweeper. Taking his three fleet destroyers with him, he steered the *Cairo* to her assistance.

Shortly before 2 PM the Italian cruisers came in sight and Hardy prepared to renew the unequal battle. At this moment, however, he saw them turn away to the westward and open fire at some target out of sight beyond his horizon. As he surmised, this was the *Bedouin* and *Partridge* for whom he could do nothing. Forced to leave them to their fate, he turned back to rejoin the convoy.

It was indeed the two destroyers on which Da Zara, having given the *coup de grâce* to the *Kentucky* and the *Burdwan*, had turned his guns. Lieutenant-Commander W. A. F. Hawkins of the *Partridge* at once slipped the tow, made smoke to screen the *Bedouin* and stood away to draw the enemy's fire. The *Bedouin* was doomed however, and her end was only hastened when at 2.25 PM an Italian aircraft put a torpedo into the easy target. The *Partridge* survived to reach Gibraltar. Da Zara, recalled, shaped course for his base.

Though the convoy was attacked by aircraft twice more

before dark, no further damage was suffered from that source. But its ordeal was not yet over. Through an error in signalling it steamed into unswept water while approaching Valetta. The *Orari* and several escorts exploded mines, but fortunately only a 'Hunt' class destroyer was sunk, the remainder suffering no more than minor damage. Thus only two, out of the six transports which had set out, reached Malta with 15,000 tons of desperately needed supplies.

From the strategic point of view, the Italian decision to send surface forces to break up the convoy was one long overdue in the protracted campaign over Malta. Tactically, the Italian admiral had failed to act with the boldness necessary to make the destruction of the convoy complete; but by delaying the convoy in waters at the extreme limit of fighter range from Malta and by drawing off the escorts, he had opened the way for Italian and German aircraft to a degree of success that they rarely achieved in the face of determined opposition.

The lesson was taken in by the Italian naval high command, but not by the Luftwaffe or the Regia Aeronautica who took all the credit for such success as had been gained; so that when a similar situation arose two months later the Italian surface ships would be denied the air cover they needed to participate. In consequence what might have been total defeat of an effort to re-supply Malta would be frustrated.

'Harpoon' had proved a costly operation for the British. Two destroyers had been lost, a cruiser, three destroyers and a minesweeper damaged. But Malta was saved at a time when starvation was very near. The island's condition would have been a great deal more satisfactory, however, if the 'Vigorous' convoy had achieved as much as 'Harpoon'. Its failure has, unfortunately, to be recorded. We left it early on June 14th making its way through 'Bomb Alley'. Its escort, commanded by Rear-Admiral Vian in the *Cleopatra*, comprised 7 cruisers and 26 destroyers besides anti-submarine corvettes and minesweepers with little fighting value. Admiral Harwood, the Commander-in-Chief, had no battleships to oppose the Italian battle squadron should it intervene. As a somewhat desperate bluff the ancient and virtually unarmed battleship *Centurion*, which had served before the war as a wireless-controlled target, was sailed with the convoy.

The real substitutes for battleship strength, some 50 'strike' aircraft of various types, were gathered on Malta and at Egyptian bases. In addition nine submarines would maintain a screen to the north of the convoy's route. This plan accorded with the developments in naval warfare which had come with the improved striking power of aircraft; but the means available to implement it were unsatisfactory in two vital points – the number of aircraft was insufficient and it was impossible to coordinate their attacks owing to the wide dispersal of their bases. Six months earlier the *Prince of Wales* and *Repulse* with a screen of four destroyers had been sunk by the massed attack of some 80 Japanese bombers and torpedo planes. The Royal Air Force in the Mediterranean after nearly three years of war could muster only 50 naval strike aircraft and they were intending to throw them in, a few at a time, to attack the Italian battleships accompanied by four cruisers and 12 destroyers. Pre-war and subsequent neglect, by a nation dependent for survival on sea power, to build up its maritime air force was once again coming home to roost.

By nightfall on June 14th, the 'Vigorous' convoy had undergone seven air attacks by a total of some 60 or 70 Stukas and Ju 88s. The majority had been foiled by the gunfire of Vian's ships and by long-range fighters, but one freighter, the *Bhutan*, had been sunk. Darkness brought little relaxation. Aircraft repeatedly illuminated the force with flares, and German E-boats, sighted at dusk, prowled round the outskirts of the formation awaiting a suitable moment to attack.

By 11 PM Vian knew that daylight must bring an encounter with the Italian fleet. That his cruisers and destroyers could not hold it off during the long summer day he also knew. To his inquiry whether he should retire, the Commander-in-Chief replied that he should hold on until 2 AM and then reverse course. In the interval perhaps Iachino might have been weakened or even halted by air and submarine attack. Vian complied. The inevitable temporary confusion, resulting from such a manoeuvre by 50 ships of widely varied types, gave the E-boats the opportunity for which they had been waiting. The cruiser *Newcastle* and the destroyer *Hasty* were both torpedoed. The former remained capable of steaming at 24 knots, but the destroyer had to be abandoned and sunk.

Meanwhile, in the joint operations room at Alexandria the two Commanders-in-Chief waited tensely for news from the four torpedo-carrying Wellingtons of No 38 Squadron which had taken off from Malta at midnight, and from a further force of nine Beauforts of No 217 Squadron which followed three hours later. By 5.25 AM nothing had come in – and, in fact, the Wellingtons, met by the usual Italian defensive measure of a dense smoke-screen, had achieved nothing. Harwood nevertheless hoped for good news from the Beauforts, and from the submarines which should be met by the Italian fleet at dawn. He ordered Vian to turn back westwards again.

Dawn did, indeed, break for the Italians in a wild flurry of excitement as the Beauforts streaked in to the attack. It was witnessed through his periscope by Lieutenant Maydon, commanding the submarine *Umbra*, who described it as

a fantastic circus of wildly careering capital ships, cruisers and destroyers; of tracer shell streaks and A/A bursts. At one period there was not a quadrant of the compass un-occupied by enemy vessels weaving continuously to and fro. It was only possible to count the big ships; destroyers seemed to be everywhere.

It was not surprising that out of such a mêlée Maydon was unable to pick a target for his torpedoes; or that the airmen were uncertain of what they had achieved. They had, in fact, hit and disabled the cruiser *Trento* but thought and reported that both Iachino's battleships had been torpedoed.

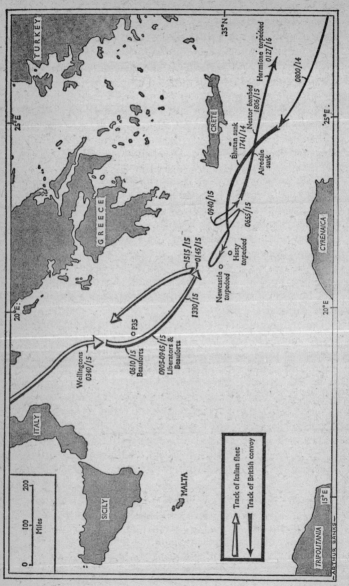

Operation 'Vigorous,' June 14th–16th, 1942

Not until well on in the forenoon did this claim reach Harwood and in the meantime a reconnaissance plane had reported the Italian fleet, at 8.28 AM, still intact, holding on southward and now within 150 miles of the convoy. Once again, therefore, Vian was ordered to turn back on to an easterly course to await results from the attacks being mounted from Egypt. This marching and counter-marching in 'Bomb Alley' exacted its toll. When 20 Stukas pounced during the forenoon, six of them concentrated on the *Birmingham*, narrowly missing her, bomb explosions causing her to whip so fiercely that several of her turrets were displaced and put out of action. In the afternoon, out of 30 dive-bombers, 12 picked the little 'Hunt' class destroyer *Airedale* for their target. When the smoke and spray subsided, she lay dead in the water, completely disabled, and had to be sunk. Fortunately, many of the enemy pilots were lured to attack the *Centurion*'s impressive bulk. The sturdy old veteran was not only well able to take their blows but had enough close-range armament to hit back. For the loss of four of their number the Stukas only succeeded in slightly damaging her.

Nevertheless, when at 1.45 PM Vian received Harwood's order, given two hours earlier and based on the Beaufort's optimistic report, to turn yet again for Malta, he disregarded it, correctly considering that it had been overtaken by a more recent air report from which it was clear that Iachino was still coming after him in undiminished strength. The air attacks dispatched from Egyptian bases had in fact neither slowed nor weakened the Italian fleet. The first to arrive had been the American Liberators. From 14,000 feet they planted their bombs with admirable accuracy all round the battleships – but only one of them hit, on the armourplate of the forward turret of the *Littorio*, doing negligible damage. To the airmen, however, it seemed that both big ships had been heavily hit and they reported accordingly. Before they left the scene they saw – as they thought – further damage inflicted by the Beaufort torpedo planes.

Twelve Beauforts of No 39 Squadron had taken off from

Sidi Barrani to synchronize their attacks with those of the Liberators. Jumped by Me 109s, two had been shot down and five more damaged and forced to return. The remainder carried on and pressed home their attacks in the face of a daunting volume of gunfire. They believed they too had hit a battleship but in fact all their torpedoes were avoided.

Around the British convoy air attack had been following air attack with scarcely an interval between them. Ammunition was being used up fast and the distance to Malta was being steadily increased. Iachino had thus achieved his object by the time the perennial preoccupation of the Italian fleet – the need to avoid night action – reared its head. At 3 PM, in accordance with his instructions, he turned his fleet away making for Navarino where he was to wait in readiness to challenge any fresh attempt by the British to break through to Malta on the following day.

On learning of this Harwood assumed the Italian fleet was returning to Taranto and signalled jubilantly to Vian that 'Now is the golden opportunity to get convoy to Malta', provided the smaller ships of the escort had enough fuel and ammunition. It was too late – perhaps fortunately, considering Iachino's orders. In the midst of some of the heaviest air attacks of the day, while his heavier guns were blackening the sky around formations of high-level bombers and the automatic weapons were shooting away their ammunition in voluminous streams at the dive-bombers, Vian sought the answer to Harwood's question. Meanwhile it was impossible to turn his unwieldy force. By 6.30 PM enough information had come in to make it clear that ammunition stocks were too low. His decision to hold on to the eastward was soon confirmed by the Commander-in-Chief who recalled the whole force to Alexandria.

The effort to relieve Malta from the east had been a dismal failure. Before Vian's squadron reached harbour it suffered further casualties. The cruiser *Hermione* was torpedoed and sunk by U-205 during the night. The Australian destroyer *Nestor*, damaged by air attacks, had to be scuttled. On the Italian side the cruiser *Trento*, crippled by the dawn attack by Beauforts, was torpedoed a second time and sunk by the *Umbra*. During its withdrawal Iachino's fleet was again attacked by the Wellingtons from Malta. Smoke-screen tactics nearly saved it as before. The baffled pilots had only dimly-seen, fleeting targets at which to aim; but one torpedo struck home on the *Littorio* near her bow. The damage put her into dockyard hands for more than two months.

So ended a desperate and gallant episode in the battle for the Mediterranean. Out of 17 supply ships which had been loaded for Malta, only two, with 15,000 tons of cargo, arrived, at a heavy cost in ships, aircraft and lives. The Italian naval historian Commander Bragadin, counts it 'a great battle won by the Italian Armed Forces and in particular by the Italian Navy'. Had Da Zara's squadron acted with proper vigour and so prevented the *Troilus* and *Orari* from getting through to Malta such an estimate would have been justified. But their cargoes were just enough to keep the Maltese people and garrison meagrely fed until another convoy could be fought through. The elimination of Malta and, as a result, the protection of the supply line to Libya, was the one vital task of the Italian Navy. An essential preliminary was the prevention of supply ships reaching the island, a task for which the Italian Navy and Air Force could at this time bring a decisive superiority to bear at the vital point. In this they failed and in doing so must accept a major responsibility for the final outcome of the battle for the Mediterranean.

10

The Turn of the Tide

JUNE 1942, it will be remembered, saw not only the failure of the 'Vigorous' operation to relieve Malta but also the withdrawal of the Eighth Army from the Gazala line, a retreat which continued until, on the 28th, Rommel's army was at Mersa Matruh with the Luftwaffe occupying airfields within 160 miles of Alexandria. Faced with the prospect of fighter-escorted bomber raids and even the loss of Alexandria itself, Admiral Harwood took the decision to disperse his fleet to Haifa, Port Said and Beirut, move all ships not required for active operations south of the Canal and transfer his own headquarters to Ismailia.

The evacuation, with its ominous implications and its implicit doubts in the Eighth Army's ability to hold the El Alamein position, spread an air of gloom. There was almost a taint of panic amongst the personnel, male and female, of the Alexandria base and administrative staffs as they crowded into Suez and Port Tewfik seeking accommodation. The loss of the submarine depot ship *Medway* to the torpedoes of U-372, on her way to Haifa on June 30th, probably marked the nadir of British fortunes in the Mediterranean. Sinking in a few minutes she took with her 90 spare torpedoes. The resultant loss of refit and replenishment facilities brought the work of the submarines almost to a halt for some time, and during July the Italian tonnage sunk by them was reduced to a single ship of 792 tons.

That British fortunes had indeed reached their lowest ebb and that the tide was on the turn, though this was far from apparent to the protagonists at the time, can be discerned from a general survey of the situation. On land, Rommel had been brought to a halt and forced on to the defensive. As

General Alexander (who relieved General Auchinleck as Commander-in-Chief on August 15th) wrote in his dispatch on the African Campaigns: 'On July 2nd, 1942, the Eighth Army defeated the enemy's most desperate efforts to break through ... the old Desert Army gained the vital time necessary for the arrival of the fresh divisions and improved tanks which were to turn the tide of battle.' The new tanks to which he referred were the 'General Sherman', 300 of which, together with 100 105-mm self-propelled guns, had been allocated to the Middle East by President Roosevelt and which were to give the Eighth Army for the first time armoured formations as well equipped as the Panzer Army and in far greater strength..

While the Eighth Army was gathering strength, the Panzer Army, except for the reinforcements hastily flown in from Sicily in the middle of July, was stagnating. Rommel was dissatisfied with the flow of men, vehicles and supplies, all of which were available in Italy but were not reaching him in sufficient quantity or in the right order and proportions. Although, as a result of the German Navy's assumption of responsibility for the coastal supply route, supplies reaching the German Army in July amounted to 26,000 tons, including 12,000 tons of fuel and 1,370 vehicles, Rommel complained that this only met the daily needs and that no reserves were being built up. The position was made worse by the raids of British cruisers and destroyers against the harbour and approaches to Mersa Matruh during July, as a result of which three supply ships were sunk. In the same month a Royal Air Force raid on Tobruk hit and destroyed the fuel storage depot there. Rommel's situation was to deteriorate still further as the attacks on the Libyan supply ships were resumed.

The resurgence of Malta, since the middle of May, as an offensive base, had led to the recall, at the beginning of July, of a number of units of Fliegerkorps II to Sicily and a renewed attempt to neutralize the island. Concentrated bombing attacks on the island's airfields, during which over 700 tons of bombs were dropped, succeeded in destroying

17 aircraft on the ground and damaging many more; but the bombers were now met by a powerful fighter defence and the brief 'blitz' cost the Axis air forces 65 aircraft against a British loss of 36 Spitfires. By July 15th the attackers had been forced to fall back on tip-and-run raids by fighter-bombers.

Already, on July 5th, Vice-Admiral Leatham, commanding at Malta, had reported that he considered the island could again be used by submarines. By July 12th the swept channel had been cleared of mines and on the 20th the first submarine, *Unbroken*, arrived. Results became apparent during August when submarines sank seven supply ships totalling 40,043 tons.

In the air the Middle East Air Force had at last reached a rough parity with the Axis air strength in the Mediterranean, though the equipment of many of the fighter squadrons with Hurricanes I and II gave the Luftwaffe a qualitative advantage. In addition there were coming into action units of the United States Army Air Force, flying Liberators, Fortresses, Mitchells and Kittyhawks.

Thus, everywhere British strength was growing and there were signs that the period of endurance in the face of superior strength was coming to an end. Not least among the omens of approaching victory was the Anglo-American agreement, reached in the middle of July, to launch an expedition through French North Africa in October. Nevertheless much time was needed for the British Eighth Army, situated at the end of its immensely long line of communications round the Cape of Good Hope, to receive the reinforcement and fresh equipment it needed before it could take up the offensive again. The earliest date estimated for this was mid-September, an estimate which was far from acceptable to Mr Churchill and had its influence on his decision to relieve Auchinleck of the Command-in-Chief. Under his successor, in the event, the British offensive did not open until October 23rd.

On the other hand time was on the side of the Eighth Army. Its lines of communication, long as they were, were

reasonably secure. For Rommel, time was running out as
losses on the Libyan route mounted in August to 34 per cent.
The longer he remained passive the stronger his enemy would
become while he himself would not. Retreat was unthinkable
in view of his past sanguine utterances. He would therefore
be forced to throw his army, in one last desperate gamble
'to win or lose it all', against the vast and powerful defences
of the excellent defensive position of El Alamein.

Only in one direction was delay seriously embarrassing to
the British. Malta was starving and must be fed. A relief
convoy in August was essential. So long as the whole of
Cyrenaica was in Axis hands, the experience of the 'Vigorous' operation showed that it was not possible to run a
convoy to the island from the east. All efforts must therefore
be concentrated on fighting a large one through from
Gibraltar. A main escort powerful enough to oppose the
Italian battle-fleet was to be assembled, while the Force 'X'
which would take the convoy through the Sicilian Channel
would this time include modern cruisers and a strong force
of destroyers. At the same time the air forces at Malta were
to be strongly reinforced for the occasion from Great
Britain and from Egypt. The code-name given to the
operation was 'Pedestal'.

The Italian Naval Staff had information well in advance,
from intercepted radio messages, that an important British
operation was impending in the western Mediterranean, and
it was not difficult to guess its nature. Consequently, when
further information came in during the 9th and 10th of a
convoy passing through the Straits of Gibraltar, a huge air
fleet of 784 German and Italian bombers, dive-bombers and
torpedo-planes, besides scouting aircraft which brought the
total to about 1,000, had already been assembled in Sardinia
and Sicily. Six Italian and three German submarines had
been stationed between the Balearic Islands and Algiers
athwart the route to Malta, 11 Italian submarines thronged
the approaches to the Narrows and another lurked off
Malta. A fresh, temporary, minefield was laid close off Cape
Bon in an area that had hitherto always been kept clear for

use by Italian convoys for Libya. South of Cape Bon 23 MTBs would be waiting in ambush. Finally a force of three heavy, three light cruisers and 12 destroyers would intercept the convoy south of Pantellaria. This formidable and versatile assembly of air and sea power, which might with some confidence have been expected to bar effectively the passage of any convoy to Malta, was certainly to bring about the most hard-fought convoy battle of the war. Though it proved tactically disastrous for the British, dogged courage and seamanlike skill, particularly on the part of the crews of the merchant ships involved, wrung from it a strategic success which was finally to dispel Axis hopes of victory in North Africa. It is, therefore, worthy of examination in some detail.

In the small hours of August 10th, 1942, the convoy of 14 merchant ships for Operation 'Pedestal', with its large fleet escort commanded by Vice-Admiral E. N. Syfret, passed through the Straits of Gibraltar and headed eastwards. It was an impressive armada. The merchantmen were all fast, modern ships, 13 of them freighters carrying mixed cargoes of which, in every case, the main items were flour, petrol stored in five-gallon cans and ammunition – the last two uneasy shipmates on a voyage with such an evil reputation. Two of these ships, the *Santa Elisa* and *Almeria Lykes*, were American-owned and manned. The remainder, the *Port Chalmers*, flying the broad pendant of the Convoy Commodore, Commander A. G. Venables, R N, the *Rochester Castle*, *Deucalion*, *Glenorchy*, *Empire Hope*, *Wairangi*, *Waimarama*, *Melbourne Star*, *Brisbane Star*, *Dorset* and *Clan Ferguson*, comprised some of the finest ships of Britain's Merchant Navy. Finally, there was one large tanker, the *Ohio*, American owned, but chartered by the British Ministry of War Transport, manned by British seamen and commanded by Captain D. W. Mason of the Eagle Oil & Shipping Company. She carried 11,500 tons of kerosene and oil-fuel, as vital to Malta's survival as the foodstuffs in the freighters.

As on previous occasions, the convoy was to enjoy powerful protection as far as the Sicilian Narrows. Against submarine attack there were two dozen destroyers. To fend off the bombers and torpedo planes there were 46 Hurricanes, 10 Martlets and 16 Fulmars aboard the carriers *Victorious*, *Indomitable* and *Eagle*, backed by the gunfire of the battleships *Nelson* and *Rodney*, the anti-aircraft cruisers *Sirius*, *Phoebe* and *Charybdis* and the cruisers *Nigeria*, *Kenya* and *Manchester*. Beyond that point, however, there would be only the three cruisers, the anti-aircraft cruiser *Cairo* and half the destroyers.

The passage of this force through the Straits of Gibraltar was known immediately by the Italian high command. Their counter-measures went at once into motion. When the first reconnaissance aircraft gained contact, at 10.10 AM on the 11th, the convoy and escort were already threading their way through the first of the five ambushes awaiting them – the nine submarines spread across the route north of Algiers. It was Lieutenant Rosenbaum of the German U-73 who had the fortune to find himself placed squarely in the way. Skilfully working his way through the destroyer screen and under the convoy columns he put four torpedoes into the *Eagle*. Within eight minutes she had gone down, taking more than 200 of her crew with her.

That evening the convoy came within range of strike aircraft on the Sardinian airfields. Thirty-six Ju 88 dive-bombers and Heinkel 111 torpedo planes timed their attack for the half-light, as dusk was settling over the calm sea. Thus they evaded the patrolling fighters; but, met by a storm of gunfire, they achieved nothing and lost four of their number. While they were away, their base airfields at Elmas and Decimomammu were struck by 10 Beaufighters from Malta which machine-gunned and destroyed five Italian torpedo planes and damaged 14 more, a loss which the Italian air commander, General Santoro, was to hold in some degree responsible for the lack of success on the following day. On the other hand, he was lucky in that American Liberators, which raided the airfields during the night, dropped their loads of delayed-action bombs wide, most of them falling in the open countryside.

Meanwhile, Admiral Syfret's force moved on through the night unmolested. Dawn of August 12th broke over the convoy, still at full strength and steaming in admirable order in four columns. Soon after 6 AM the fighter patrol of 12 took off from the carriers and it was not long before Martlets from the *Indomitable* had chopped out of the sky the two Italian shadowing aircraft. But, with only about 70 miles to come from their Sardinian bases, the enemy aircraft could have no difficulty in finding their target. Soon after 9 AM they arrived, 19 Ju 88s. They had a very rough reception being intercepted by 16 British fighters. On board the ships men waiting tensed for their ordeal were heartened by the sight of twin-engined aircraft smoking and spiralling down to crash in the sea. Others dropped their bombs wide and fled. Six of the German aircraft were missing when their comrades got back to base.

There was grim satisfaction in the fleet and convoy but no illusion about what was yet in store. And, indeed, at that moment the Regia Aeronautica was preparing to launch its most ambitious coordinated assault by more than 100 aircraft of all types. The first wave, whose primary object was to distract the defences from the torpedo planes following it, was composed of 10 Savoia bombers, eight Caproni fighter bombers and an escort of 14 Macchi fighters. The Savoias were carrying a new weapon, the 'motobomba', a torpedo which, after floating down by parachute, set off on a zigzag or circling course impossible to predict and difficult to avoid. Ingenious as it was, dropped ahead of the convoy it was no serious threat to one so well drilled and alert as this. At sight of the falling parachutes, the ships turned smartly together 90 degrees to starboard to 'side-step' the danger area, manoeuvring perfectly together in spite of having to fight off simultaneously the Capronis dive-bombing and machine-gunning.

It may be that this unexpected manoeuvre upset the 43 torpedo planes which, while it was in progress, swooped down in two groups, one from each flank. Or they may have been put off by the Sea Hurricanes and Martlets, some of

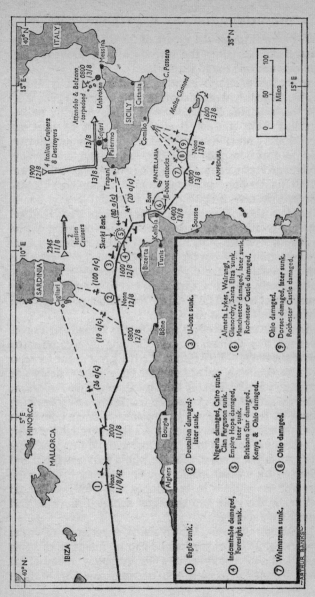

Track of British convoy in Operation 'Pedestal', August 11th–13th, 1942

T—H

which broke through the escort of 26 Re 2001 fighters to harass them. Certainly the torpedoes were fired at long range and not one found its mark.

The big Italian effort was petering out ineffectually. However, the Italians had other shots in their lockers. The first of these was a Savoia 79, loaded with a heavy bomb, radio-controlled from a Cant float-plane, a sort of pilotless 'Kamikaze'. Unfortunately for them, this ingenious device failed to function. The S 79 flew off inland and finally crashed and exploded in Algeria. The other consisted of two Re 2001 fighter-bombers, single-engine monoplanes resembling Hurricanes, each carrying a special heavy bomb designed to cause havoc amongst a carrier's deck load of aircraft. The *Victorious*, engaged in landing-on some of her Hurricanes, saw two of them, as it seemed, approaching and took no action till, from their bellies, bombs fell away. One landed squarely on the flight deck and would have had a disastrous effect if it had exploded; but fortunately it broke up on impact and did little harm. The Italian pilots escaped without a shot fired at them.

For all the massive effort made by the Italian Air Force, it was left to a formation of 37 German dive-bombers to achieve the only positive results. Arriving just as the torpedo planes were retiring, only 11 managed to evade the defending fighters and attack. Picking the Blue Funnel ship *Deucalion*, a veteran of the Malta run, which was leading the port wing column of the convoy, they concentrated their bombs on her. Only one hit her and this passed right through the ship; but others fell and exploded so close around her, smashing a lifeboat in the process, that the whole ship was lifted and shaken as by a giant hand. Captain Ramsay Brown rang down for the engines to be stopped and lifeboats cleared away while the mate and carpenter sounded the wells and inspected the damage.

It was not Ramsay Brown's first experience of being damaged while in convoy and he had no intention of being left behind if he could help it. Unfortunately, many of his seasoned crew had recently been replaced; and now, without orders, some greasers and assistant stewards in panic lowered two of the lifeboats and pulled away in them. When it was found that the damage was by no means fatal and the ship could get under way again, these two boats and their crews had to be recovered, which caused an hour's delay. Left far behind, the *Deucalion*, escorted by the destroyer *Bramham*, turned towards the Tunisian shore, hoping to avoid the attention of the enemy by following the coastal route. Ramsay Brown's plan came near to success. Though towards evening the ship was again attacked by two dive-bombers and the resultant near misses again lifted and shook her, her sturdy construction saved her and as dusk came down she was still plodding along at 12 knots. But, with the last of the light, two torpedo planes found her. A torpedo burst against her side. Aviation petrol and kerosene caught fire, sending flames up to twice the height of her masts. The ship was an inferno and it was only a matter of minutes before the explosives in her hold would blow up. Abandon ship was ordered and the crew rescued by the *Bramham*.

In the meantime, much had been happening around the convoy. Having beaten off, for the loss of the *Deucalion*, the enemy's major effort of the day, Syfret's force had reached the approaches to the Sicilian Narrows thronged with Italian submarines. The glassy calm summer sea provided the worst possible conditions for asdic detections, as temperature layers in the water deflected the sound beams to give faulty indications and a multitude of false alarms. Throughout the afternoon destroyers were engaged sniffing suspiciously at contacts and from time to time dropping depth-charges to scare off the hidden attackers. At 4.40 PM suspicions were confirmed when from the *Tartar* a torpedo track was seen. Then the *Lookout* astern of her sighted a periscope. In the hunt which followed the submarine *Emo* was shaken and damaged by the depth-charges; but the destroyers could not linger for long and she escaped with nothing worse.

At almost the same time, away on the other side of the widespread concourse of ships, the *Ithuriel* also spotted a periscope and the top of a conning tower as a submarine broke surface momentarily. Racing to the spot her depth-charges caused such damage that the submarine *Cobalto* was forced to come to the surface where she was rammed and sunk. While the survivors were being picked up a fresh air attack by a small force of Caproni fighter bombers was developing. Intercepted by the fleet's Hurricanes and daunted by the volume of fire reaching up towards them they preferred to take on the solitary destroyer. *Ithuriel*'s gunners were ready for them and the Capronis retired with nothing achieved.

So far the losses suffered by the British, grievous as they were, represented a failure on the enemy's part to take advantage of the tactical situation presented by his successful concentration of aerial and underwater forces. Brushing aside the repeated efforts of submarines and bombers to get at the all-important merchantmen, the British force had swept steadily onwards, the convoy maintaining its compact rectangle in good order. This state of affairs was shortly to be dramatically transformed.

By 6.30 PM the convoy had come within reach of the Sicilian airfields and therefore of the deadly Stuka dive-bombers. Twenty-nine of these now arrived simultaneously with 14 Italian torpedo planes, the whole escorted by a swarm of fighters. In a perfectly synchronized attack, the torpedo planes came in from either flank while the Stukas screamed down from ahead and astern. One group of dive-bombers concentrated on the *Indomitable*, diving down to 1,000 feet to make sure of a hit. Three bombs burst on her flight deck making it unusable, her fighters subsequently having to land on the *Victorious*. The remaining Stukas achieved nothing, while the torpedo planes' only victim was the destroyer *Foresight* which, with her stern blown off, had to be sunk.

The convoy steamed on undiminished. But now had come the critical time as, towards the end of the day, Syfret's battleship and carrier force had to turn back from the restricted waters of the Skerki Channel ahead. At the same time Commodore Venables' well-drilled, compact convoy had to become a long double line in order to thread its way through the narrow channel, a manoeuvre which inevitably led to some loss of unity in the convoy and of cohesion with the escort.

With all this to distract the escorts, the slender periscopes of two Italian submarines, turning their baleful eyes on the busy scene, went unobserved. They were the *Axum*, commanded by Lieutenant Renato Ferrini, and the *Dessie*, Lieutenant Renato Scandola. Ferrini had had his first sight of the British force, dimly in the distance, at 6.20 PM and had steered, submerged, to close it. Twenty minutes later two columns of smoke and anti-aircraft bursts in the sky confirmed the nature of his sighting. Let his logbook take up the story here.

18.41 Alter course North to close.
18.50 Observe bearing of smoke now 300 degrees. Dive to 20 metres and steer course 030 at full speed.
19.27 Periscope depth. Enemy formation spread between bearings 290–010 degrees, distance 8,000 metres, course 110°. Alter course parallel to study situation.
19.33 Fresh observation. Enemy's course 140. *ie*, enemy has altered course in the interval 30° to starboard. Alter course to starboard to 180°. Am able meanwhile to establish that the formation comprises about 15 steamers, two cruisers and numerous destroyers. They are in three columns with the steamers divided amongst the three lines, the two cruisers in centre and the destroyers spread on an outer line. Note further, but imprecisely because masked by other units, a ship with three lattice masts, similar to those of American battleships. Able to take a quick general view only as in the flat calm the feather of the periscope is conspicuous even at minimum speed.
19.37 Fresh estimate of distance 4,000 metres. Course of

enemy 140. Speed 13. Alter course starboard to 220 to reach firing position.

19.42 After a quick look at periscope depth, dive to 15 metres and go half speed ahead on both engines to close.

19.48 Periscope depth. Angle of sight of cruiser in the second line 28 degrees. In the nearer line, ahead and astern of the cruiser are respectively a destroyer and a large merchant ship.

19.55 Fire bow tubes in order 1, 4, 3, 2 of which 1 and 2 straight, 3 and 4 angled respectively 5° to starboard and 5° to port.

Directly after firing, disengage. Distance at firing from first line 1300 metres, from cruiser 1,800 metres.

63 seconds after firing hear first explosion. 90 seconds after firing, two explosions close together. This leads me to assume a hit on a unit in the first line and successively on one in the second line. Calculating from speed of torpedoes, distance on firing was less than estimated, being actually about 1,000 metres from the first line and 1400 from the second.

4 m. 30 sec. after firing, while at 65 metres depth, the hunt begins with a pattern of depth charges; dive to 100 metres and stop all machinery. The hunt continues with deliberate attacks for two hours, patterns of depth charges being fired. It is noticed that each time the boat rises to between 80 and 90 metres the transmissions of the asdics are clearly heard, followed immediately by depth charges. Decide to remain between 100 and 120 metres, particularly as at 21.35 a destroyer passes overhead from bow to stern and besides the noise of the propellers is clearly heard another like a vibrating wire leading me to think it comes from an explosive sweep.

After 22.15 the hunt draws away.

22.50   Surface. 3,000 metres ahead is a big ship in flames.
         On starboard bow another burning with much
         smoke. 70° on port bow a third ship already burnt
         out from which still comes, however, the charac-
         teristic dense grey-black smoke. The flames of the
         first ship clearly illuminate me and immediately
         afterwards I see two destroyers in motion and sig-
         nalling; since it is essential for me to replenish air
         bottles and recharge batteries, I submerge to avoid
         being further hunted and leave the area.

Although the *Dessie* fired torpedoes at almost the same
moment, the *Axum*'s torpedoes probably hit three ships, the
Nigeria, flagship of Rear-Admiral Burrough commanding
the 'through escort', the *Cairo* and the tanker *Ohio*. This
simultaneous triple catastrophe in the gathering dusk not
unnaturally threw the whole force into considerable confusion. Destroyers of the escort scurried this way and that,
going to the assistance of the stricken cruisers and seeking
the hidden assailant. In the convoy the *Ohio*'s sudden halt
forced the *Empire Hope*, astern of her, to reverse engines in
order to avoid collision. Other ships swung aside independently to 'comb' the torpedo tracks. All order was for the
time being lost. And, in the middle of it, out of the dark
eastern sky roared a mixed force of German Ju 88s and
Italian torpedo-carrying Savoias. Guns blazed wildly in
every direction but with little effect – perhaps fortunately as
one of the targets selected was a formation of long-range
Beaufighters from Malta, come to take the place of the
carrier fighters.
    Confusion mounted to chaos as the *Empire Hope*, hit by
bombs, burst into flames and had to be abandoned; *Clan
Ferguson* and *Brisbane Star* shuddered to a stop, hit by
torpedoes either from the submarine *Alagi* or from the
torpedo planes.* Certainly it was a torpedo from the *Alagi*

* The *Clan Ferguson* sank; *Empire Hope* remained afloat until
nearly midnight when she was sunk by a torpedo from the submarine
Bronzo. The *Brisbane Star* was got under way again.

which at this time hit the *Kenya* and damaged her, but not so badly as to put the cruiser out of action.

This is how the savage scene had appeared to Lieutenant Sergio Puccini, Captain of the Italian submarine:

09.00   Begin to hear explosions which during the course of the day become louder and more frequent. Steer for the south-eastern part of the patrol area where it is estimated the convoy will be at sunset.

20.00   Through periscope can see on a bearing 300° a tall column of smoke and, a little later, the masts of ships distant about 20,000 metres. Alter course towards.

20.20   Convoy attacked by aircraft. Violent anti-aircraft reaction. All ships alter course together to starboard, steering south. A destroyer is hit by a bomb. I can count 15 ships comprising cruisers, destroyers and freighters.

20.40   Ships alter course again and reform; almost at their head is a cruiser of the *Southampton* class. Range 8–10,000 metres. Manoeuvre to attack this ship.

21.00 (about)   Third air attack begins, more violent than the others and two merchantmen are hit and set on fire. A destroyer stops near them, perhaps to render help. A storm of bombs near the other ships raises tall columns of water, some of them not more than 3 or 4,000 metres from the submarine. The cruiser which has a merchantman very close ahead of her seems to have reduced speed to keep with the convoy, scattered by the violent bombardment.

21.05   Course 214°, range 1,500–2,000 metres, launch four bow torpedoes at the cruiser . . . While disengaging hear three explosions quite different from those heard during the bombing. Since, owing to the spread, the cruiser could not have been hit by three torpedoes, I think I must have hit the merchantman immediately ahead of her . . . Disengage and settle on bottom at 90 metres.

21.26 Hear a very violent explosion. Meanwhile, on the hydrophones are heard other units passing through the area. It must be a second group of ships steering towards Cape Bon.

23.13 Surface. The horizon between bearings 180° and 240° is a continuous line of flame from the burning, sinking ships.

23.50 A burning ship blows up.

Meanwhile, amongst the survivors of the harried British force, after the confused sound and fury of the simultaneous air and underwater attack, a sudden quiet had settled down with the darkness. Astern of them the night was lit by the lurid glare of blazing ships.

Destroyers sped hither and thither rounding up the un-injured ships and shepherding them into some sort of order. After transferring to the destroyer *Ashanti*, the Admiral had ordered the crippled *Nigeria* to return to Gibraltar. The *Ohio*, with a hole 24 feet by 23 in her side, had come to a stop, on fire. Officers and men had set to, however, extin-guished the fire and shored up bulkheads in the first of a succession of damage repairs which were to make the story of the *Ohio* an epic of the sea. By now she was under way again, limping after the convoy as best she could, steering by emergency means and without a serviceable compass. The *Cairo* was so damaged that she had to be sunk.

The largest organized group at this time consisted of the cruisers *Kenya* and *Manchester* followed by the American ship *Almeria Lykes* and the *Glenorchy*, the whole led by two destroyers with mine sweeps streamed. The remainder were coming on alone or in company with shepherding destroyers of the escort. Coming up from astern carrying the Admiral, the *Ashanti* overtook the *Ohio* and, at the request of the Master, Burrough sent the destroyer *Ledbury* back to guide the compass-less ship through the narrow channel. By day-light the sturdy tanker, the twisted, buckled plates of her damaged hull groaning at the strain on them, would have worked up to 16 knots and rejoined what was left of the convoy. Besides the *Ohio*, another crippled ship had been able to get under way again. This was the *Brisbane Star* whose resourceful master, Captain Riley, finding himself left far behind, had decided to hug the Tunisian shore and try to make his own way to Malta as opportunity offered. In this he was to be successful. By fine seamanship and resource he overcame all difficulties to reach Valetta with the majority of his desperately needed cargo unharmed.

About midnight the various groups and single ships rounded Cape Bon. Lying in wait, their engines stopped, invisible in the darkness against the loom of the land to the southward, were the German and Italian E-boats. The calm sea was ideal for them. Their youthful captains proceeded to make the most of it. From 1 AM the next four hours saw a succession of confused mêlées marked by the sudden glare of searchlights, the bright coloured streams of tracer bullets, the deep-throated roar of E-boat motors and from time to time the boom of exploding torpedoes. It is impossible to extract a clear and detailed picture of events from the accounts of the many attackers and their victims.

Certainly it was two Italian boats, Ms 16 and Ms 22, commanded by Lieutenant-Commander Manuti and Sub-Lieutenant Mezzadra, which had the first success, each of them putting a torpedo into the *Manchester* which wrecked her propellers and left her immobilized, to be abandoned and scuttled the following day. The *Almeria Lykes* was the next to go, torpedoed by an invisible assailant, and soon on her way to the bottom. Her crew were rescued by the destroyer *Somali* which also saved the survivors of the *Wairangi*, another E-boat victim. Soon after 2 AM the *Glenorchy* was suddenly illuminated by a searchlight, turned at once towards it, but was hit almost immediately by two torpedoes which tore open her hull and flooded the engine room. The ship was abandoned at the order of the Master, Captain G. Leslie, who himself stoutly refused to leave in spite of repeated appeals by his officers and men. The boats were finally rowed to the nearby Tunisian coast and the majority of the crew interned by the Vichy French. The Mate, Mr

Hanney, with a volunteer boat's crew went back at daylight to the *Glenorchy* to try once again to persuade the Captain to leave; but as they approached the ship they saw her turn over and sink. At this moment the Ms 31 (Lieutenant Calvani), which had torpedoed the *Glenorchy*, returning to the scene of his success, came upon the boat and took its occupants prisoner. Captain Leslie was not seen again.

Two other ships were torpedoed before the coming of dawn brought the attacks to an end – the American *Santa Elisa* and the *Rochester Castle*. The former, trailing astern owing to engine defects caused by near bomb misses on the previous day, beat off one E-boat with her machine guns, but a second came in unseen on the other side. The torpedo exploded amongst the canned petrol and set off an uncontrollable blaze. The crew abandoned her barely in time before the flames reached the explosives and she blew up. Her survivors were taken aboard the destroyer *Penn*.

Captain Richard Wren of the *Rochester Castle* had already managed to elude a number of attacks, weaving in and out of torpedo tracks, when at last a torpedo reached his ship, tearing a huge hole in her side abreast the forward holds. But the ship was a credit to her builders. The bulkheads held, her engines continued to function and at daybreak Captain Wren found himself leading the undamaged survivors of the convoy – the *Waimarama* and *Melbourne Star*, followed at a little distance by the *Ohio* and farther astern the *Port Chalmers* and *Dorset*.

It was to the sky that the haggard eyes of all in the British force were now lifted, knowing full well what they must expect. Beaufighters and long-range Spitfires were coming from Malta; but with both the fighter-direction ships *Nigeria* and *Cairo* gone, their capabilities would be much reduced. There was time for all hands to eat their breakfast before the first alarm at 8 o'clock, though not many can have had much stomach for it.

For Rear-Admiral Harold Burrough, in the *Ashanti*, there was another preoccupation as August 13th dawned, besides the certainty of a massive air attack. On the previous evening a reconnaissance aircraft from Malta had reported an enemy force of six cruisers and 11 destroyers in the Tyrrhenian Sea steering south. A simple calculation showed that they could reach the convoy south of Pantellaria by dawn, in just the way Da Zara's squadron had done in June – but in much greater force than on that occasion. And though Syfret had sent the light cruiser *Charybdis* and two destroyers to Burrough's aid, the arrival of such an enemy squadron could mean nothing less than the annihilation of the convoy.

The fate of the British force, of Malta and, it may well be, of British fortunes in the Middle East hung, indeed, by a thread. The intervention of their cruiser-squadron had been an integral part of the plan of the Italian Naval Staff, who had absorbed the lesson of the June convoy. But past experience also gave them a healthy respect for British torpedo planes. They had, therefore, secured promises from both Kesselring and the *Comando Supremo* of fighter cover for their ships in the Sicilian Channel.

When the chiefs of the two Air Services – Luftflotte II and the Regia Aeronautica – realized that by the end of the second day their huge and costly efforts had contributed so comparatively little to the destruction so far achieved, they were determined that a maximum effort should be made on the 13th. To mount it, every available fighter would be required to escort the strike aircraft. None could be spared for the Italian Navy – for which, in truth, the airmen had developed considerable contempt since Da Zara's failure in June.

To inter-service rancour, which had dogged the Italian Navy and Air Force throughout the war, were added the demands of political expedience when Mussolini was appealed to by the Naval Staff. Unwilling to offend Kesselring and through him Hitler, he decided in favour of the Air Forces. The decision robbed the Italian Navy, already almost immobilized through lack of oil-fuel, of its last chance to win a decisive victory. It also saved Malta. At 1.30 AM the Italian cruiser squadron was recalled. The following morning it was intercepted by the submarine *Unbroken*, commanded by Lieutenant Alastair Mars. Firing four torpedoes, Mars achieved a remarkable success. The heavy cruiser *Bolzano*, hit amidships and set ablaze, had to be beached. The light-cruiser *Attendolo*, with her bows blown off, managed to reach Messina. Neither ship was able to play any further part in the war. As for the *Unbroken*, in spite of a counter-attack lasting eight hours during which Mars counted 105 depth-charge explosions, she emerged un-scathed to return in triumph to Malta.

At the very moment that Mars was thus engaged, the ordeal of the convoy, now south-east of Pantellaria and 200 miles from Malta, had begun at 8 o'clock, when 12 Ju 88s dived on the merchant ships. The *Waimarama* was hit, the aviation petrol in her cargo blazed up and in a moment the ship had disintegrated in a monstrous explosion. Captain MacFarlane of the *Melbourne Star*, following close astern, was just able to steer clear of the flames though he was driven to take cover from the searing heat and the hail of debris falling aboard. Thirty-six of his crew, imagining it was their own ship which had blown up, had leaped over-board. Together with the tragically few survivors of the *Waimarama*, they were rescued by the *Ledbury* from the flame-covered sea. In the *Ohio*, next in the line, burning debris started a fire in her cargo of kerosene which was with difficulty extinguished.

An hour later another formation of enemy aircraft was sighted, eight of them with the characteristic gull-wing of the deadly Stuka. These were Italian-manned planes, how-ever, and the pilots were no doubt unfamiliar with the technique. Their bombs missed; one was shot down by a Spitfire; another, hit by gunfire, crashed into the *Ohio*'s starboard side, parts of it falling on board; its bomb failed to explode. The solitary tanker was inevitably the favourite target. Near misses shook up her machinery and defects were accumulating. When the next attack by a mixed force of Ju 88 and 87 came in at 10.50 AM a salvo of six bombs, all near misses, brought her long-suffering machinery to a shuddering stop.

The same attack had started a fire in the *Rochester Castle* but had not stopped her. The *Dorset*, however, had been crippled and lay immobilized. Admiral Burrough sent the destroyer *Bramham* to stand by her and the *Penn* to the *Ohio*. There now began a heartbreaking struggle to take the huge, unwieldy, deeply laden tanker in tow, a struggle in which only the desperate need to get at least some of her cargo of oil to Malta led her rescuers to persist long after all hope seemed to have vanished. For a time the *Penn* alone tried to get her moving, but it was impossible. While the efforts were being made, bombers swooped again and again and further near misses increased the damage and flooding. At 2 PM the *Ohio* was temporarily abandoned, the crew going aboard the *Penn* to await darkness and further help.

One last attack had meanwhile descended on the main body – by Italian torpedo planes, some carrying 'moto-bomba'. Their weapons were prudently launched at long range and no tracks were seen. Nevertheless, the Commodore's flagship, *Port Chalmers*, which had throughout borne a charmed life amidst countless bombs and torpedoes, had yet another miraculous escape.

One torpedo passed directly beneath her; another was seen passing close up her starboard side. Soon afterwards her starboard paravane wire began to vibrate violently, indicating some object caught up by it. The ship was stopped and the paravane hoisted out of the water to reveal a torpedo firmly entangled with it, its deadly warhead swaying to and fro a few feet from the ship's hull. Delicately it was lowered into the water and the paravane wire was slipped while the ship hastily backed away. After an interval which gave the ship time to get clear, there was an explosion which seemed to lift her out of the water as the torpedo hit the sea bottom; but she escaped damage.

By now this main body, three merchantmen and escort, was nearing Malta and the minesweeping squadron under Commander Jerome came out to take charge, one of them, the *Rye*, being sent to join the *Penn* and *Ohio*. Admiral Burrough could now take his depleted Force 'X' to rejoin

Syfret to the westward, running the gauntlet of the Narrows again in the reverse direction. E-boats, submarines and aircraft all tried to bar his way, but without any further success.

During the afternoon the *Rye* and two motor launches joined the *Penn*. The combined efforts of the warships at last got the *Ohio* moving at some five or six knots and under a precarious control. Hardly had this been achieved when once again there came attack from the air, one bomb falling close under the tanker's stern, another plunging down into the engine room where it exploded. Other bombs fell close alongside the *Penn* and *Rye*. The tanker's crew were again taken off.

At this time, 70 miles away, to the frenzied cheers of the people and garrison of Malta, the *Port Chalmers*, *Rochester Castle* and *Melbourne Star*, their scarred and blistered sides providing evidence of the ordeal they had survived, were sliding slowly between the arms of the breakwater of Valetta Harbour. Yet Malta's survival could still hang on the outcome of the valiant fight being made for the life of the *Ohio*.

During the night, while the crew of the *Ohio* lay in the deep sleep of the utterly exhausted, Lieutenant-Commander Swain of the *Penn* and Lieutenant J. A. Pearson, RNR, of the *Rye* concocted some ingenious and unorthodox methods of getting the huge tanker moving, and at one time had succeeded in achieving four knots with her; but then the towing wires parted and all was to do again. Further help now joined in the shape of the destroyers *Bramham* and *Ledbury*. The *Bramham* had been standing by the *Dorset*, but the crippled merchantman had made an easy target when Stukas had swooped on her and three bombs had sent her to the bottom. Lieutenant-Commander R. P. Hill had brought the *Ledbury* back after an unsuccessful search for the scuttled *Manchester*. By 10.45 in the morning of August 14th, the *Ohio* was moving again with the *Rye* towing, the

Penn lashed alongside and the *Ledbury* secured to her stern to keep her heading in the right direction. Gathered round protectively were the *Bramham* and the minesweepers *Speedy*, *Hebe* and *Hythe*.

Then came again the growl of aircraft engines – Ju 88s coming in for a final effort to deny Malta the oil without which she could not survive. Spitfires streaked down to engage them. The German formations broke up. Some came flaming down. Others loosed their bombs wide, but one bored doggedly on, its 1,000-lb bomb bursting close under the tanker's stern, tearing yet another hole in her hull. The *Rye*'s towing wire parted.

This was the last attack to get through the fighter defences. From then on the problems were confined to salvaging the slowly sinking tanker. Not the least was the exhaustion of the men of the little warships, the *Rye* still towing and the *Penn* and *Bramham* lashed on either side of the *Ohio*. Time and again the wires parted, only be be renewed by the sleep-starved sailors. Other difficulties, too many to be recounted, were dealt with by splendid seamanship. It was, indeed, by little short of a miracle of skill and endurance that the *Ohio* was finally got into the Grand Harbour of Valetta. The 10,000 tons of fuel oil and kerosene salved from her torn hull set the final seal on Operation 'Pedestal'. Malta was saved.

In his report, Admiral Syfret said that he and all officers of the Royal Navy who saw 'the steadfast manner in which [the merchantmen] pressed on their way to Malta through all attacks . . . will desire to give first place to the conduct, courage and determination of their Masters, officers and men' – a judgement with which the passage of time has brought no reasons for disagreement.

11

Rommel's Supply Crisis

MUSSOLINI'S RETURN to Italy on July 20th, disappointed of the early triumphal entry into Cairo in which Rommel's rash boasts had led him to believe, was an acknowledgement of the blighting of the bright hopes which were animating the Axis commands at the beginning of the month. At the same time Rommel himself was admitting failure in a long report to the German High Command. His losses in the fighting on the El Alamein line had reduced his effective strength to 30 per cent. Replacements were not fully trained. Reinforcements were urgently needed to prevent the British breaking through. As previously mentioned, these were being formed from the forces which had been standing by for Operation 'Hercules'.

Above all, Rommel was anxious about the supply situation. Men could be flown across to Africa, and, indeed, were, to the number of 36,500 during July and August; but tanks, armoured cars, guns, vehicles and fuel had to come by sea in the ever-diminishing Italian merchant fleet. Already at the end of July, a month when cargoes unloaded in North Africa reached the highest figure for some time and losses were kept down to 6 per cent, he was complaining that supplies only equalled consumption and no reserves could be accumulated. In fact, his gamble had failed and he was feeling the consequences.

Both armies had now reached a state of exhaustion after the long period of heavy and costly fighting in the horrible conditions of midsummer in the desert. With the men pestered by the plague of flies, parched with thirst, suffocated by sandstorms, roasted in tanks under a pitiless sun and subject to loathsome desert sores, morale on both sides was

wearing thin. A period of rest and recuperation was essential
before either side could resume the offensive. The month of
August 1942 thus saw a stalemate in North Africa, but it was
a stalemate of which the British were able to make better
use than Rommel.

Reinforcement, re-equipment and the accumulation of
large reserves of fuel, ammunition, aircraft and vehicles
were all pre-requisites of an offensive. The British, with their
supply line secure and the products of American industrial
expansion coming to their aid, were certain of all these
things eventually; but they needed time for them to arrive
via the 14,000 miles of the Cape route. Auchinleck, constantly pressed for an early offensive, gave the middle of
September as his earliest estimate. Rommel's prospects being
far less satisfactory, his only chance of success lay in striking
first, before the convoys bringing the fresh troops and new
tanks to the Eighth Army could reach Suez. This, and the
need for moonlight for his preliminary moves, set the date
as the latter part of August. It also meant stepping up the
rate of supply, particularly of petrol, at the very time that
the British were able to resume their attacks on the Italian
convoys.

The supplies which did reach North Africa were further
subjected to ceaseless attack on their way to the front. As
Rommel bewailed,

> Since the end of July the RAF had shifted the main weight
> of its activity to our lines of communication between the
> African ports and the front, where they were shooting up
> our transport columns and sinking one barge and coastal
> vessel after the other. No ship lying in the harbour at
> Bardia and Mersa Matruh, and frequently even at Tobruk,
> was safe from the attentions of the British bombers. . .
> The coastal waters were also being harassed by British
> naval forces.

In spite of appeals to the *Comando Supremo* and of
Italian promises, as August drew on, Rommel's reserves of

supplies, far from building up, actually diminished. Of this time he was to write:

> The fact that the German formations of the Panzer Army consumed between the 1st and 20th August almost double the supplies that were brought across the Mediterranean in the same period, tells its own story. . . At the end of this period the German forces were below strength to the extent of 16,000 men, 210 tanks, 175 troop carriers and armoured cars and – at a low estimate – 1,500 other vehicles. If we had not had the big British dumps in the Marmarica and Western Egypt to fall back on we should never have been able to exist at all. Rations were miserable and so monotonous that we were sick of the sight of them. The petrol and ammunition situation was as serious as ever and we were having to exercise the strictest economy. We were frequently compelled to put a complete ban on all forms of harassing fire merely in order to save ammunition. The British, on the other hand, were able to exercise their artillery for hours on end at our troops, who were forced to endure frightful hardships in the heat and desolation of our positions.

Rommel appreciated that his correct course was to make a strategic retreat, at least to the Egyptian frontier, thereby yielding to the British nothing but miles of useless desert and inflicting on them an equal burden of lengthy communications. Neither Hitler nor Mussolini, however, would hear of such a thing.

Faced, under these conditions, with the absolute necessity to attack and advance or accept inevitable eventual defeat, it is not surprising that the health of even the ebullient 'Desert Fox' was breaking down. A long-standing stomach complaint was so aggravated by these anxieties after the weeks of mental and physical strain in a trying climate, that on August 22nd he informed the German Supreme Command that he was ill and must be relieved before the coming offensive. Told that no Panzer General was available and disliking the command proposals made by Hitler under which Kesselring would have assumed supreme command in Africa, Rommel replied that he now felt well enough to command the operation under medical supervision but would then have to go home for a cure.

In contrast, on the British side, advantage of the lull was at this time being taken to revitalize the higher command. Winston Churchill arriving in Cairo early in August en route to a conference with Stalin in Moscow, took the opportunity to study the situation at first hand. He came to the conclusion that a drastic and immediate change was needed in order to impart a new and vigorous impulse to the Army. The result was the appointment of General the Hon Sir Harold Alexander to supersede General Auchinleck, and Lieutenant-General Bernard Montgomery to command the Eighth Army.

These two Generals at once set about reviving the morale, confidence and enthusiasm of the Army. How well they succeeded has been told and re-told elsewhere. It is sufficient here to quote from Mr Churchill's telegram to the War Cabinet on August 21st, after he had spent two days with the Eighth Army on his return from Moscow.

A complete change of atmosphere has taken place . . . the highest alacrity and activity prevails . . . our army will eagerly meet the enemy should he attack and I am satisfied that we have lively, confident, resolute men in command working together as an admirable team under leaders of the highest military quality.

Such was the Army which Field-Marshal Rommel was preparing to attack in a mood which sadly lacked his old fire and lively confidence. No longer were his eyes set on the goal of the Suez Canal. 'Because of the general shortage of supplies', he was to write, 'planning had to be limited to striking a blow at the Eighth Army in the Alamein line and taking possession of the territory around Alexandria and Cairo.'

If even this less ambitious offensive were to be mounted at the end of August, it would be necessary for 6,000 tons of fuel and 2,500 tons of ammunition to reach Libya between August 25th and 30th. The *Comando Supremo* dispatched seven ships carrying 10,000 tons of fuel, half for the Panzer Army and half for the Luftwaffe, to be followed by others a few days later. Only three of them got through to Tobruk carrying about 1,500 tons. Of the others, the *Ogaden* of 4,553 tons and the *Lerici* of 6,070 tons were both sent to the bottom by the submarine *Porpoise* commanded by Lieutenant L. W. A. Bennington, on her first combat patrol after a long period of employment as a petrol and supply carrier to Malta. Another, the *Rosolino Pilo* of 8,325 tons, was bombed and damaged by RAF aircraft from Malta when south of Pantellaria. The submarine *United* (Lieutenant T. E. Barlow) was sent to finish her off. So effectively did he do so that the *Pilo* blew up with such violence that a 12-foot length of iron frame landed on the surfaced submarine, partially wrecking her bridge and steering gear and forcing her to return to base for repairs. Finally, Beaufighters of No 227 Squadron intercepted the 5,000-ton tanker *San Andrea* and sank her. Two thousand four hundred tons of petrol for the Panzer Army went with her.

All Rommel's plans were in jeopardy. Appeals to Marshal Cavallero brought renewed promises of further tankers on the way under heavy escort. Kesselring promised to help the Panzer Army out of the Luftwaffe stock and, if necessary, to institute an airlift to bring petrol in. Nevertheless, to attack was to gamble.

In the hope that the promise would be fulfilled [Rommel later wrote], and trusting to Marshal Kesselring's assurance that he would fly across up to 500 tons of petrol a day in an emergency – but above all, in the certainty that if we did not act during this full moon, our last chance of an offensive would be gone for ever, I gave the order for the attack to open on the night August 30th–31st.

* * *

In this spirit of desperation, therefore, the Battle of Alam el Halfa was launched by the ailing 'Desert Fox'. Rommel's plan was bold and simple, and relied on his favourite gambit of a wide encircling movement. It was as much a gamble tactically as the whole conception of an offensive was strategically. Rommel's armoured formations were given the task of covering by night in seven hours a distance of 30 miles of unreconnoitred, mined territory so that they would be ready by daylight to strike northwards behind the British defensive positions. Once this wildly optimistic programme had been fulfilled, surprise was essential for the success of the next move.

As regards the latter, the plan had from the first been doomed to failure. Montgomery had confidently predicted it and, with the Alam el Halfa Ridge, running east and west, strongly held and fortified, welcomed the opportunity it gave of defeating the Panzer Army. Thus, even if the timetable for the advance could have been kept to, Rommel's armour would still have been forced to expend its strength in a battle in which all the advantages were held by the enemy.

In the event the Panzer Army's move soon fell far behind schedule owing to mines, bad 'going', harassing attacks from the air (which began even before the striking forces had reached their assembly points), and an unexpectedly stiff resistance by the fully alerted British. By daylight Rommel was already having doubts about continuing. General Fritz Bayerlein, who was at that moment acting as commander of the Afrika Korps in place of General Nehring, severely wounded during the night, has said that:

> The Desert Fox had not lost his flair, his subtle sixth sense which had always stood him in such good stead. As soon as he realized that he had not succeeded in taking the enemy by surprise, he wished to break off the attack. I was personally responsible for persuading Rommel that he let me continue the attack towards Alam el Halfa.

The attacks which followed made no progress against the

well-chosen and powerfully defended British positions. Nightfall found the Panzer divisions firmly held south of the ridge and running short of petrol. With darkness the Royal Air Force, hampered during the day by dust-storms, swarmed out to smother Rommel's concentrations of transport with a night-long hail of bombs, by the light of flares from Fleet Air Arm Albacores of Nos 821 and 826 Squadrons. Immense damage was done and the German soldiers' morale and fighting capacity shaken by the continuous bombing and lack of sleep.

Of the countless vehicles set ablaze, the petrol carriers were Rommel's chief concern. For not only was the immediate supply to his tanks being destroyed, but the flow of fuel across the Mediterranean was still far below his requirements. Of this time he was to write:

Consequently on the morning of September 1st, I found myself compelled to give up any attempt at major action for the moment; all large-scale movement of the motorized forces had to be avoided and the most we could permit ourselves was a few local, limited objective attacks. Acting on this decision, the Afrika Korps attacked on the morning of September 1st with the 15th Panzer Division only; after shooting up a number of British heavy tanks, the division's main force managed to reach the area just south of Hill 132 (the summit of Alam el Halfa Ridge) where, with their petrol almost exhausted, they were forced to call off even this local advance.

To complete the Panzer Army's discomfiture, the Royal Air Force swarmed over it to deliver intensive and repeated attacks throughout the day and night which followed, inflicting heavy casualties and leaving the desert studded with burning vehicles.

The wheel had indeed, come full circle, since the day when the British Army (and Navy) had had to submit to the unopposed assaults of the Stukas. Meanwhile, as Rommel was to record 'Still no drop of the promised petrol had arrived in Africa. That evening the Panzer Army had only one petrol issue left, and one issue, even with the greatest economy, could only suffice to keep our supply traffic going for a very short time . . .'

The next day Rommel admitted failure by ordering a gradual withdrawal to the westward of the British minefields. An attempt by the British to close the gaps in the minefields behind the enemy's striking force failed at the cost of heavy casualties. The Battle of Alam el Halfa was over.

Making allowances for the natural inclination of a defeated General to ascribe any reverse to circumstances outside his own control, and taking into account General Montgomery's accurate forecast and skilful anticipation of his opponent's movements, it seems fair to say that the assault on Rommel's supply lines, strategically by British naval and air forces in the central Mediterranean and along the coastal route to the front, and tactically on the field of battle, was a major cause of Rommel's failure at Alam el Halfa. Axis losses and casualties were certainly higher than those of the British, except in the air, but no more than to be expected from an assault on well-sited fixed defences. Very few of Rommel's tanks were put out of action by bombing, though tank-busting fighters did make a successful début at this time. On the other hand, hundreds of vehicles, and with them the precious petrol, were set ablaze. The attack ground to a halt principally because Rommel's troops were immobilized by the RAF's round-the-clock bombing in terrain which offered no cover and because petrol supplies for his armoured divisions were exhausted.

Rommel was palpably shaken and dismayed by the RAF's new-found superiority in the air – he had some narrow personal escapes. But in discussing the matter, it was the effect on his supply columns which he accentuated.

Whoever enjoys command of the air is in position to inflict such heavy damage on the opponent's supply columns that serious shortages must soon make themselves felt . . . an assured flow of supplies is essential;

without it the army becomes immobilized and incapable of action.

Where the supply line is partly over the sea, the same, of course, applies to command of the sea, whether it is exercised by ships, submarines or aircraft.

Rommel's realization that insufficient petrol was reaching Africa even to maintain a local offensive finally forced him to withdraw, a decision strengthened by news, on September 2nd, of the sinking by RAF Beaufort torpedo planes of the tanker *Picci Fassio*, and the crippling of the *Abruzzi*. It had been the announcement of the impending arrival of these two ships that, according to Westphal, had persuaded Rommel reluctantly to open his offensive. Two more ships, the *Bianchi* and the *Padenna*, were sunk on September 4th by combined air and submarine attack. Other convoys were less unlucky and, in spite of incessant attack from above and below, ships did get through. A convoy with four ships, for instance, sailed early on September 6th with an escort of no less than 12 destroyers and, by day, seven Ju 88s, five Macchi 200s, and one Cant Z506. Beauforts from Malta broke through the escort to torpedo one ship, the *Manara*, though she did not sink and was towed to a Greek anchorage. When the submarine *Ultimatum* attacked on the next day, a premature explosion of one torpedo gave the alarm. The attack was avoided and the *Ultimatum* was lucky to survive the ensuing counter-attack. All that day and during the night aircraft tried to stop the convoy – American Liberators by day and RAF torpedo planes by night – but the only result was a destroyer damaged by near misses.

By the 8th, in Rommel's words,

the supply situation had reached crisis proportions largely because the quantities sent to us had never once come up to the agreed target; during the first eight months of 1942 we had received approximately 120,000 tons – only 40 per cent of our absolute minimum needs. . . More and more tonnage was being lost and less and less ships were being provided by the Italians for the Africa run. . . Sinkings were going up steadily. Ten ships had been sunk by enemy action in the period from February until the end of July; between the end of July and the middle of October it was twenty.

Thus the Panzer General paid tribute to the dominant influence of sea power, a factor to which his own dazzling success at Tobruk had temporarily blinded him. Since then he had found himself caught up inexorably in the toils fashioned by himself when he insisted on the postponement of the assault on Malta. 'Malta has the lives of many thousands of German and Italian soldiers on its conscience', he was to write. It would have been more accurate to lay these lives on the consciences of those who failed to launch the assault on Malta – initially the Italian High Command in the early months of the war and subsequently Hitler and the German Supreme Command and, for one brief, fatal moment after Tobruk, Rommel himself.

In spite of promises by Cavallero and *Comando Supremo*, the supply situation improved very little in September. Though a greater tonnage was off-loaded in North African ports and losses were reduced to 20 per cent, Rommel complained that too much of it consisted of equipment and supplies for a fresh Italian division stationed in Cyrenaica, that the Italians took too great a share of the remainder and that the German element of the Panzer Army was neglected. Even food was insufficient and the health of the Afrika Korps was suffering.

To add to the Axis logistic difficulties, Allied heavy bombers made repeated daylight raids on the North African ports with strong fighter escort, which proved far more effective than the rather hit-or-miss efforts by night. On September 23rd an ammunition ship was blown up in Benghazi harbour, destroying the main unloading jetty.

On September 25th, on the orders of Hitler, Rommel flew home on leave for a course of medical treatment. General Stumme arrived from the Russian front to act as deputy commander during his absence. Both in Rome and at Hitler's headquarters in the 'Wolf's Lair', Rommel tried to hammer home the overriding importance of the supply problem. At the latter he found 'an atmosphere of extraordinary confidence'. Hitler assured him that the supply problem would be solved within the next few weeks by the employment in vast numbers of Siebel ferries. Encouraging statistics of current arms production were produced and promises made of the early dispatch of a brigade armed with a new, heavy multiple rocket projector with 500 barrels, as well as 40 of the newest 'Tiger' tanks to be followed by several assault gun units.

Rommel found little comfort in these sanguine promises. Even while he was at the Wolf's Lair a convoy of two of Italy's most modern, fast ships, the *Francesco Barbaro* and the *Unione*, was being broken up off the coast of Greece. With an escort of six destroyers they had sailed on the 26th bound for Tobruk. The familiar sequence of events repeated itself. Reconnaissance aircraft located and shadowed during the 27th, their reports enabling the submarine *Umbra* to intercept that afternoon. From her salvo of torpedoes one hit the *Barbaro* and brought her to a stop, disabled. A destroyer took her in tow for Navarino, while others ineffectively hunted the submarine. At dark Lieutenant Maydon was able to set off in chase. A second attack sent the *Barbaro* to the bottom with 545 tons of oil, 21 tanks, 151 vehicles, 1,217 tons of ammunition and 2,334 tons of general supplies. Meanwhile the airmen had swooped on the surviving ship. Soon after midnight the *Unione* was torpedoed. As her bows dipped until almost awash, her crew abandoned ship but were ordered back on board by the escort commander. A tow was eventually passed and the *Unione* brought into Navarino – a feat of remarkable seamanship under the circumstances; but 3,562 tons of petrol and 192 vehicles had failed to get through to the Panzer Army.

Early in October Kesselring's arrangements to carry out Hitler's orders to weaken or paralyse Malta had been completed by the transfer of aircraft from North Africa – further

enhancing the RAF's local superiority over Cyrenaica –
until a force of more than 300 German and Italian bombers
had been assembled. To meet the new threat, Malta could
put up 100 Spitfires and 13 Beaufighters.

These inflicted such heavy losses on the attackers that,
during the nine-day battle which took place, each day saw
the proportion of fighter escorts to bombers increase. One
raid, indeed, consisted of 14 bombers escorted by 98 fighters.
On October 16th the battle was almost continuous from
9 AM until sunset, during which time the enemy bombers
flew 200 sorties and at one time more than 90 aircraft were
in combat ten miles north of the island. By October 19th
some 70 German and Italian bombers had been shot down
for the loss of 30 Spitfires, 17 of whose pilots were rescued,
and Kesselring admitted defeat by forbidding any further
sorties by twin-engined bombers.

The chief target had been Luqa airfield, but at no time
was it put out of action for more than half an hour. Nor was
the island's air striking power eliminated, as the Fleet Air
Arm squadrons demonstrated at the height of the 'blitz' by
torpedoing three valuable supply ships in the Sicilian
Channel. Two of these were part of an important convoy on
which, as though in defiance of the Luftwaffe's efforts to stop
them, Malta's submarines and aircraft concentrated. As a
result of their combined efforts the convoy was almost wiped
out, one freighter and a crippled tanker being the only
survivors.

The October casualty rate of ships sunk or damaged on
the Libya route rose to 40 per cent. Out of 32,000 tons of
supplies shipped for the German elements of Rommel's
command, only 20,000 tons arrived. As to the all-important
fuel, out of 10,000 tons loaded, less than 4,000 tons reached
North Africa. The Panzer Army remained as critically short
as ever. And all the time the Eighth Army was building up
its huge superiority in men, tanks, guns, aircraft and supplies. General Montgomery, determined to destroy the
Afrika Korps once and for all, could afford to wait.

*   *   *

Out in the Atlantic a number of large convoys, assembled and sailed in the greatest secrecy from American and British ports, were steering by devious routes, the Americans for Casablanca, the British for the Straits of Gibraltar. Others, composed of faster ships, were loading and gathering for the same destinations. Aboard them were some 70,000 assault troops with their appropriate equipment, weapons, ammunition and supplies. They were scheduled to assault and capture simultaneously, on November 8th, the three ports of Casablanca, Oran and Algiers prior to the occupation of French Morocco, Algeria and Tunisia.

By October 23rd Montgomery was satisfied, as well he might be. At 9.40 PM the whole of the Eighth Army artillery, nearly 1,000 guns, opened fire simultaneously and the Battle of El Alamein had begun.

12

British Sea Power Victorious

IN THE present volume there is no place for a detailed description of the Battle of El Alamein or of the subsequent events of the campaign on land, but only of the salient features as seen against the background of the struggle for the Mediterranean as a whole. After two days of fierce fighting the British XXX Corps succeeded in making a breach six miles wide in the enemy's defences which directly threatened the centre of his communications. The X Corps had succeeded in deploying into a position in the north, where it could threaten an envelopment of the enemy's line or meet any counter-attack with its massive array of 700 tanks and powerful artillery, while the XIII corps had, by diversionary tactics in the south, kept the main body of the Afrika Korps' armour from intervening at the decisive point.

Nevertheless, when Rommel, hastily recalled from leave, resumed command late on October 25th, after General Stumme had been killed, the Eighth Army was far from achieving a breakthrough. Difficulty had been experienced in opening paths through the minefields wide enough for the British armour to advance *en masse*. Rommel at once appreciated the necessity to concentrate his armour against the main British thrust, which was now clearly being developed in the north. So short of petrol was the Panzer Army, however, that he hesitated. Passing through Rome on his journey, he had been given the catastrophic news that only sufficient fuel for three issues existed in North Africa. Ammunition was equally scarce.

Before hurrying on, Rommel had demanded that all available submarines and destroyers of the Italian fleet be pressed into service to carry these vital supplies. But meanwhile the

situation was calamitous. On October 26th the tanker
Proserpina, bringing petrol to Tobruk, was bombed and sunk
outside the harbour. Thus Rommel found himself unable to
take advantage of what seemed to him Montgomery's ex-
cessively cautious tactics on encountering a stout and gallant
resistance from the outnumbered Panzer Army, which was
forced to send its tanks piecemeal against the British
armoured columns. To bring the 21st Panzer Division from
its position in the south to meet the British thrust would
dangerously deplete its petrol supplies. Once moved, there
would be insufficient fuel for a return journey.

Rommel's hesitation was, therefore, understandable; but
it did not continue for long. His only chance to defeat the
British was by exploiting the often-demonstrated mobility of
his armour. The 21st Panzer Division was ordered north,
and by its intervention forced Montgomery to pause and
regroup before resuming his attack. For a time Rommel had
grounds for hoping that in spite of the overwhelming odds
the Afrika Korps might yet again save the day. But then, on
October 29th, 'at about half past eleven, I received the
shattering news that the tanker *Louisiana*, which had been
sent as replacement for the *Proserpina*, had been sunk by an
aerial torpedo. Now we were really up against it.' And,
indeed, from that moment onwards the outcome of the
battle could never really be in doubt. Though Kesselring
organized an air lift for Army fuel from Crete, this could
only have a minor effect on the situation. The Italian Navy
responded to Rommel's appeal by employing six destroyers,
four submarine transports as well as armed merchant cruisers and small craft to bring fuel across, but the majority of
these unloaded at Benghazi, several days' travel, under
constant air attack, from the front line.

By November 3rd the Panzer Army was at the end of its
resources; but on that same day came Hitler's crazy exhortation to Rommel to 'show his troops no other road than
that to victory or death'.

In spite of our unvarnished reports [the ill-used Field-

Marshal was to write], it was apparently still not realized at the Fuehrer's Headquarters how matters really stood in Africa. Arms, petrol and aircraft could have helped us, but not orders. We were completely stunned, and for the first time during the African campaign I did not know what to do.

The Panzer Army had done all that dogged courage and gallantry could do faced by a crushing superiority in men, guns, tanks and aircraft and crippled by a hand-to-mouth supply of fuel and ammunition. Nothing remained but to save those units still mobile, less than a third of the Axis forces engaged. It meant the abandonment of the majority of the Italian formations. Ten thousand Axis soldiers had died, 15,000 were wounded, 30,000, including nine Generals, were to be captured. By November 5th the Afrika Korps was streaming westwards. But they had inflicted 13,500 casualties on the Eighth Army before conceding victory to the British. They left more than 500 tanks disabled or destroyed; they had in reply disabled 500 of the British tanks, though the majority of these could be repaired.

Nevertheless, the victory at El Alamein was total and decisive because the British, with their immensely greater local resources and superiority of numbers, could afford the losses and casualties. The Germans and Italians, their lines of communication strangled, could not. Though from time to time Rommel was able to turn at bay and face his pursuers while they prudently allowed their supplies to catch up, he could never again hope to do more than delay the Eighth Army as it swept westwards to recapture Cyrenaica and upper Tripolitania.

While the Afrika Korps was turning westwards from the field of El Alamein, the assault convoys for Algiers and Oran were already inside the Mediterranean, their composition, size and destination quite unknown to the Axis Supreme Commands. Dönitz's U-boats in the Atlantic, busy harassing a convoy homeward bound from West Africa, had caught no glimpse of them. Unusual activity at Gibraltar had been ascribed to preparations for a Malta convoy. Even when the invasion fleets were reported in the Straits of Gibraltar on November 5th, no suspicion of their real destinations entered German minds and the German Naval Staff was subsequently to confess that they 'were completely outwitted in the intelligence game'. Light came to them only when a BBC announcement on the 8th gave Algiers as a destination. Not until midday on the 8th did the first air attack on the invasion force develop. On the 11th, Hitler gave orders 'to establish a bridgehead in Tunisia before enemy units have time to advance there from Algiers'. Three German Divisions, including an Armoured Division and two Italian Divisions, were assigned to the task.

The consequences of adding the burden of transportation and logistic support for an army in Tunisia to the shoulders of the already overwhelmed Italian Navy could, in the long run, end only in disaster. Hitler, however, was temperamentally incapable of accepting a voluntary strategic withdrawal, a characteristic which was to prove disastrous on a number of occasions. In this case, though the Italian Navy rose nobly to the occasion, sailing to Tunisia before the end of November no less than 90,000 tons of shipping without loss, carrying fuel, supplies, tanks and guns for the five Divisions (the men were mostly transported by air), the effort was made largely at the expense of supplies for Rommel in Tripolitania.

For the time being the Axis forces flown in to Tunisia, aided by the torrential rains and initial shortage of transport which slowed up all movement, were able to halt the Anglo-American army under General Anderson advancing eastwards from Algiers and so deny the port of Bizerta to the Allies. Thereafter the Axis armies were to hold out doggedly for another five months before final defeat – a defeat always inevitable sooner or later from the moment Hitler and Mussolini decided to try to hold Tunisia.

Nevertheless, suicidal as Axis strategy proved to be, the

deployment of the German and Italian army in Tunisia must be respected as a logistic feat of no mean order. Between December and March inclusive, the Axis Air Forces flew 7,371 sorties by Ju 52 transport planes, 434 by the giant Me 323s and 151 by Savoia 82s. More than 40,000 military passengers and 14,000 metric tons of supplies were safely delivered. Italian destroyers, between November and April, transported 51,935 troops.

Though the route to Tunisia did not at first come under the notice of Malta's naval and air striking force, this was soon to change. For with the airfields of Cyrenaica now again in British hands it had been possible to run a replenishment convoy through to Malta, and its safe arrival on the 20th marked the island's final relief from siege. Furthermore not only could the number of submarines and strike aircraft based there be increased but it was now again possible to maintain a surface striking force of cruisers and four destroyers, which, assuming the designation Force 'K', promised to emulate the devastating feats of its famous predecessor.

Another cruiser and destroyer force was based on the Algerian port of Bône within easy striking distance of the convoy route. All this boded ill for the Italian seamen burdened with the responsibility of maintaining supplies to the Axis armies trapped in Tunisia.

Meanwhile between November 10th and the end of the month only four ships with cargoes for the Afrika Korps, now back on the Tripolitanian frontier, reached Tripoli. Thirty-two thousand tons of shipping were sunk on passage, another 25,000 tons damaged and forced to turn back. By December 3rd the Italian Naval Staff was reporting that:

The Tripoli route is now exposed to such peril from Malta-based naval forces and aircraft that there is little point in continuing with our convoys. Only the Air Force can alter the situation.

Rommel, fettered by a totally unrealistic directive from

Mussolini that forbade him to withdraw farther, in spite of enormous British superiority both on the ground and in the air and of his own serious shortage of ammunition, was again facing catastrophe. In desperation he flew to Hitler's headquarters to protest.

There he flatly declared that in his view the general military situation and the resources available made any further tenure of Libya or Tunisia impossible, and he appealed to the Fuehrer to withdraw the Panzer Army to Italy through Tunisia before it was too late. His suggestion was curtly rejected. North Africa was to be defended in all circumstances and no matter what the cost, Hitler declared, in order to keep Italy in the war. Rommel was permitted, in case of extreme emergency, to withdraw to Buerat, but there a final stand had to be made. The last chance for the Axis to avoid a catastrophic military disaster in North Africa thus passed.

Sick at heart and deeply depressed, Rommel returned to his command. On December 7th indications that the Eighth Army was about to outflank his position by a wide encircling move led him to withdraw the Italian infantry units to Buerat. Six days later he moved back his motorized units, abandoning the El Agheila position in the nick of time. By the time the withdrawal was complete all his motorized units were at a standstill with, for the time being, no drop of fuel remaining.

Rommel continued to press for permission to withdraw at least into Tunisia, protesting that with the scanty stocks of fuel and ammunition available a major battle, even a defensive one, was beyond his resources. He was met by refusals from the *Comando Supremo* as well as from the German Supreme Command which can only be ascribed to a wilful refusal to face the facts of the situation at sea. For already the bitter ordeal that Italian and German seamen were to suffer during the next five months had begun.

During December 1st a convoy of four ships, loaded with armoured vehicles, munitions and a number of troops, and escorted by five destroyers, was located by air reconnaissance and its position and route were passed to the newly formed

Force 'Q' out of Bône, consisting of the cruisers *Aurora*, *Argonaut*, *Sirius*, and the destroyers *Quentin* and *Quiberon*, commanded by Rear-Admiral Harcourt whose flag flew at the masthead of the *Aurora*. Harcourt's flag-captain was well experienced in the task which lay ahead, for he was none other than Captain 'Bill' Agnew who, with Force 'K' from Malta, had annihilated an Italian convoy a year earlier.

With all the advantages of superior radar and gunpower, Force 'Q' fell upon the Italian convoy in devastating fashion. Once again Tunisian waters were aflame with blazing, exploding ships as the convoy and one of the destroyer escorts were wiped out in a brief overwhelming cannonade – but this time they were Italian ships, instead of British merchantmen and warships trying to get through to Malta. Their whirlwind assault completed, the British cruisers and destroyers withdrew, having suffered no damage from the ineffectual efforts of the escorts to protect their flock. Even while this holocaust was taking place off Cape Bon, farther north to the westward of Sicily the Italian tanker *Giuliano* laden with the fuel so desperately needed in Tunisia, had been located by an Albacore of the Fleet Air Arm from Malta and set ablaze by a torpedo hit amidships. During the next two nights that graveyard of Axis ships off the Kerkenah Bank saw the parachute flares hanging in the sky over Italian ships and flames shooting up, as four more ships succumbed to the torpedoes of Albacores. There, too, the Italian destroyer *Lupo*, veteran of so many convoy battles, remaining to help a crippled merchantman, was caught by destroyers of Force 'K' out of Malta and sent to the bottom.

Wellingtons and Beauforts, armed with torpedoes, added their quota of supply ships set upon and sunk by night at this time, so that night passages of the Sicilian Channel became too costly to be continued. The Italians now tried daylight passages under cover of heavy fighter escort. At the same time they laid two long minefields across the Narrows from Tunisia flanking the route to Bizerta and Tunis on either side, leaving a fairly narrow channel. This certainly countered the operations of the British naval surface striking forces which could still not afford to operate during daylight for lack of fighter protection. But it was promptly answered by the sowing of British mines in transverse lines across the chosen Italian route, by the fast minelayers *Abdiel* and *Welshman*, by submarines and by aircraft. The result of the Italian move was thus not only to cost them a number of ships blown up by mines, but by restricting their convoys to a strictly limited route made their location much more certain.

The convoys all had to pass through a comparatively restricted area off the north-west corner of Sicily – roughly between the islands of Ustica and Marittimo – during the night so as to enter the channel between the minefields at daylight. This area now became the hunting ground for the British torpedo planes and submarines and was soon yielding as heavy a bag as the Kerkenah Banks had done previously.

During December, in fact, though the Italian Navy and Merchant Marine strove valiantly to supply the armies in North Africa, reaching their highest ever total of tonnage sailed, 212,500 tons, no less than 68,000 tons were sunk and 15,000 tons damaged – a casualty rate of 40 per cent. Most of what got through went to maintain the forces in Tunisia. It is not surprising, therefore, that Rommel continued to advocate a withdrawal of the Panzer Army from Tripolitania. This was, however, too bitter a political pill for Mussolini to swallow, and, even when Rommel's previous order to stand fast was rescinded by the *Comando Supremo* on December 29th, it was only a partial withdrawal – to the Tarhuna-Homs line – that was permitted. Kesselring had been assuring the German Supreme Command that it would be possible to supply the armies in North Africa with 80,000 tons monthly even though only 24,000 tons had reached them in December.

January was to be an even worse month. To the aid of the RAF Naval Cooperation squadrons and the Fleet Air Arm came the United States XII Air Force under General Spaatz. Their initial lack of success owing to inexperience in naval warfare was transformed by the attachment of naval observers from the British Fleet Air Arm and soon they were running up a tally of transports, tanker and escort vessels left burning and sinking.

Their technique, the deadly but hazardous one of high-speed, low-flying attack with bombs, proved its efficacy from their first encounter on January 20th, when the 5,000-ton tanker *Saturno* blew up and sank.

Out of 51 ships sailed for North Africa during January, 11 were sunk by submarines, four by surface vessels, two by mines and seven by aircraft, while another seven were seriously damaged by air attack – a casualty rate of 55 per cent. The Italians pressed into service every kind of small craft to swell the trickle of supplies getting through, but these too were intercepted by submarines and MTBs and sunk by gunfire, or set upon by the swarms of American aircraft now coming into action as Algerian airfields were occupied and equipped. It is little wonder that to the Italians the route to Tunisia was known as 'the death route'. It is more astonishing that seamen were found to accept its fearful hazards again and again till they met their inevitable fate at the hands of submarines or aircraft.

Their heroism succeeded during the winter months in keeping enough supplies passing to the Tunisian army to enable it to hold off the greatly superior Allied army of General Eisenhower while the winter rains persisted. Little could be done for Rommel's Panzer Army and it says much for the tactical genius of the 'Desert Fox' that it was not until the middle of February that it finally evacuated Tripolitania to make a last stand on the Mareth Line. This, indeed, was the end of the Panzer Army as a unit. In a regrouping of forces, the German part of it, the old Afrika Korps, combined with Italian units to form the Italian 1st Army under General Messe. This new army and the German 5th Army, under General von Arnim, holding Tunisia in the west, combined to form Army Group, Africa, under the supreme command of Field-Marshal Rommel. On March 9th, in response to repeated demands by the Italians, who had lost confidence in him, Rommel was recalled by Hitler and the supreme command assumed by von Arnim.

In the last week of March the British Eighth Army succeeded in turning the Mareth Line position and resumed its victorious advance into Tunisia until halted by the mountainous country north of Enfidaville at the end of April. Here they were instructed to stand until the Allied armies broke through from the west.

Meanwhile, with the steady build-up of Allied air power to overwhelming proportions, the massacre of Italian shipping mounted continually. Indeed, its virtual extinction would have been achieved early in 1943 but for 120,000 tons of Vichy French shipping transferred to the Italian flag. By March, four-engined bombers of the US Army Air Force were available in large numbers to bring daylight massed raids to smother Italian harbours. In one such raid by 22 Flying Fortresses on Palermo four freighters were destroyed. The blast from one of them as it exploded, blew two 600-ton ships bodily on to the Santa Lucia pier. In another raid by 84 Fortresses, Italy's last two heavy cruisers, the *Trieste* and the *Gorizia*, were attacked in the harbour of La Maddalena, Sardinia. The *Trieste* was sunk and the *Gorizia* put out of action for the rest of the war. During February, 34 ships set out for Tunisia, but only 20 arrived. In March, 23 ships out of the 44 which sailed were sunk or severely damaged.

By this time von Arnim had been forced to report to the blindly stubborn Fuehrer that his position was hopeless, with both food and fuel for his trapped armies running short. Even Kesselring, ever loyal in his support of Hitler's demands, however impracticable, was advising that Tunisia could not be held and that the time had come to see whether at least a partial evacuation could be achieved. Hitler again flatly rejected any such idea and insisted that the Army must fight on 'to the last man'. At a meeting with Mussolini early in April he brought his Axis partner round to the same unrealistic point of view. The last chance of minimizing the inevitable approaching catastrophe thus passed.

To the Italian Navy and the *Comando Supremo*, the

hopelessness of the situation and the uselessness of the sacrifices being made were clear enough. But to their objections to throwing away further lives and ships, Kesselring invoked Mussolini's authority to demand renewed efforts and the use of every available destroyer and motor torpedo boat, as well as merchant ships, to transport men and supplies to Tunisia. The Italian Navy bowed to the inevitable and the slaughter went on. During April no less than 60 per cent of all shipping was sunk or crippled.

Long before the end of the winter rains allowed the superior Allied armies to advance to capture Tunis, the Axis forces were on siege rations of food and largely immobilized on account of lack of fuel. By the end of April they were virtually sealed off. Even air reinforcement ceased when American fighters intercepted a large fleet of escorted Ju 52s and destroyed them all or forced their pilots to crash land.

Yet with a dogged persistence and a fatalistic disregard of the facts of the situation, long past hope of salvation, merchant ships continued to attempt the passage of the Sicilian Channel. As late as the night of May 3rd, the destroyers *Nubian*, *Petard* and *Paladin* from Malta intercepted a large ship of 8,000 tons off Cape Bon, escorted by a torpedo boat. Both were sunk. The mighty explosion with which the transport, laden with ammunition, bombs and land-mines, blew up may well be taken as marking the end of the Battle for the Mediterranean.

On May 7th, with the Axis land front everywhere crumbling, the German Naval Commander in Tunisia reported that no more ships could be accepted. Yet Hitler and Dönitz continued to call for every possible ship to be dispatched. That evening the last three German cargo ships sailed for Cape Bon and actually succeeded in crossing the Sicilian Channel safely only to find no harbour left in Axis hands in which to unload. As they steamed forlornly up and down the Tunisian coast they were set upon by swarms of Allied aircraft. They ran themselves aground and were there blown to pieces by bombs.

By this time the Army Group, Africa, was penned in to the

Cape Bon peninsula, cut off from escape by sea, control of which had finally passed securely into Allied hands after three years of struggle. To the British destroyers off the coast for Operation 'Retribution', Admiral Cunningham signalled in terms reminiscent of the eighteenth-century naval wars, 'Sink, burn and destroy. Let nothing pass'. Very few tried to. The pathetic stream of motor, sailing or rowing boats, even rafts and rubber dinghies, which the destroyer men called the 'Kelibiah Regatta' yielded about 1,000 prisoners. A quarter of a million prisoners surrendered on shore when the last Axis resistance ceased on May 12th.

For another year or more the northern shores of the Mediterranean were the scenes of bitter fighting by land, in Italy, the Balkans and the South of France. In the Aegean, Axis air power would for a long while continue to dominate. But, with the passing into Allied hands of the whole of the North African shore, the Mediterranean as a whole became a sea open to the passage of Allied ships throughout its length. U-boats continued to lurk in its waters, but their numbers were steadily whittled down and their threat reduced to a minor and occasional hazard. Locally the Luftwaffe would continue to dispute the ability of the Allied Navies to use the sea to transport their Armies where they wished to go and thereafter to support them; but in no case was control of even the local areas lost by the Allies.

Thus, though battles in the Mediterranean area there continued to be, the Battle for the Mediterranean can be said to have been finally won when the Axis forces in Tunisia laid down their arms on May 12th, 1943.

Select Bibliography

OFFICIAL HISTORIES

Cocchia, Admiral Aldo (and others), *La Marina Italiana nella Seconda Guerra Mondiale*, Rome, 1959.

Playfair, Major-General I. S. O. (and others), *The Mediterranean and the Middle East*, HMSO, 1954.

Roskill, Captain S. W., *The War at Sea*, HMSO, 1954.

OTHER BOOKS

Bayerlein, Lieutenant-General Fritz, *The Fatal Decisions* (*El Alamein*), Michael Joseph.

Bernotti, Admiral, *La Guerra sui Mari nel Conflitto Mondiale*, Società Editrice Tirrena, Livorno, 1948.

Bragadin, Commander, *The Italian Navy in World War II*, US Naval Institute, 1957.

Cunningham, Admiral of the Fleet, Lord, *A Sailor's Odyssey*, Hutchinson & Co Ltd, 1951.

Liddell Hart, Captain B. H. (Ed.), *The Rommel Papers*, Wm Collins Sons & Co Ltd.

Lloyd, Air Marshal Sir Hugh, *Briefed to Attack*, Hodder & Stoughton Ltd, 1949.

Roskill, Captain S. W., *A Merchant Fleet in War*, Wm Collins Sons & Co Ltd, 1962.

Index

Aagtekirk, Dutch supply ship, sunk, 157

Abdiel, HM minelayer, 64, 122, 213

Abruzzi, 54; crippled, 201

Adriatico, Italian auxiliary cruiser, sunk, 115

Afrika Korps, 13, 24, 46, 52–9, 83, 116, 198

    convoys, British attacks on, 87ff., 98, 105–9, 110–15, 193ff., 212, 213–14

    withdrawals to El Agheila for regrouping, 117, 131

    its offensive to the Gazala Line, 131, 132

    at Mersa Matruh, 170

    in eclipse, Chapter 11

    retreats to Tripoli, ceases to exist as a unit, 210, 214

Agnew, Captain W. G., 111, 112, 113, 212

Airedale, sunk, 167

Ajax, 28, 33, 55, 62, 64, 65, 71, 78, 129

Alagi, Italian submarine, 183

Alam el Halfa, Battle of, 198–200

Albacore aircraft, 77, 103, 114, 124, 133, 134, 137, 199, 212

Alexander, General, succeeds Auchinleck, 171

Alexandria, 15, 16, 17, 24, 25, 29, 34, 35, 55, 64, 65, 66, 76, 77, 78, 83, 91, 98, 125, 135, 154, 165, 170

Algeria, 205

Algiers, 208

Almeria Lykes, USS, 174, 185 sunk, 186

Andrea Doria, 38

Andrea Gritti, sunk, 105

Antelope, 158

Anti-aircraft defences at Malta, 26

Anti-aircraft cruisers, 28, 156, 160, 162, 175, 183, 185, 187

Antonietta Laura, Italian transport, sunk, 88

Arcturus, German transport, sunk, 89

Arethusa, 19, 101

Argonaut, 212

Argus, 27, 28, 57, 138, 156, 160

Ark Royal, 19, 39, 40, 41, 42, 47, 48, 57, 64, 65, 101, 103, 104, 126

    sunk, 118

Armando Diaz, torpedoed and sunk, 53, 87

Army of the Nile, 42, 45, 52, 61, 64

Arnim, General von, 214, 215

Arta, German transport, destroyed, 89

Asdic, Italian lack of, 92

Ashanti, 185, 187

Athens, 62

Attendolo, damaged, 189

Auchinleck, General, 149
  succeeded by Alexander, 171, 172, 196

Aurora, 110, 111, 112, 123, 125, 212

Australian Forces, 70

Axum, Italian submarine, 181, 183

Back, Captain (of H M S *Orion*), killed, 80

Badoglio, Marshal, 30

Badsworth, H M destroyer, 162

Bagnolini, Italian submarine, sinks *Calypso*, 17

Baleno, destroyed, 58

Bande Nere, 87, 139; sunk, 141

Barbaro, torpedoed, 105

'Barbarossa', Operation, 83

Bardia, 18, 31

Barham, 34, 55, 64, 77
  bombed, 77
  torpedoed and sunk, 119

Bari, 45

Barlow, Lieutenant T. E., 197

Bastico, General, 116

'Battleaxe', Operation, 98

Bayerlein, General Fritz (Afrika Korps), 198

Beatrice Costa, bombed and sunk, 94

Beaufighters, 64, 160, 175, 183, 197

Beaufort torpedo-carrying planes, 45, 133, 137, 156, 165, 167, 201, 212

Bedouin, 160, 161, 162
  sunk, 162

Beirut, 170

Benghazi, 58, 64, 98, 110, 114, 123, 207
  bombarded, 66
  retaken by Axis forces, 132

Bennington, Lieutenant L. W. A., 197

Bergamini, Admiral, 134

Bernotti, Admiral, *La Guerra sui Mari nel Conflitto Mondiale* (qu.), 29–30

Berwick, 34, 40, 41, 42

Bhutan, 164

Bianchi, 'Charioteer', 128

Bianchi, Italian supply ship, sunk, 201

Bir Hacheim, defence of, 151
  Line, 132, 148

Birmingham, 167

Bisciani, Captain, 112, 113

Bizerta, 212

Blenheim bombers, 28, 84, 91, 93, 94, 95, 97, 103, 106, 133, 137

Bolzano, 54; torpedoed and beached, 189

'Bomb Alley', 77, 100, 156, 163, 167

Bomba, 31
  Gulf of, 125

Bombay transport planes, 28

Bonaventure, 47

Bône, 210, 212

Borghese, Lieutenant-Commander Valerio, 126
Bragadin, Commander, *The Italian Navy in World War II* (qu.), 29, 169
Bramham, 179, 190, 191, 192
Brarena, Italian tanker, sunk, 97
Breconshire, supply ship, 64, 102, 122, 123, 124, 129, 130, 135, 138
  damaged, 142
Brindisi, 45
Brisbane Star, 174, 183, 186
British convoys, *see* Malta convoys
British Eighth Army, *see* Eighth Army
Brivonesi, Vice-Admiral Bruno, 111, 112, 113
Bronzo, Italian submarine, 183
Brown, Captain Ramsay, 178, 179
Buerat, 211
Burdwan, 156; sunk, 162
Burrough, Rear-Admiral H., 104, 183, 187, 190
Bush, Captain, 140

Caffaro, Italian ammunition ship, blown up, 106
Cagliari, 156
Cairo, 153
Cairo, A/A cruiser, 156, 160, 161, 162, 175, 183
  sunk, 185, 187
Calcutta, 28, 62, 71
  sunk, 80
Calvani, Lieutenant, 187
Calypso, sunk, 17
Campbell, Colonel I. R., 70

Campioni, Admiral Inigo, 20–23, 29, 32, 33, 34, 35, 37, 40, 41, 42, 46
Canea, 69
Cant Z501 seaplane, 15, 94, 178
  Z506, 201
Canzoneri, Rear-Admiral F., 91
Cape Bon, 32, 85, 120, 212, 216
Capo Faro, sunk, 115
Capo Vita, Italian transport, sunk, 87
Capponi, Italian submarine, sunk, 88
Caproni '42' fighter, 94, 95, 106, 176, 180
Caralis, Italian auxiliary warship, 86
Carline, Lieutenant G. A., 36
Casablanca, 205
Carlisle, 62, 71, 74, 123, 129, 135, 138
Cassiopaea, 114
Catania, 43
Cavagnari, Admiral, 15, 45
Cavallero, General, 132, 153, 154, 197, 202
Cavour, 20, 38
Cayley, Lieutenant-Commander R. D., 87
C. Damiani, Vichy French tanker, sunk, 89
Centurion, 164, 167
Cesare (*Giulio Cesare*), 20, 21, 37, 40, 45, 47, 123
Chant, USS, 156; sunk, 161
'Chariot' (2-man torpedo), 125, 126
Charybdis, 156, 175, 188

Churchill, Winston, 149, 150, 172, 196

Cigno, Italian torpedo-boat, 120, 121

Clan Campbell, 135, 136, 138; sunk, 142

Clan Chattan, 135; sunk, 136

Clan Ferguson, 174; sunk, 183

Cleopatra, 139, 140, 144, 163

Cobalto, Italian submarine, sunk, 180

Collett, Lieutenant A. F., 87

Comiso airfield, 43

Conte Rosso, Italian troop liner sunk by Wanklyn, 91, 107

Convoys, British; see Malta, Operation Italian, see Libya, Tunisia

Corbett, Lieutenant-Commander J. W. S., 134

Corfu, 126

Costa Rica, British troopship, sunk, 62

Coventry, 28, 62, 76

Crete, 33, 34, 57, 60, 63
  defence of, 68
  Germans capture, 69ff.
  German losses at, 81
  map showing losses from the campaign, 72

Cripps, Sir Stafford, 149

Cristoforo, Commander Pietro, 58

Cunningham, Admiral Sir Andrew, 15, 16, 17, 24, 25, 26, 29, 32–5, 38, 44, 57, 63, 64, 78, 119, 130, 138, 217
  on Stuka dive-bombing (qu.), 49

Curteis, Vice-Admiral, 104, 156, 160

Cyrenaica, 45, 52, 61, 67, 204
  Axis driven from, 116
  retaken by Eighth Army, 208
  airfields, 149

Da Barbiano, sunk, 120, 121

Da Mosto, Italian destroyer, sunk, 115

Da Zara, Admiral, 157, 160, 161, 162, 169

Decimomammu, 175

Decoy, damaged, 80

De la Penne, Lieutenant, 127, 128

'Demon', Operation, 61

Denby Dale, tanker sunk by 'chariot', 126

Dentz, General, 82

Derna, 151

Despatch, 40

Dessie, Italian submarine, 181, 183

Destroyer Flotilla, Fifth, 84

Deucalion, 174, 178
  bombed and burnt out, 178, 179

Di Giussano, sunk, 120, 121

Diamond, sunk, 63

Diana, Italian auxiliary warship, 126, 127

Dido, 71, 73, 78, 80, 129

Dive-bombing, 48, 49

Dodecanese, 83

Doria, 123

Dorset, 174, 187; crippled, 190

Duca degli Abruzzi, torpedoed, 114

Duilio, 38, 123

Duisburg, 85, torpedoed by Upholder, 86

'Duplex pistol' (torpedo device), 36

Eagle, carrier, 16, 19, 23, 24, 29, 34, 138, 146, 156, 158, 175

E-Boats, 146, 165, 186

Edinburgh, 101

Egypt, 28, 83, 103
  Italian invasion of, 31

Eighth Army, British, 13, 113
  retreats from Benghazi to Gazala Line, 131-2, 148
  retreats to El Alamein and strikes back, 154
  gets self-propelled guns and Sherman tanks, 171
  lines of communication, 172
  revitalized by Montgomery, 196
  X Corps, 206
  XIII Corps, 115, 206
  XXX Corps, 115, 206

El Agheila, 117, 131

El Alamein, 13, 120, 153, 193
  Battle of, 205

El Gazala, 117, 132, 148

Elmas airfield, 175

Emo, Italian submarine, 179

Empire Hope, 174
  bombed and abandoned, 183

Empire Song, mined and sunk, 65

Enfidaville, 215

Esperia, Italian troop liner, 90, 97; sunk, 107

Eugenio di Savoia, 157

Euro, 19, 112

Euryalus, 122, 129, 140
  damaged, 140

'Excess', Operation, 46

Faggioni, Lieutenant, 126

Fearless, HM destroyer, sunk, 101

Ferrini, Lieutenant Renato, 181

Fiji, 64, 65, 75
  bombed and sunk, 75

Fiume, 54, 56

Fleet Air Arm:
  813 Squadron, 19, 31
  815 Squadron, 36
  819 Squadron, 36
  821 Squadron, 199
  824 Squadron, 31
  826 Squadron, 134, 199
  828 Squadron, 103, 114, 124
  830 Squadron, 19, 26, 45, 59, 105, 114

Fliegerkorps II, transferred from Russia to Sicily, 119, 120, 130
  makes all-out attack on Malta, 132, 138, 143, 144, 145, 158
  reinforced, 171

Fliegerkorps VIII, 60, 61, 67, 81, 83
  transferred to Russian Front, 83

Fliegerkorps X, 43, 46, 47, 51, 52, 54, 55, 60, 61, 68, 81
  reduced in strength, 80, 83, 84, 91, 100, 117, 119, 132, 143

Fliegerkorps XI, 67, 68, 81

Flying Fortress, 133, 137, 172, 215

Force 'B', 119

Force 'H', 18, 20, 34, 39, 40, 45-8, 64, 65, 101, 102, 104, 119, 138

Force 'K', 111, 113, 114, 115, 119, 120, 121, 122, 123, 131, 136, 212

Force 'Q', 212

Force 'X', 101, 102, 104, 173ff.

Foresight, H M destroyer, sunk, 180

Formidable, 53, 55, 56, 64, 66, 69, 77

badly damaged, 77, 118

Foscarini, bombed, 93

France, 15, 18, 27

Francesco Barbaro, sunk, 203

Freccia, 90

Free French forces, 151

French North Africa, Allied invasion of, 205

Freyberg, General, 69, 115

Frogmen, Italian, 125

Fulmar aircraft, 25, 28, 48, 51, 65, 66, 69, 77, 86, 101, 158, 175

Fulmine, sunk, 112

Furious, 103

Galatea, 122

Galilea, torpedoed, 88

Gallant, 48, 144

Garibaldi, 54

Garside, Captain, 20

Gavdo Island, 55

Gazala, 148

Battle of (May 1942), 151

Line, 170

Geister, General der Flieger, 43

Genoa, 47

Georgiopolis, 70

German Air Force, *see* Luftwaffe *and* Fliegerkorps

German Army Group Africa, 214

Afrika Korps, *see* Afrika

Fifth Army, 214

12th Army, 61

Panzer Army, 154, 171, 197ff.

15th Panzer Division, 199

21st Panzer Division, 207

German Navy, 67, 151

Third E-Boat Flotilla, 146

MTBs, 174

Gibraltar, 18, 34, 43, 46, 57, 104, 118, 126, 209

Giorgioni, Flotilla Commander, 126

Giuliano, Italian tanker, sunk, 212

Glasgow, 34

Glaucos, Greek submarine, sunk, 145

Glenearn, 62

Glengyle, 62, 129, 130

Glennie, Read-Admiral I. G., 71, 73

Glenorchy, 174, 185; sunk, 186, 187

Glenroy, 77

Gloster-Gladiator aircraft, 16, 26, 28, 51, 68

Gloucester, 20, 47, 48, 49, 55, 75

burnt out, 75

Gloxinia, minesweeper, 65

Gondar, Italian submarine, sunk, 126

Göring, Marshal, 68, 110

Gorizia, 139; disabled, 215

Graziani, Marshal, 31, 42

Grecale, Italian destroyer, 112, 113

Greece, Mussolini declares war on, 33, 34, 45
  Germans invade, 56
  British evacuation from, 61ff.
  map showing losses from the campaign, 72
Greyhound, bombed and sunk, 75
Grohman, Rear-Admiral Baillie, 62
Guggenberger, Lieutenant, 118

Haifa, 170
'Halberd', Operation, 104
Hale, Lieutenant-Commander J. W., 36
Hal Far airfield, 84, 86
Hampton, Captain T. C., 74
Harcourt, Rear-Admiral, 212
Hardy, Captain C. C., 160, 161, 162
'Harpoon', Operation, 156–63
Harwood, Admiral, 157, 163, 167, 168
Hasty, 165
Havelock, 125
Havock, 141
Hawkins, Lieutenant-Commander W. A. F., 162
Hebe, 161, 162, 192
Heinkel '111', 51
Heraklia, sunk, 88
Heraklion, 68, 70, 73, 77–8
'Hercules', Operation, 132, 149, 152, 153, 154
Hereward, sunk, 79
Hermione, 101, 168
Hezlet, Lieutenant A. R., 107
Hill, Lieutenant-Commander R. P., 191

Hipper, German cruiser, 47
Hitler, Adolf, 43, 88, 110
  doubts necessity or advisability of taking Malta, 132
  agrees with Mussolini on a date for Rommel's offensive, and for assault on Malta, 149
  decrees that Panzer Army must fight to the last man, 215
Hood, 19
Hotspur, 79
Hurricane aircraft, 26, 27, 28, 45, 51, 53, 68, 77, 101, 103, 133, 155, 172, 175
Hurricanes, Sea-, 158, 176
Hutchison, Captain C. A. G., 142
Hyperion, sunk, 45
Hythe, minesweeper, 192

Iachino, Admiral Angelo, 46, 54, 55, 104, 123, 139, 140, 142, 156, 157, 160
Illustrious, 25, 28, 32, 33–7, 39, 44, 45, 48, 50, 51, 53, 86
  badly damaged by dive-bombing, 49, 118
Imperial, damaged, 78; sunk, 79
Imperial Star, sunk, 104
Indomitable, 118, 175, 176
  out of action, 180
Ingo, sunk, 85, 86
Iraq, 82
Iride, 31, 125
Iridio Mantovani, Italian tanker, sunk, 115

Isaac Sweers, Dutch destroyer, 120

Ismailia, British Naval HQ moves to, 170

Italian Air Force, 15–16, 20–25, 32, 35, 39, 41, 42, 54, 101, 178, 188
Army, 27, 52
Navy, 15, 19, 29, 32, 35, 54, 65, 74, 99, 102, 104, 110–15, 151, 155, 156, 173, 179, 180, 188, 207; 10th Light Flotilla, 126, 127

Italian convoys, 53, 91–8, 110, 112, 113, 131, 133, 216, 217

Ithuriel, 179, 180

Janus, 57

Jerome, Commander, 190

Jervis, 57, 58

'Judgement', Operation, 34, 36

Junkers '52', 76, 94, 139, 210, 216
'87', *see* Stuka
'88', 48, 51, 91, 134, 140, 146, 158, 164, 175, 183, 189, 201

Juno, sunk by bombing, 71

Kalamata, 62

Kandahar, 75, 125; sunk, 125

Kashmir, sunk, 76

Kaso Strait, 78, 79

Keighley-Peach, Commander Charles, 16, 24

Kelly, sunk, 76

Kelvin, damaged, 80

Kent, 32

Kentucky, USS, 156
disabled, 161, 162

Kenya, 156, 175
damaged, 184, 185

Kerkenah Bank, 58, 85, 86, 87, 89, 106, 212, 213

Kesselring, Field-Marshal, 119, 132, 143
decides that Malta is neutralized and withdraws part of Luftwaffe, 146–7, 148
agrees to Rommel's advance as far as El Alamein, 153
advises Hitler that Tunisia cannot be held, 215

Kimberley, 79

King, Admiral E. L. S., 71, 73, 74, 75

Kingston, 75, 141, 144

Kipling, 76

Kithera Channel, 75

Kittyhawk planes, USAAF, 172

König, General, 151

Königsberg, 50

Kriegsmarine, *see* German Navy

Lampedusa Island, 97

Lampo, put out of action, 58
salvaged, 59

Lance, 111, 125

Laura Corrado, sunk, 88

Leatham, Vice-Admiral, 172

Ledbury, HM destroyer, 185, 189, 191, 192

Legion, 120
damaged and beached, 142

Lerici, Italian supply ship, sunk, 197

Leslie, Captain G., 186, 187

Leverkusen, German transport, sunk, 89

Libeccio, sunk, 113

Liberator aircraft, 156, 157, 167, 172

Libya, 23, 27, 30, 32, 52, 56
convoys, 53, 92, 93–5, 109, 113, 114, 131, 133

Liguria, 19

Littorio, 18, 29, 38, 104, 120, 123, 139, 140, 141, 156, 167

Lively, 111, 125

Liverpool, 32, 156
damaged, 158

Lloyd, Air Vice-Marshal, 93, 142

Löhr, General, 68, 70

Longmore, Air Chief Marshal Sir Arthur, 27, 45, 52, 57, 103

Lookout, 179

Lörzer, General, 119

Louisiana, Italian tanker, sunk, 207

Luftflotte II, 119, 146, 188
IV, 68

Luftwaffe, 25, 43, 44, 64, 65, 66, 67, 89, 102, 110, 217

Lupo, 73, 114; sunk, 212

Luqa airfield, 204

Lysander aircraft, 28

Lyster, Rear-Admiral, 33, 45

Macchi fighter aircraft, 176, 201

MacFarlane, Captain, 189

Mack, Captain Philip, 57, 84

Maddalena Odero, sunk, 97

Maestrale, 111, 112

Malaya, 34, 38, 44, 45, 47, 48, 156

Maleme, 68, 69, 70, 71, 77

Malocello, 161

Malta, 14, 16, 18, 19, 20, 21, 25, 27, 30, 32, 34, 40, 43, 44, 49, 53, 65, 111
its vital role, 26
aircraft strength in August 1941, 103
convoys, 42, 46, 64–6, 100ff., 122, 129, 135, 138, 142, 155–69, 173–92
respite from air attack, 84
resumes its value as base against Rommel's convoys, 91ff.
renewed Luftwaffe assault on, 122ff.
the suppression of, Chapter 8
Axis plans capture of, 132
under all-out air attack, 132, 142–3,
acquires Spitfires, 138, 146
its work as submarine base brought to a standstill, 145
big Spitfire reinforcements redress the balance, 147, 155
airfields bombed, 171
first British submarine arrives back, 172
again under air attack, 204

Manara, disabled, 201

Manchester, 40, 101, 175, 185
crippled, 101, 186
sunk, 186

Manuti, Lieutenant-Commander, 186

Manxman, fast minelayer, 101

Maori, 120, 144

Maori troops, 71

Marceglia, Antonio, 127, 128
Marco Polo, Italian troop liner, 90, 97
Mareth Line, 215
Maritza, German transport, sunk, 114
Marne, 161
Mars, Lieutenant Alistair, 189
Martellotta, Vincenzo, 127, 128
Martlet aircraft, 175, 176
Maryland aircraft, 28, 33, 34, 35, 45, 103, 111
Mason, Captain D. W. (of *Ohio*), 174
Matapan, Battle of, 55, 56 Cape, 54
Matchless, 161
Maydon, Lieutenant, 165, 203
Mediterranean, Map of, 10–11
Mediterranean Fleet experiences success, Chapter 6 in eclipse, Chapter 7
Medway, submarine depot ship, sunk, 170
Megara, 62
Melbourne Star, 174, 187, 189, 191
Merano, 53
'Merkur', Operation, 81
Mersa Matruh, 31, 153, 154, 170
Messe, General, 214
Messerschmidt '109', 138, 146, 151, 168
'110', 51
'323', 210
Messina, 122 Straits, 54, 90, 105, 111
Mezzadra, Sub-Lieutenant, 186

Micklethwait, Captain, 141
Middle East Air Force reaches parity with Axis, 172
Milos, 71
Mitchell bombers, USAAF, 172
Mohawk, 48, 57 torpedoed and sunk, 58
Monemvasia, 62
Montecuccoli, 157
Montello, Italian ammunition ship, sunk, 94
Montezemolo, Colonel, 116
Mongomery, Lieutenant-General Sir Bernard, 196, 198, 205
Morea, 62
Moriondo, Vice-Admiral, 87
'Motobomba', 176, 190
Motor torpedo ships, Italian, *see* E-Boats
Mountbatten, Captain Lord Louis, 76
Mountain Division, 5th German, 70, 74 Regiment, 100th, 70
Mussolini, 33, 44, 149, 154 authorizes advance to Suez Canal, 153 forbids Rommel to retreat beyond Tripoli, 213

Naiad, 64, 65, 71, 74, 122, 129 torpedoed, 139
Napier, damaged, 80
Naples, 45, 104
Napoli, damaged, 124
Navarino, 168, 203
Nauplia, 62, 63
Naval Cooperation Group, Alexandria, 103

Nehring, General (Afrika Korps), 198
Nelson, 101, 104, 126, 175
Nembo, 19
Neptune, mined and sunk, 125
Neptunia, Italian troop liner, 97, 107
sunk, 108
Nestor, HMAS, damaged and scuttled, 168
Newcastle, 165
Newton, D. and A. C. Hampshire, Taranto, 37
New Zealand forces, 70, 115
New Zealand Star, 65
Nicolo Odero, sunk, 107
Nigeria, 175
torpedoed, 183, 185, 187
Nizam, 78
Norman, Lieutenant E. D., 53, 87
Norway, 18, 43, 50
Nubian, 57
destroys Baleno, 58
damaged by bombing, 77
again in action, 216
Nye, Lieutenant-General, 149

Oceania, Italian troop liner, 97, 107
torpedoed and sunk, 108, 109
Ogaden, Italian supply ship, sunk, 197
Ohio, US tanker, 174, 186
torpedoed, 183, 185, 189, 190
reaches Malta, 191, 192
Operation:
'Barbarossa', 83
'Battleaxe', 98

'Demon', 61
'Excess', 46, 47
'Halberd', 104
'Harpoon', 156, 157–63
'Hercules', 132, 149, 153
'Judgement', 34, 36
'Merkur', 81, 173–92
'Pedestal', 173–92
'Retribution', 217
'Tiger', 64, 65, 66
'Vigorous', 156, 157, 163ff.
Oran, 205
Orari, 156, 162, 169
Oriani, 113
Orion, 22, 55, 62, 64, 71, 78
badly damaged with big casualties, 80
Orione, Italian torpedo boat, 86
Ostro, 19

P32, HM submarine, lost, 92
P33, HM submarine, lost, 92
P36, HM submarine, 139; damaged, 144
P39, sunk, 144
Pack, Captain S. W. C., Battle of Matapan, 55
Padenna, Italian supply ship, sunk, 201
Paladin, 216
Palermo, 43, 102, 157, 160, 215
British minefield off, 88
Wellington raids on, 135
Pampas, 138, 142, 143
Pandora, sunk, 144
Pantellaria, 45, 95, 160, 174, 188, 189
Panzer Army, 154, 171, 197ff.
Division XV, 199
Division XXI, 207
Partridge, 161

Patch, Captain Oliver, R M, 31, 125

Pearl Harbor, 128

Pearson, Lieutenant J. A., 191

'Pedestal', Operation, 173–92

Penelope, 110, 123, 125, 136, 139, 144

Penn, 187, 190, 191, 192

Pennland, British troopship, sunk, 62

Persiano, Italian tanker, sunk, 88

Perth, HMAS, 55, 62, 64, 71, 73

  severely damaged, 80

Petard, 216

Petrol, Rommel's lack of, 195, 199, 200, 204

Phoebe, 62, 175

Picci Fassio, Italian tanker, sunk, 201

Pola, 45, 54; sunk, 56

Poland, Captain, 141

Porpoise, HM submarine, 197

Port Chalmers, 174, 187, 190

  survives to reach Malta, 191

Port Said, 84, 170

Port Tewfik, 170

Pound, Admiral of the Fleet Sir Dudley, 16

Preussen, German ammunition ship, sunk, 97

Pridham-Wippell, Vice-Admiral H. D., 46, 55, 62

Prince of Wales, 104, 128, 164

Procida, German supply ship, sunk, 114

Proserpina, Italian tanker, 207

Puccini, Lieutenant Serigio, 184

Queen Elizabeth, 64, 65, 77, 99, 119

  damaged by 'chariot', 128

Quentin, 212

Quiberon, 212

Raeder, Grand Admiral, 53, 132

Ramillies, 34, 38, 40, 41

Raphina, 62

Raphtis, 62

Rawlings, Rear-Admiral, 44, 74, 78, 79, 80

Re '2001' fighter-bombers, 178

Reggio Calabria, 43

Renown, 40, 41, 47, 64, 65, 101

Repulse, 128, 164

Resolution, 19

Retimo, 70

'Retribution', Operation, 217

Rhodes, 44, 54

Riccardi, Admiral Arturo, 45, 54

Riley, Captain (*Brisbane Star*), 186

Rochester Castle, 174

  torpedoed, 187, 190

  but arrives at Malta, 191

Rodney, 104, 175

Rommel, General Erwin, 13, 24, 61, 66, 83, 102, 103, 113, 115, 116, 117, 148, 149

  attacks Auchinleck, 150

  takes Tobruk and wants to continue offensive, 151, 152, 153

  his supply crisis, Chapter 11

  dissatisfied with supplies received, 171

wishes to retreat but Hitler forbids, 195
retreats to Tarhuna-Homs, 213
recalled by Hitler, 215
Rorqual, HM minelaying submarine, 88
Rosenbaum, Lieutenant, 175
Rosolino Pilo, sunk, 197
Rowallan Castle, 135; sunk, 136
Royal Air Force, 19, 26–8, 39, 93, 98, 100, 201
   38 Squadron, 165
   39 Squadron, 167
   105 Squadron, 93
   107 Squadron, 93
   148 Squadron, 51, 57, 84
   217 Squadron, 165
   227 Squardon, 197
   252 Squadron, 64, 129
   272 Squadron, 129
   431 Flight, 33
Royal Naval Cooperation:
   Group 201, 129, 130, 133, 137, 139
   Group 205, 137
Royal Sovereign, 22
Ruhr, German supply ship, torpedoed, 88
Russia, 110, 118
Rye, HM minesweeper, 190, 191, 192

Sabaudia, blown up, 58
Sagittario, 73, 74
Sagona, tanker, damaged by Italian 'chariot', 128
San Andrea, Italian tanker, sunk, 197
Santa Elisa, USS, 174
   sunk, 187

Santoro, General, 175
Sardinia, 41, 46, 65, 156, 175,
Savoia '79' aircraft, 48, 51, 139, 176
   '82', 210
Scandola, Lieutenant Renato, 181
Scarlett, Lieutenant N. J., 36
Scarpanto airfield, 77, 78
Schergat, 'charioteer', 128
Schuster, Admiral, 73
Sciré, Italian submarine, 126
Scurfield, Commander, 160
Sea Hurricanes, 158, 176
Sheffield, 40, 47, 64
Sicilian Narrows, 40, 64, 104, 179
Sicily, 32, 40, 41, 43, 89, 110, 213
Sidi Barrani, 31, 153, 168
Sidi Rezegh, 115
Siebel ferries, 203
Sikh, 120
Simpson, Captain, 145, 146
Sirius, 175, 212
Sirte, Second Battle of, 139–41
Skerki Channel, 101, 160
Skua aircraft, 50
Slamat, troopship, sunk, 63
Sokol, Polish submarine, 145
Somali, 186
Somerville, Vice-Admiral Sir James, 18, 34, 39, 47, 64, 65, 101, 104
Southampton, 40, 47, 48–9
   bombed and sunk, 49
Speedy, minesweeper, 192
Spezia, 141
Sphakia, 80
Spitfires, 138, 143, 146, 147, 155, 160
   long-range, 162

Stampalia, 44

Stokes, Commander G. H., 120

Student, General Kurt, 67, 69, 70

Stuka dive-bombers, 48, 52, 158, 161, 164, 167, 168, 178

Stumme, General (Deputy CIC of Afrika Korps), 202; killed, 206

Submarines, British, 53, 59, 92, 135
  as transports, 100
  withdrawn from Malta, 146
  'P' and 'R' Class, 85, 92, 144, 197
  Triton class, 85, 88
  'U' class, 53, 85–92, 107, 108, 109, 113, 114, 122, 144, 145, 165, 172, 188, 197, 201
  Dutch, 91
  German, 15, 67, 110, 173; *see also* U-boats
  Greek, 145
  Italian, 15, 31, 88, 125, 173, 179, 180
  Polish, 145

Suda Bay, 33, 37, 44, 62, 63, 71, 73, 77

Suez Canal, 64, 83, 102

Sunderland aircraft, 28, 45, 55, 86

Swain, Lieutenant-Commander, 191

Swordfish aircraft, 16, 19, 24, 26, 29, 31, 34, 36, 37, 57, 59, 60, 84, 86, 91, 101, 105, 106, 114, 133
  get radar, 97

Sydney Star, damaged, 101

Syfret, Rear-Admiral, 101, 138, 174, 176, 188, 192

Syria, campaign in, 82

Takoradi, 103

Talabot, 138, 142
  scuttled, 143

Tanimbar, Dutch freighter, 156
  sunk, 158

Tanks, 66, 151
  'Sherman', 171
  'Tiger', 203

Taranto, 20, 33, 34–9, 45, 107, 122, 156, 157, 160, 168
  Battle of, 36ff.

Tarhuna-Homs Line, 213

Tarigo sinks *Mohawk* before being sunk, 58

Tartar, 179

Tedder, Air Marshal, 157

Tembien, Italian motorship, damaged, 95

Tesei, Lieutenant, 125, 126, 127

Tetrarch, HM submarine, 88

Thermopylae, sunk, 129

Ticino, Italian tanker, sunk, 88

Tiesenhausen, Lieutenant-Commander von, 119

'Tiger', Operation, 64, 65, 66

'Tiger' tanks, 203

Tobruk, 19, 52
  siege of, 83, 84, 98, 115, 116, 132, 197, 207
  British surrender, 152
  German fuel tanks destroyed by bombing, 171

Tolon, 62

Tomkinson, Lieutenant E. P., 92, 146

Torpedo, airborne, 32, 36, 37, 39

Toscano, Admiral, 121

Toschi, Lieutenant, 125

Tovey, Vice-Admiral John, 22

Trapani, 43

Trento, 54, 111, 139
 disabled, 165
 sunk, 169

Trieste, 54, 111
 torpedoed, 114
 sunk in harbour by bombing, 215

Tripoli, 19, 45, 58, 66, 86, 87, 89, 90, 107, 114, 131

Tripolitania, 52, 116, 208

Troilus, 156, 169

Tunisia, 209, 214
 convoys, hopeless situation of, 213, 215

Tyrrhenian Sea, 91, 188

U-73, torpedoes and sinks *Eagle*, 175

U-81, sinks *Ark Royal*, 118

U-331, sinks *Barham*, 119

U-372, sinks *Medway*, 170

U-557, sinks *Galatea*, 122

Ulster Prince, sunk, 62

Ultimatum, 201

Umbra, HM submarine, sinks *Trento*, 169, and *Barbaro*, 203

Unbeaten, HM submarine, 107, 108, 109
 damaged, 144

Unbroken, HM submarine, arrives at Malta, 172, 188, 189

Undaunted, HM submarine, lost, 92

Unione, Italian battleship, disabled, 203

Unique, HM submarine, 85, 87

Unison, HM submarine, lost, 92

United, HM submarine, 197

United States Army Air Force, 156, 172, 213, 215

Upholder, HM submarine, 86, 88, 89, 90, 91, 92, 107, 108, 109, 113
 sunk, 145

Upright, HM submarine, 53, 87, 88, 107, 109, 122

Urge, HM submarine, 92, 122, 141
 mined, 146

Ursula, HM submarine, 108, 109

Usk, HM submarine, lost, 92

Ustica, 213

Utmost, HM submarine, 87, 88, 114

Valiant, 19, 28, 32, 34, 44, 48, 55, 64, 99, 119
 disabled by 'chariot', 128

Valona, bombardment of, 44

Venables, Commander A. G., 174, 181

Venice, unsuccessfully bombed, 93

Verde, Italian tanker, mined, 88

Vian, Rear-Admiral, 123, 124, 127, 129, 136, 138, 139, 140, 141, 156, 158

Victoria, Italian troop liner, 90, 97
 sunk, 134

Victorious, 175, 178, 180

'Vigorous', Operation, 156, 157, 163ff.

Vittorio Veneto, 18, 29, 37, 47, 54, 55, 104, 120, 122, 156 torpedoed, 56, 122

Vivaldi, bombed and set on fire, 161

Vulcania, Italian troop liner, 97, 107, 109

Wachtfels, German supply ship damaged, 95

Waimarama, 174, 187; blown up, 189

Wairangi, 174; sunk, 186

Wanklyn, Lieutenant-Commander M. D., 88, 89, 90, 91, 107, 108, 109 sunk, 145

Warspite, 21, 22, 23, 32, 34, 44, 48, 55, 64, 74

Wasp, US Carrier, 145, 146

Wavell, General Sir Archibald, 27, 31, 42, 61, 63, 68, 77, 98

Wehrmacht, *see* German Army

Weichold, Admiral, 110

Wellington Bomber aircraft, 45, 51, 57, 84, 103, 107, 114, 124, 133, 135, 137 night torpedo planes, 156, 165, 169, 212

Welshman, minelayer, 147, 157, 213

Western Desert, 150

William-Powlett, Captain, 75

Williamson, Lieutenant-Commander Kenneth, 36, 38

Wilson, General Maitland, 68

Woodward, Lieutenant, 108, 109

Wren, Captain Richard, 187

Wryneck, sunk, 63

York, 28, 126

Zara, 54, 56

Zeffiro, 19

Zulu, 136

BRITISH BATTLES SERIES (cont.)

THE BATTLE FOR NORMANDY (30p) 6/–
Eversley Belfield and H. Essame
'The last great set-piece of the Western World'—
THE OBSERVER.

CORUNNA (30p) 6/–
Christopher Hibbert
The battle in the Peninsular War which saved a British
Army from annihilation.

AGINCOURT (25p) 5/–
Christopher Hibbert
'A straightforward and absorbing account of this
astounding battle and the campaign that so improbably
led up to it'—THE OBSERVER.

WATERLOO (25p) 5/–
John Naylor
'No commanders were ever better served by their men,
British, French and Prussian'—BRITISH ARMY REVIEW.

THE SOMME (30p) 6/–
Anthony Farrar-Hockley
One of the most bloody and protracted battles in history.

YPRES 1914: Death of an Army (30p) 6/–
Anthony Farrar-Hockley
A magnificent and moving story of the old British
Regular Army.

BATTLES OF THE INDIAN MUTINY (35p) 7/–
Michael Edwardes
'Lucknow relieved . . . Cawnpore avenged, Delhi stormed
. . . all excellently recounted using much unpublished
material'—THE SUNDAY TIMES.

THE BATTLE FOR THE MEDITERRANEAN
Capt. Donald Macintyre   (30p) 6/–
Achieves an excellent balance between the strategic and
the operational features of the campaign'—RUSI JOURNAL.

Chaucer

THE NUN'S PRIEST'S TALE	8/–
THE PARDONER'S TALE	8/–
THE CLERK'S TALE	8/–
THE PRIORESS'S TALE	8/–
THE PROLOGUE TO THE CANTERBURY TALES	8/–
THE CANTERBURY TALES	8/–

Literature

EMMA Jane Austen	8/–
NORTHANGER ABBEY Jane Austen	8/–
PERSUASION Jane Austen	8/–
PRIDE AND PREJUDICE Jane Austen	8/–
LORNA DOONE R. D. Blackmore	8/–
JANE EYRE Charlotte Brontë	8/–
WUTHERING HEIGHTS Emily Brontë	8/–
THE PLAGUE Albert Camus	8/–
THE STRANGER Albert Camus	8/–
HEART OF DARKNESS Joseph Conrad	8/–
LORD JIM Joseph Conrad	8/–
GREAT EXPECTATIONS Charles Dickens	8/–
A TALE OF TWO CITIES Charles Dickens	8/–
ADAM BEDE George Eliot	8/–
THE MILL ON THE FLOSS George Eliot	8/–
MIDDLEMARCH George Eliot	8/–
SILAS MARNER George Eliot	8/–
TOM JONES Henry Fielding	8/–
MADAME BOVARY Flaubert	8/–
THE GUN C. S. Forester	8/–
A PASSAGE TO INDIA E. M. Forster	8/–
LORD OF THE FLIES William Golding	8/–
THE VICAR OF WAKEFIELD Oliver Goldsmith	8/–
THE POWER AND THE GLORY Graham Greene	8/–
FAR FROM THE MADDING CROWD Thomas Hardy	8/–
THE MAYOR OF CASTERBRIDGE Thomas Hardy	8/–
FOR WHOM THE BELL TOLLS, FAREWELL TO ARMS Ernest Hemingway	8/–
THE OLD MAN AND THE SEA Ernest Hemingway	8/–
THE SUN ALSO RISES Ernest Hemingway	8/–
BRAVE NEW WORLD Aldous Huxley	8/–
PORTRAIT OF THE ARTIST AS A YOUNG MAN, James Joyce	8/–
SONS AND LOVERS D. H. Lawrence	8/–
ANIMAL FARM George Orwell	8/–
1984 John Orwell	8/–
THE GRAPES OF WRATH John Steinbeck	8/–
THE PEARL John Steinbeck	8/–
THE ADVENTURES OF HUCKLEBERRY FINN Mark Twain	8/–

THE ADVENTURES OF TOM SAWYER Mark Twain   8/–
THE HISTORY OF MR POLLY H. G. Wells   8/–

Drama

WAITING FOR GODOT Samuel Beckett   8/–
A MAN FOR ALL SEASONS Robert Bolt   8/–
THE WAY OF THE WORLD William Congreve   8/–
MURDER IN THE CATHEDRAL T. S. Eliot   8/–
SHE STOOPS TO CONQUER Oliver Goldsmith   8/–
ANDROCLES AND THE LION, MAJOR BARBARA
               George Bernard Shaw   8/–
MAN AND SUPERMAN George Bernard Shaw   8/–
SAINT JOAN George Bernard Shaw   8/–
SCHOOL FOR SCANDAL, THE RIVALS Sheridan   8/–

Poetry

WORKS Robert Browning   8/–
MAJOR POEMS AND PLAYS T. S. Eliot   8/–
POETRY John Keats   8/–
PARADISE LOST John Milton   8/–
THE FAERIE QUEENE Edmund Spenser   8/–
PRELUDE William Wordsworth   8/–

General Science

GENERAL SCIENCE, PARTS 1 & 2   8/–
BIOLOGY NOTES   10/–
BOTANY NOTES   8/–
INTRODUCTION TO CHEMISTRY   8/–
MATHEMATICS NOTES, PARTS 1 & 2   8/–
ALGEBRA-MATHEMATICS NOTES   8/–
SENIOR GEOMETRY NOTES   8/–
SENIOR MATHEMATICS   8/–
HOW TO SOLVE PHYSICS PROBLEMS   10/–

Geography

PHYSICAL AND HUMAN   8/–
AFRICA, AUSTRALASIA, BRITISH ISLES   8/–

New Forum House

AN OUTLINE OF 17TH CENTURY ENGLISH LITERATURE
Edited by John Henderson   10/–
AN OUTLINE OF RESTORATION & 18TH CENTURY
LITERATURE
by John C. Stumpf   8/–
AN OUTLINE OF 19TH CENTURY ENGLISH LITERATURE
by John C. Stumpf   8/–
AN OUTLINE OF THE RENAISSANCE DRAMA
by John C. Stumpf   8/–
AN OUTLINE OF BRITISH LITERATURE SINCE 1900
by Thomas B. Flanagan   10/–
THE ENGLISH NOVEL FROM DICKENS TO CONRAD
by Alfred Johnson   8/–

THE ENGLISH NOVEL FROM DEFOE TO SCOTT
by Alfred Johnson 8/-
AN OUTLINE OF PRINCIPLES OF GENETICS
by Arthur Portland 12/-
CHAUCER: POET OF MIRTH AND MORALITY
by Helen Storm Corsa 20/-
AN OUTLINE OF THE WORKS OF DYLAN THOMAS
by Richard Morton 10/

Forum House—Stock Titles

MAJOR BRITISH ROMANTIC POETS 20/-
G. B. SHAW—CREATIVE ARTIST 15/-
MODERN ENGLISH POETS 10/-
D. H. LAWRENCE: A CRITICAL SURVEY 20/-

The Man and His Works

SAMUEL BECKETT edited by Frederick Hoffman 15/-
T. S. ELIOT Eric Thompson 15/-
E. M. FORSTER Norman Kelvin 15/-
F. SCOTT FITZGERALD Richard D. Lehan 15/-
CHRISTOPHER FRY Emil Roy 15/-
JAMES JOYCE Joseph Prescott 15/-
D. H. LAWRENCE Harry T. Moore 20/-
HENRY MILLER edited by George Wickes 15/-
EUGENE O'NEILL John Henry Raleigh 20/-

History of English Literature Series

ANGLO-SAXON AND MIDDLE ENGLISH LITERATURE 8/-
RENAISSANCE PROSE AND POETRY 8/-
CONTEMPORARY AMERICAN NOVELISTS 15/-
CONTEMPORARY BRITISH NOVELISTS 15/-
CONTEMPORARY EUROPEAN NOVELISTS 15/-

The Man and His Plays

SEAN O'CASEY Jules Koslow 8/-

General Reference Titles

HOW TO USE THE SLIDE RULE 8/-
DEVELOP YOUR SPEED READING POWER 8/-
DICTIONARY OF SYNONYMS AND ANTONYMS WITH
DISCRIMINATIONS 15/-